Dangerous Voices

Dangerous Voices

Women's laments and Greek literature

Gail Holst-Warhaft

For Philip & Ruth & all of you dear Holmes — we will miss you — don't stay away long! Love Gail & Jack Ithaca 6/23/94

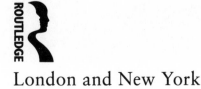

Routledge

London and New York

First published 1992
by Routledge
11 New Fetter Lane, London EC4P 4EE

Simultaneously published in the USA and Canada
by Routledge
a division of Routledge, Chapman and Hall Inc.
29 West 35th Street, New York, NY 10001

Typeset in 10/12pt Bembo by
Ponting–Green Publishing Services, Berkshire
Printed in Great Britain by
T J Press (Padstow) Ltd, Padstow, Cornwall

British Library Cataloguing in Publication Data
Holst-Warhaft, Gail
Dangerous voices: women's laments and Greek literature.
I. Title
393.9

Library of Congress Cataloging-in-Publication Data
Holst-Warhaft, Gail,
    Dangerous voices: women's laments and Greek lit-
erature / by Gail Holst-Warhaft.
        p. cm.
    Includes bibliographical references and index.
    1. Greek literature–History and criticism. 2. Literature
and Society–Greece–History. 3. Women and literature–
Greece–History. 4. Mourning customs–Greece–History.
5.   Women–Greece–Social conditions. 6. Mourning customs in   literature. 7. Laments–Greece–History.
8. Laments in literature. 9. Death in literature.
I. Title.
PA3074.H64   1992
880.9'001'089–dc20   91-40115

ISBN 0–415–07249–2

For my son, Sacha Ambrose Warhaft,
January 1985–October 1988

'my little ear of wheat, winnowed and reaped unripe'
(Greek lament)

Contents

Acknowledgements

Part of the contents of chapter 6 appeared in the *Journal of Modern Greek Studies*, October 1991. I am grateful to the editors for permission to use the material in this book.

The frontispiece was reproduced by kind permission of The Metropolitan Museum of Art, Rogers Fund, 1954.

I thank all my friends and colleagues who have given me material, discussed my work with me and offered their insights. They include Fred Ahl, Martin Bernal, Wayles Browne, Calum Carmichael, Sotiris Chianis, John Chioles, David Curzon, Vangelis Fambas, Steven Feld, Helene Foley, Sandor Goodhart, David Grossvogel, Janet Hart, Rudolf Käser, Lucia Lermond, Jean Lewis, David McCann, Kathryn March, Philip Mitsis, Charina and Francis Oeser, Jeff Rusten, Marcia and Barry Strauss, Karen Van Dyck, Kostas Vantzos, Ingeborg Wald and Olga Zissi. The Western Societies Program at Cornell University, under the imaginative guidance of Susan Tarrow and Sander Gilman, provided me with travel and study grants to complete my research.

I particularly want to thank three of my dear friends: Chana Kronfeld, whose painstaking criticism and encouragement helped me structure my own lament; Margaret Alexiou, whose work on lament was in large part the inspiration for this study and who gave my manuscript a generous, insightful reading; and Mariza Koch, who taught me how Greek women turn tears into ideas.

Zellman, Zoe and Simon helped put an end to laments.

A note on transliteration and translation

For some reason, the question of transliteration seems to arouse more angry debate than almost any other issue in Greek studies. I apologize in advance for having adopted what seemed to me to be a useful working compromise. Rather than attempt to abide by a strict system of transliteration that approximated modern Greek pronunciation for Greek words, I have tried to follow generally acceptable English practice based on the spelling of the original Greek or on common usage. This means that I have used *moirolói* rather than *miroloy*, *epitaphios* rather than *epitàfios*. Similarly I have used Maniot rather than Maniat (see Seremetakis 1991) because books like Patrick Leigh-Fermor's *Mani* have made the former familiar to the English reader. Unless otherwise acknowledged, translations of ancient and modern Greek texts are my own and I bear full responsibility for them.

Introduction
Dangerous voices: women's laments and Greek literature

Mourning is universal, its rituals manifold. Among them, one of the most interesting and least understood is lament. When we speak of lament, we are speaking of many different genres. A lament is an expression of mourning, but it is not necessarily mourning for the dead. A whole class of laments, including those of the biblical book of Lamentations, are songs for the fall of great cities. In cultures where forced emigration is common, we often find laments either for those who have gone into exile or composed by émigrés for the homeland and family they have left behind. In Finland, China and Greece, laments are sung by the bride's family, and often by the bride herself, as she leaves to become a member of her husband's household.[1]

The form laments take is just as varied as their subject. Anything from an elaborate poem to 'tuneful weeping' can be classified as a lament. In this investigation I am particularly interested in laments for the dead, and since the two cultures I will be looking at closely are ancient and modern Greece, I will be looking at a variety of forms of lament, from the *kommos* of classical tragedy to the folk laments of Mani and Epirus.

LAMENT AS AN ART OF WOMEN

What is common to laments for the dead in most 'traditional' cultures is that they are part of more elaborate rituals for the dead, and that they are usually performed by women. In these cultures, as in our own, women and men are perceived and expected to mourn in different ways. Men and women may both weep for their dead, but it is women who tend to weep longer, louder, and it is they who are thought to communicate directly

with the dead through their wailing songs. Frequently, in these
cultures, laments are led or sung by a skilled, even professional
class of women who are regarded as being especially gifted at
improvising and performing songs for the dead. There is
evidence, even in traditional societies, that it is more shameful
for men to weep over their dead than women.[2] When we come
to lament as a western literary genre written mostly by men, we
are reminded that women and men mourn in their own ways,
and that while in early literary texts such as the Bible and the
Homeric poems it was proper for men to weep and be wept
over, it later became unacceptable:

> There our murdered brother lies;
> Wake him not with women's cries;
> Mourn the way that manhood ought –
> Sit in silent trance of thought.
>
> Write his merits on your mind;
> Morals pure and manners kind;
> In his head, as on a hill,
> Let Virtue place her citadel....

So writes the Irish poet Willian Drennan (1754–1820) in *The
Wake of William Orr*. It is not simply saying that men and
women mourn differently, but that one is better than the other,
especially in the context of a funeral of a man who dies, as Orr
did, a hero. A hero's death, it seems, should be marked by
praise, not women's cries, that may 'wake the dead'. If their
cries have such power, women must be capable of some direct
communication with the dead. What is meant by 'waking the
dead'? Simply disturbing their peace, or stirring them to revisit
the living, perhaps to take revenge for an unjust death?

In societies like nineteenth-century rural Ireland, or like
Greece today, there is a clear division between laments performed as part of a funeral service in a traditional village
setting, and the formal, composed lament in verse or prose
which may form part of a religious or civic ceremony, or may
simply be an artistic composition inspired by bereavement or
loss. At the village level, it seems, women play a dominant role
in the rituals of death, as they do in the rituals of birth. In
societies where most deaths are deaths of small children, it may
seem 'natural' for the mother who tends the small child from

birth to bury it. From this it may also be natural to assume that women should lead the weeping over the dead, that this weeping should develop into a form of song that is associated with women. Since they are usually addressed directly to the dead, laments enable the members of the family or small community to tell the dead they are missed, sometimes to berate them for abandoning the living.[3] Laments may also, by a sort of possession on the lamenter's part, enable the dead to address the living, and either assuage their grief or call on them to redress real or imaginary grievances suffered in life.

THE THREAT POSED BY WOMEN'S LAMENTS

Such a dialogue with the dead places a certain power in the hands of women. It is a power that may be effective in societies like those of rural Sicily, of Mani, or the Bedouin of Saudi Arabia, where blood feuds are, or have until recently been, fuelled by the violent rhetoric of funeral laments. Potentially, such power poses a danger to the order of the more complex social unit of the city or city-state in at least three ways. First, it can be used as a means of inciting an uncontrolled sequence of reciprocal violence (a potential which the state may conceivably co-opt to its own advantage). Secondly, by focusing as it does on mourning and loss rather than praise of the dead, it denies the value of death for the community or state, making it difficult for authorities to recruit an obedient army (in chapter 4, I will deal specifically with this threat and how the Athenian state attempted to resolve it). Thirdly, in a patriarchal society where women are consistently undervalued, it leaves in the hands of women, who, both as child-bearers and midwives already have a certain control over birth, potential authority over the rites of death.

In classical Greece, from the sixth century BC onwards, legislation was introduced in Athens and a number of the more advanced city-states aimed at the restriction of what is viewed as extravagant mourning of the dead.[4] The new laws were particularly severe on women mourners, a fact which suggests that women must have played a leading part in the funeral ceremony. Evidence from the Byzantine period and from modern anthropologists working in Greece in this century, however, suggests that despite opposition from the state in antiquity, and from the church in the Christian era, women have continued to be the self-appointed mourners of the dead, composing and singing laments to express their grief and often their rage at losing their loved ones.

In 1943, at Kalavrita in the northern Peloponnese, the entire male population of the village was executed in reprisal for the killing of a German officer. The women were locked in the village school and forbidden to bury or lament their dead. They managed to escape and risk their own lives to tend to them. It is a story familiar to us from classical tragedy, and I suspect that classical tragedy was composed in a society where such an occurrence seemed normal. *Antigone*, like a number of Greek tragedies, is a play about new institutions that come into conflict with older values. The great *agōn* between Antigone and Creon has been read by critics from Hegel onwards as defining the limits of state and of male authority over the private and familial rights of burying the dead. But should Creon be seen as embodying the values of the *polis* as an 'ethical power' (*eine sittliche Macht*)?[5] His apparent readiness to deny burial not only to Polynices but to all the enemy dead makes his behaviour seem excessive, if not blasphemous, by Attic standards. Nor is Antigone a representative of what might be considered normal family rights. I will consider the play in some detail in chapter 5, but here it is enough to point out that Sophocles and the other tragedians were acutely aware of the traditional authority of women over the rites of the dead, and the potential for violent action inherent in interfering with mourning. We must listen to Antigone's lines with care, not reading into them so much a woman's side to the conflict over the right to control death, but perhaps the tragedian's awareness that there is in the Athenian state, that embodiment of contemporary civilized *man*, a danger in interfering with traditional customs and the family's relationship to its dead.

If legislation against female mourning is not effective, and there is evidence, apart from the tragedies themselves, to suggest that it was not wholly so,[6] then how can the power of the lament be counterbalanced? How can men take at least partial control of death? Greek literature offers us, I believe, a partial solution. Two literary genres that are, in Nicole Loraux's phrase, 'the invention of Athens': the *Epitaphios Logos*, or encomium, delivered at the tomb, and the tragedy, are both, I suggest, appropriations of the lament and of its great antiphonal dialogue with death. In the case of the *Epitaphios Logos*, both the appropriation and its function are more obvious. The (male) funeral oration for those who die in battle makes a virtue of death, provided it is death in the service of the state. This is in direct opposition to the lament of the female relatives, who, if we are to take the folk laments of Greece and other modern cultures as representative, mourn their personal loss in terms of emotional, economic and social deprivation, and look on death as an enemy. The tension between public and private burial can only be resolved when the state, as it has done many times in modern European history, convinces the families, particularly the mothers of soldiers, that the glory of dying for the fatherland outweighs private grief, and compensates them for their loss.

Once any state has need of a standing army, it must condemn the negative, bitter pain of traditional lament; otherwise how will it recruit volunteers and keep their loyalty? Similarly, once a state has established courts of law, how can it tolerate the cycle of revenge such as the one triggered by female lamenters at the tomb of Agamemnon, or the threat of anarchy posed by laments like that of the widow Vrettis from Mani in the Peloponnese, who, when her only son was killed by neighbours, pulled out her knife in the courtroom, bit it and said:

– Mr President,
if you don't condemn them
to death or a life sentence
you see this dagger?
I'll go to the upper quarter
and if I can't find a grown-up
I'll grab a small child
and I'll slay him like a lamb
for mine was an only child
and they cut him to pieces.[7]

Laments give vent to passionate feelings. As Vico put it: 'Men vent great passions by breaking into song, as we observe in the most grief-stricken and the most joyous' (*The New Science*, LIX). In most cultures, it has been women, not men, who have broken into a song of grief.[8] If we can judge by the folk laments of Mani, where vendettas were common at least as late as the 1950s, laments can quickly be transformed from songs of grief to songs of anger that call for or describe revenge. To our modern western sensibility calling narratives of revenge 'laments' may seem a misnomer, but in Mani there is no clear distinction between the songs that express grief and those that inspire revenge. In fact the movement from one emotional state to the other frequently occurs within the same lament. It is not surprising that such laments could be seen as posing a threat to the order of the state. But what happens then to the expression of grief and anger that has been the traditional response to death for centuries?

I have suggested that the state of Athens may, consciously or unconsciously, have channelled the passion of lament into its two great rhetorical inventions, the funeral speech and the tragedy. Similarly, the early Christian fathers may have diverted the subversive potential of private mourning, controlled by women, into the central focus of a ritual controlled by male priests in which the Virgin's lament for her dead son becomes a symbolic substitution for the worshippers' personal grieving. However it has been achieved, traditional women's lament has been almost eliminated from the modern western world. Only in isolated pockets – remote areas of Greece and Yugoslavia, rural Ireland, Scotland, the Ingrian villages of Finland and Russia – can we find, usually in the memory of the older women, some last remnants of the songs for the dead that were once improvised at every funeral.

THE LAMENTER AS AN ARTIST

With the disappearance of lament, women have lost more than their traditional control over the rites of mourning the dead. Women lamenters were, and still are in places where lament survives, folk poets, composers, actors. Not every woman can sing laments – it is always recognized as an art demanding musical and verbal skills in combination with an ability to transform one's own or another's pain into a work of art. This art of lament, an art perfected by women, is something that underlies and can frequently be discerned in various other forms of poetry, including epic, elegy, lyric, tragedy and narrative. Occasionally an example of a woman mourner's lament has survived to remind us that it can be a brilliant art form in its own right.

The British poet Peter Levi, in his inaugural lecture as the

Professor of Poetry at Oxford in 1984, chose to read an example of that art, a lament he described as 'the greatest poem written in these [the British] islands in the whole eighteenth century'.[9] It was a lament for Arthur O'Leary, composed by O'Leary's widow, Black Eileen, for the second burial of her husband, who died in 1773. Since the Irish original, copied down after surviving for many years in the oral tradition, would have been incomprehensible to most of his audience, Levi read the poem in an English translation by Eilis Dillon. Eileen O'Leary, was the daughter of a poet and her family had been patrons of traditional Irish wandering poets, so there may be elements of unusual sophistication in this lament, but it is clearly informed by and composed in a traditional form. It begins with a lamentation at the death of O'Leary, who was shot on the run as an outlaw by a soldier, Abraham Morris. It continues with a quarrel over the wake between Eileen and O'Leary's sister with comments by the dead man's father, followed by the lamentation before burial, and two stanzas for the second burial. Here is the section beginning just before Eileen learns of her husband's murder:

> My friend and my love!
> Of the blood of Lord Antrim
> And of Barry of Allchoill,
> How well your sword suited you,
> Hat gold-banded,
> Boots of fine leather
> Coat of broadcloth
> Spun overseas for you.
>
> My friend you were forever!
> I knew nothing of your murder
> Till your horse came to the stable
> With the reins beneath her trailing,
> And your heart's blood on her shoulders
> Staining the tooled saddle
> Where you used to sit and stand.
> My first leap reached the threshold
> My second reached the gateway,
> My third leap reached the saddle.
>
> I struck my hands together
> And made the bay horse gallop

As fast as I was able,
Till I found you dead before me
Beside a little furze-bush.
Without Pope or bishop,
Without priest or cleric
To read the death psalms for you,
But a spent old woman only
Who spread her cloak to shroud you –
Your heart's blood was still flowing;
I did not stay to wipe it
But filled my hands and drank it.

My love you'll be forever!
Rise up from where you're lying
And we'll be going homewards.
We'll have a bullock slaughtered,
We'll call our friends together,
We'll get the music going.
I'll make a fine bed ready
With sheets of snow-white linen,
And fine embroidered covers
That will bring the sweat out through you
Instead of the cold that's on you!

How eloquently we are led through the gamut of emotions that pass through the widow's head – her pride in her husband's noble ancestry, his fine clothes, then the horror of the riderless horse, still reminding her, with its 'tooled leather', of his past glory! The drama of Eileen's ride, the wonderful transformation of the pitiful death – the 'little furze bush', the 'spent old woman' who has to substitute for the hierarchy of the church – leads to an act that fills us with horror and breaks the boundaries between the living and the dead, enabling the lamenting woman to call up her husband and invite him to feast and lie with her again.

LAMENT AS PART OF THE COMMUNITY'S RESPONSE TO DEATH

Most of the songs women have composed over the centuries to mourn their dead are sung on a particular occasion and soon forgotten. Only if they are sufficiently admired within the community do they pass into the folk memory, becoming part of an oral tradition that can be reused on other occasions. Eileen O'Leary's song, like the laments of rural Greece or the highlands of New Guinea, is an example of the art of the female lamenter who articulates the inarticulate, forming a bridge between the living and the dead that is recognized by the community. Some residue of this art is found in the tragic poetry of every age. Its mark is clear, as I will demonstrate, in the tragedies of fifth-century Athens. But as it is articulated by male poets removed from a ritual context, it loses its functional quality as a communal expression of grief. Laments are perceived by those who perform them as well as by those who hear them as an essential part of the grieving process. They have been banned or restricted, I suggest, as part of an urban, more sophisticated attitude to death: what Philippe Ariès, in his discussion of changing attitudes towards death in western Europe, characterizes as the movement from *mort apprivoisée*, death tamed and integrated into community life through ritual, to *mort sauvage*, death that is feared as impure and so kept at a distance.[10] What happened in the Greek city-states, as in France of the late eighteenth and nineteenth centuries, is a change in the symbolic categorization of death, one that is familiar to us because it corresponds in many ways to our own sensibility.

RECENT RESEARCH INTO DEATH

Since the mid-1960s there have been an increasing number of studies of death by anthropologists, sociologists and social historians. Herminio Martins, in his introduction to *Death in Portugal*[11] summarizes the main lines of recent research into death in the western world under four headings: (1) The hospitalization and medicalization of death, (2) the deritualization of death, (3) the decay of language or discourse about death, and (4) the meaninglessness of death. As evidence of the deritualization of death, Martins contends that mourning has all but disappeared from some sectors of western society. This is not, he explains, a function of secularization, but is reflected in changes in the Catholic liturgy, where the traditional sacrament of Extreme Unction has been altered and renamed the Unction for the Sick. In post-Salazar Portugal, 'enlightened' modernizers within the church replicate political modernizers who dismiss peasant custom as 'superstitious' and 'backward'. Such an attitude on the part of priests who have traditionally officiated at funerals within the framework of village custom is likely, Martins observes, to divorce the church 'from oral tradition, ascriptive communities and the received natural symbols of age and gender'.[12]

Closely linked to the deritualization of death in the west is the disappearance of a ritualized language in which to speak about it. As Martins says, 'before the ineffable and unspeakable the resources of illocutionary or performative speech-acts are strained to the utmost, and the ritual languages of the past which rendered allusively, through tropes and metaphorical observances, that which defies expression, have become attenuated.'[13] Martins's view of the decay of ritual and ritual language in the west, particularly in the case of present-day Portugal, presupposes the centrality of the Catholic liturgy to that culture. But ritual and religious language are not necessarily one and the same. In rural Greece, for example, beliefs about death and the afterlife expressed in women's laments for the dead often conflict with the beliefs of the Greek Orthodox Church. They do, however, provide the community with a ritualized language for speaking about death, and as the *moirologhístres*, the traditional performers of lament, die out, modern Greek discourse about death may become as clichéd and impoverished as it is in most western societies.

CONCLUSION

The fact that death has become, in recent years, a popular subject for research, and that laments for the dead are being collected and analysed in a number of different cultures, may indicate that we are in the process of re-examining our attitude to death and mourning. In the light of that re-examination, I suggest that we must consider lament not simply as a traditional female response to death, but as representative of the relationship of society to death, and so as fundamental to life. This is something that I believe the Greek tragedians understood well. The tragedians were drawing on a tradition where women addressed the dead directly, rousing them to interact with the living. Tragedy is an art preoccupied with death. It is, at least in part, an appropriation of the traditional art of women and we sense in its language, its inscrutable echoes of music and dance, an older body of ritual, a sub-stratum which informs and at times intrudes itself into an urban, male art. Similarly, the echo of women's lament informs the poetic art of societies like contemporary Ireland or Greece, where the village tradition is still sufficiently strong to preserve a ritual language of death.

In the chapters that follow I will examine laments primarily in the context of ancient and modern Greek literature. My purpose will be to show that an understanding of how laments function in societies where they constitute an important part of the rituals of death is essential to an informed reading of Greek tragedy and, conversely, that Greek tragedy can tell us much about the art of lament and why it posed a threat to society. In my discussion of modern lament, I will concentrate on Greece, although I will also examine the work of anthropologists who have studied lament in a number of other cultures. Since my own field-work has been limited to making recordings of lament outside the context of a funeral, I draw on the work of other scholars who have investigated laments in Greece and make use of anthologies of lament texts compiled by Greek researchers. Finally, I will show how modern Greek writers have drawn on and interacted with traditional funeral dirges, including the lament of the Virgin embedded in the Orthodox liturgy.

Margaret Alexiou noted in her pioneering investigation of Greek lament that what 'makes the study of Greek tradition so rewarding and exciting . . .[is the] dynamic interaction between learned and popular poetry'.[14] Such an interaction can occur only, I suspect, where a strong tradition of folk-song exists; at some point in our modern western culture the possibilities for drawing on the vital force of lament seem to have been lost. We sense its presence in the blues – perhaps the last great manifestation of lament to emerge in the west from a people more recently in touch with a folk tradition. The absence of lament has left us without a language to express not only the grief but the rage of the living in the face of death. It may be that women writers and singers have recently begun to sense the absence of such a language. Adrienne Rich, in a poem entitled 'A Woman Dead in her Forties', demands an end to the constrictions of silence in the face of death: 'from here on/ I want more crazy

mourning, more howl, more keening.'[15] In a more positive
spirit, May Sarton is similarly determined to keep the memory
of her dead alive by a return to a more traditional response of
endless lament:

> Now the dead move through all of us still glowing,
> Mother and child, lover and lover mated,
> Are wound and bound together and enflowing.
> What has been plaited cannot be unplaited –
> Only the strands grow richer with each loss
> and memory makes kings and queens of us.
>
> Dark into light, light into darkness, spin.
> When all the birds have flown to some real haven,
> We who find shelter in the warmth within,
> Listen, and feel new-cherished, new-forgiven,
> As the lost human voices speak through us and blend
> Our complex love, our mourning without end.[16]

It is perhaps no accident that one of the few artists to
confront the horror of AIDS in a head-on collision is the
American singer/song-writer Diamanda Galas. Galas, whose
own origins are Greek, draws on her ancestry in her work. She
appears on the cover of her record 'You Must be Certain of the
Devil' dressed in the traditional clothing of a Greek village
woman in mourning, with her finger on the trigger of a pistol.
The songs written for her brother and other victims of AIDS
draw on a motley of texts from Poe to Baudelaire, but it is her
ability to interweave these poetic texts with the laments of Mani
– not only with their words but the high-pitched timbre of their
voices, the spilling over from song to scream – that give her
work its compelling power. 'Let's not chat about despair,' says
Galas on the cover of the same record, 'If you are a man (and not
a coward)/ You will grasp the hand of him denied mercy/ Until
his breath becomes your own.'[17]

Laments do not chat about despair. They confront death with
open eyes. They seem always to have women's way of bearing
the unbearable. Perhaps, as women find new voices for expression in Greek and other literature, they will, like Galas, look
consciously to lament as a source of inspiration. Meantime, by
recognizing echoes and appropriations of lament in the begin-

nings of western literature, we may come to understand what the suppression and loss of women's voices as a vehicle for expressing communal grief has meant for our society.

Chapter 1

Death, tears and ideas: lament in cross-cultural perspective

LAMENT IN THE CONTEXT OF DEATH RITUALS

The current interest in death as a general topic of research – what has been termed the 'death awareness' movement (Huntington and Metcalfe 1979), began in the late 1950s and early 1960s with the publication in *Encounter* in 1955 of Geoffrey Gorer's article 'The Pornography of Death', closely followed by Jessica Mitford's book, *The American Way of Death*. Both had an immediate popular appeal and both were critical of contemporary western attitudes to death. Gorer's article claimed that as Victorian taboos about sexuality declined, they were replaced by new taboos about death. These taboos led to a sort of 'social invisibility of death' and to restrictions on outward expressions of grief and mourning. Mitford's book was directed against the funeral industry for profiteering on people's distress and creating an elaborate display that she saw as being inappropriate to the American way of life.

Since the publication of Gorer's and Mitford's writings, a vast body of literature has been published in a variety of fields about the death rituals of the west. Among the more influential scholarly approaches to the subject have been the work of two French scholars, Philippe Ariès and Michel Vovelle. In his survey of eight hundred years of thinking about death in the west,[1] Ariès denies the importance of political and ideological change affecting western attitudes to death. Instead he sees such changes taking place at a non-conceptual level, in a realm he terms *pensée confusée*. In other words we change our attitudes to death in a way which is intuitive rather than conscious. Vovelle,[2] who approaches the subject as a Marxist, claims that ideological changes, such as those of the European Enlightenment, have a direct causal relationship to the way a society views death. Conscious of the apparent contradiction in the two approaches, Vovelle has tried to reconcile his theory with Ariès' by examining how such fundamental changes in social attitudes to death relate to deep changes in the collective unconscious. In examining the case of ancient Greece (chapter 4) I will suggest that while no single explanation can account for the apparent change in attitude to death and mourning in the classical city-state, such a synthesis as Vovelle proposes may be the most useful method of approach.

Despite the contrast in their focus, both Ariès and Vovelle have examined death and its rituals in a broad interpretative framework, using literary, architectural and epigraphic evidence to support their theses. By placing attitudes to death in such a broad historical perspective, we can view changes in the rituals of death, such as those that took place in the Greek city-states or that are taking place in Greece and other European societies today, as part of a continuous process of redefinition in attitudes towards death in western society.[3] Neither Ariès nor Vovelle examines changes in attitudes to death in terms of gender difference or the relevance of the societal position of women to such changes, although such considerations are implicit in much of their work. Restrictions on lament and the appropriation of lament by other artistic and culturally functional forms of expression may be viewed as manifestations of a change in social attitude, but it is hard to escape the conclusion that like so many other 'social' attitudes, what we see here is a redefinition of a male, rather than a female, perspective.

ANTHROPOLOGY AND THE STUDY OF DEATH RITUALS

It was Greek and Roman supposed attitudes to death and the afterlife that underlay the work of the so-called 'intellectualist' or 'armchair' anthropologists of the late nineteenth century, E. B. Tyler and Sir James Frazer. They viewed man, at an earlier stage of his development, as being preoccupied with fears concerning the hereafter, a fixation which led to the concept of the soul and hence to religion. The French sociologist Emile

Durkheim criticized such a response to questions about the origin of religion as being over-simplified. Instead, he posited an approach to religion and the moral views of the society it reflects as having to do with the integration of individuals into the life of the community. Beliefs about death and the hereafter, like other communally held beliefs or 'collective representations', both unite individuals and emphasize their separate identities, leading to ambiguities and tensions within society.

The two studies that have most influenced modern anthropological views of death and death rituals are both indebted to Durkheim's school of thought. The first, by Robert Hertz, was originally published in 1907.[4] The second was Arnold van Gennep's *The Rites of Passage* (1909). Neither appeared in English translation until 1960. Since then they have had a fundamental impact on anthropological attitudes to death rituals. Hertz's originality was to analyse attitudes to death in a particular society (Borneo) by examining a single feature of the death ritual in detail. In his essay 'A Contribution to the Study of the Collective Representation of Death', Hertz examined the phenomenon of secondary burial, noting that the corpse, as it decayed, seemed to be viewed as a model for the soul. During the intermediary phase between death and reburial of the clean bones, the soul of the departed was neither dead nor alive, but existed in a miserable twilight zone where it was liable to inflict injury on the living. Its hostility had to be avoided by elaborate rituals until the 'great feast' honouring the now dry bones established the soul's arrival in the land of the ancestors and ended its desire to harm the community. From his observations of a particular ritual in its ethnographical context, Hertz went on to make a connection between secondary burial and sacrifice. Both cases, he noted, involve the destruction of an object in this world so that it may pass into the next.

What links the work of Hertz to that of van Gennep, is its focus on the transitional, or what the latter would call the *liminal* phase of death. Van Gennep's concept of 'rites of passage' is well known. He was not the first to observe the similarity between such rites in a wide variety of cultures, but he noted that the similarities could be analysed in structural terms. His structural model is based on the simple idea that any distinction creates two classes and that this binary opposition (in this case of social statuses) implies a tertiary structure, in which passage from one state to the next is mediated by a liminal stage marked by rites of passage. The innovation of his methodology was to view what had appeared to western observers as bizarre anachronistic rituals surrounding death, birth or marriage as part of a coherent system of ritual representation comprehensible in terms of transitional states. Death rituals, in particular, he saw as universally reflective of the theme of transition.

Like such classical modern studies as those of William Douglass (1969) and Jack Goody (1962), Loring Danforth's study of Greek death rituals (1982) draws on the pioneering work of van Gennep. Danforth is also indebted to the American anthropologist Clifford Geertz (1973), who saw the elaborate systems of symbols in a culture as the embodiment of structures of meaning established by society. Such structures, Geertz believes, help us to find order in the apparent chaos of the world around us. What appears to be everyday reality to a member of any society, is, according to such a semiotic theory, a social construct, arrived at through a constant interaction between the individual and other members of the society. In order to maintain his sense of order and meaning in the world, an individual must constantly reaffirm his sense of identity by an ongoing dialectic with other members of the community. The symbolic systems that maintain a person's sense of reality in a given culture are not only linguistic but include other symbolic systems such as ritual, myth, dance or art. Death rituals, like the myths that structural anthropologists, notably Lévi-Strauss, have analysed in detail, are viewed, in such a context, as expressions of fundamental contradictions perceived by man. Life and death, like the other binary oppositions such as right and left, nature and culture, are, according to Lévi-Strauss, oppositions which all mythical and ritual language tries to mediate. And since these oppositions are real, the symbolic language of myth or ritual cannot overcome the contradiction implicit in their juxtaposition. Instead, a third, mediating term is introduced to ease the conflict, and the ritual or myth must be constantly repeated in an attempt to resolve irreconcilable oppositions.

The rituals that surround death can be viewed, Danforth argues, as attempts to mediate the especially disturbing contradiction of the life/death opposition. Religion is one of the means constructed by society to confront this opposition and enable survivors to maintain a sense of reality. It appears that the rituals of death, in most societies, communicate not finality but the transcendence of death by some sort of afterlife. In an article published in the Harvard Theological Review, Calum Carmichael argues persuasively that a number of the exhortations in Deuteronomy can be understood in terms of a desire to counteract the traditional practices of the Hebrews in 'that grey area where life and death are intertwined'.[5] According to Carmichael, laws such as those prohibiting marking one's body for the dead, the seething of a kid in its mother's milk and the consumption of an animal that dies naturally, are all motivated by the desire of the lawmakers to separate life and death clearly, and the most plausible explanation for such a careful list of exhortations is that the common belief of the Israelites at the time was one they shared with most cultures, i.e. that no such clear distinction existed.[6]

Studies of death rituals in rural Greece support the notion that there is a constant shift between the religious perspective of a hereafter and a more commonsense perspective forced on the survivor by the realities of the body's decay and the attitude of other members of the community. Since the contradictions between these two perspectives cannot be resolved, attitudes to death in any community will always be, as Danforth and others have underlined, ambivalent.

Laments, in Danforth's study, are examined in the broader context of death rituals considered as rites of passage. The many parallels between marriage and death rites in Greece and other cultures, including the often identical laments sung at both occasions, confirm this structuralist analysis by seeming to mediate the opposition between life and death. The fearful mystery of death is reduced by likening it to a marriage, including the practice of dressing the corpse as a bride or groom. The funeral then becomes a wedding and the grave is likened to a new home. A popular lament recorded by Danforth in the village he calls 'Potamia' develops an elaborate metaphor of death-as-wedding. The dying man exhorts his companions not to inform his relatives he has died but rather to:

Just tell them that I have married and taken a good wife.
I have taken the tombstone as mother-in-law, the black earth as wife

and I've taken the little pebbles as brothers and sisters in law.[7]

By the use of such a metaphor, the finality of death is denied; it becomes a transition rather than a permanent state. Marriage is an appropriate mediating metaphor, since, like death, it involves separation and departure from one household to another. Within the laments, marriage and a journey to a distant land, both involving painful separation, can be seen as imperfect metaphors for the separation of death. In a number of cultures, including that of rural Greece, the death of a young person who has not yet married is regarded as especially tragic. At the funerals of such young people the links between marriage and death are usually made poignantly clear in laments. Among Iraqi Jews, as recently as the 1950s, two groups of women lamenters would chant antiphonally at such funerals, alternating wedding songs with laments.[8]

Danforth's analysis of laments extends the work done by Margaret Alexiou on Greek lament. Before summarizing Alexiou's work and more recent studies by Seremetakis, Caraveli-Chaves and others, I would like to look at laments in a cross-cultural perspective, not only in the context of the death rituals of a society, but as phenomena to be studied in their own right. It is interesting that laments and ritual wailing have, even within the study of death rituals, been generally marginalized by anthropologists. Since Hertz's study, death has been seen more as a social process than as a precise event. Laments have been considered as reinforcing the concept of liminality (Radcliffe-Brown 1964, Danforth 1982) through their metaphors of transition or as marking interrupted social relations, but other features of lament, such as their gender specificity and their relationship to the preservation of memory, have been largely neglected.

COMPARATIVE LAMENT STUDIES

Anthropologist and ethnomusicologist Steven Feld, whose work I will make considerable use of in my own analysis of laments, has suggested five lines along which laments might be explored:[9] (1) They could be considered as a form that exists on the borders of speech and song; (2) they could be analysed in terms of composition and performance, in order to establish a poetics of lament or extend the discussion of oral–formulaic theory; (3) they could be examined as a cultural expression of emotion; (4) as a gender-specific genre; and (5) as rituals giving voice to metaphors of transition. In this study I extend Feld's list to include the relationship of lament to memory, and to revenge. Since my purpose is to understand why laments have been perceived as a threat to society and how they have been subsumed and reworked in other artistic forms in Greece, I will be concerned, too, with the cultural reception of laments, and with the attitude of the non-performer towards the women who traditionally perform them.

One of the questions Feld has raised in his discussions of lament is why laments have been so long neglected. The answer, he suggests, has to do with the trivializing of emotion in modern western society (i.e. in the culture of the majority of anthropologists). Death may be kept at arm's length, but it is hard to trivialize. The weeping songs that invariably accompany it in societies where there is still a live oral tradition are seen as insignificant by a culture that eschews vocal displays of grief. From being distrusted and feared, laments have suffered a worse fate in the modern world: they have been seen as a minor element in the rituals of death, unworthy of serious attention in their own right. As anthropologists, folklorists and ethno-musicologists begin to focus on laments in other societies, they are realizing what an important part dirges play not only in the rituals of death but in the life of the community.

GENDER AND LAMENT

One point on which those who have studied lament in cultures as diverse as those of China, New Guinea, India, Greece, Saudi Arabia and Ireland agree is that laments are generally performed by women. Men and women both weep in these societies, but while men's weeping tends to be inarticulate, it is women who seem to be able to turn weeping into a controlled, often contemplative lament: 'tears become ideas,' as Feld puts it. In his work among the Kululi people of the Papuan rain forest in New Guinea, Feld notes the precise vocabulary the Kululi have for expressing the different ways men and women weep. In the lexicon of Kululi there are one general and five specific terms for what he calls 'patterned varieties of weeping'.[10] Of the three words that describe male weeping, all are immediate responses – they indicate respectively 'loud falsetto melodic weeping, startled weeping and loud, uncontrolled melodic weeping'. The two words that are used for female structured weeping are *gese-yelema*, 'a pitiful, sorrowful weeping that is particularly common when women weep to mourn children', a lament which mimics the call of the fruit-dove or *muni* (a bird linked, through the myth of 'The Boy who Became a Muni-bird', to all children's deaths), and *sa-yelema*, a more elaborate lament, again related to the call of the dove, but with a long improvised text.[11] *Sa-yelema* is considered 'the original sound form expressive of the sad state of loss and abandonment that is beyond the resources of talk'.[12] Because these two forms of weeping are considered as controlled performances, they are evaluated by other members of the tribe, and the lamenter's voice is compared with that of the dove. As Feld points out, the Kululi use the two poles of 'short out-of-control-hysterical-sad bird voice' and 'controlled-sorrowful-reflective bird voice' to characterize respectively male and female weeping. It is women, not men, in Kululi culture who are the makers of structured lament and their patterned weeping is considered to be the most moving human sound expression in their society 'because it is the closest sound to being a bird'.[13]

Kululi men's 'tuneful weeping' is frequently not a response to death, but to performances of drumming, dance or song. It takes place in the context of elaborate ceremonies such as the *gisaro*, in which men of one long-house community perform dances and songs for a neighbouring community in a ceremonial presentation of meat. Edward Schieffelin, in *The Sorrow of the Lonely and the Burning of the Dancers* (1976), describes how the men become so enraged at having been moved to tears by the song of the *gisaro* dancers that they burn the shoulders of the performers with flaming torches. The 'painful tension between grief, anger, intimacy, and violence becomes visible when someone from the audience angrily thrusts the torch out on the dancer's shoulder and then throws his arms around him, hugging him affectionately and wailing uncontrollably'.[14] Schieffelin's analysis of the reciprocity of emotion and aesthetics involved in the *gisaro* ceremony is too complex to reproduce here. It does, however, suggest why the word 'hysterical' or some cognate is used not of women's laments in Kululi, but of men's inarticulate wept song. While women's tears provoked by death and loss lead to artful song, it seems that men's tears, provoked by an art that is an interpretation or mimesis of loss, lead to anger and retribution.

Schieffelin's and Feld's research on the Kululi suggests parallels with Clifford Geertz's research on the Balinese cockfight.[15] According to Geertz, the cockfight enables the normally self-absorbed, composed Balinese men to discover what it is like to be attacked and 'driven to the extremes of fury'.[16] Geertz's concept of 'deep play' provokes a reading of the Balinese spectator sport of cockfighting that enables him to compare it to an artistic text like *Macbeth*. Just as we define ourselves in western society by playing out roles in our multiple readings of classical texts, so the cockfight becomes a model for the Balinese male 'to see a dimension of his subjectivity'.[17] According to Geertz, art or games do not merely represent experience, but affect it in turn. For the Kululi men, watching the *gisaro* seems to present a similar possibility. Their reaction to the song of the dancers provokes a more violent display of emotion than reality itself. Can it be that the 'deep play' of the cockfight, the *gisaro*, the bullfight or, say, the tragedies of Aeschylus are not so much re-enactments of life, but restructurings that give expression to what is constrained in 'real' life? Could one suggest that women, whose involvement with the dead body is an intimate one (in most societies it is women who tend the dying, wash the corpse and dress it) need no heightened retelling of the stories of death to comprehend its reality or to quicken their emotional response? They move from experience to art, from tears to ideas. Men, whose experience of death is, in many traditional societies, less physical, in that they do not tend the dying or handle the corpse except when they kill one another (a situation which demands a particular relationship to the dead-as-enemy) must re-read death in art or play in order to experience it. The movement, in this case, might be seen as the obverse of women's lamentation, one that progresses from ideas to tears.[18]

The confused welter of emotions provoked by *gisaro* dancers is not untypical of reactions to death itself among the Kululi. Death is never thought of as accidental, but is caused by enemies in the guise of witches or *seis*. This means that every death is taken to be murder. The kinsmen of the deceased are accordingly involved in a retaliatory raid to kill the *sei* considered responsible for their kinsman's death.[19] The emotions occasioned by death in such a society are a complex mixture of anger and sorrow. Similarly, among the Bedouin, death is regarded, whether justifiably or not, as caused by someone, and it provokes not only tears and laments, but long and bitter disputes over the cause of death often leading to retribution.[20] While these prolonged disputes continue, the women weep, at first in a kind of high-pitched, wordless wailing called *ayat*, and then in chanted lament.[21] Again there is a marked difference in the outward manifestation of grief between the sexes. What is described as 'crying' is, as among the Kululi, a structured lament performed by women that is perceived as deeply affecting:

> Beginning with a phrase whose English equivalent is 'woe is me,' the bereaved bewail their loss in 'crying'. Those consoling the bereaved bewail the loss of a person dear to them, usually a father or mother. . . . The special pitch and quavering of the voice, more exaggerated than in singing, along with the weeping and sobbing that often accompany it, make this heart-rending. The Bedouins do not equate 'crying' and singing, but they recognise the resemblance when questioned. The two are structurally equivalent, both being expressions of sadness that draw attention to the mourner's sorrow and bereavement.[22]

Men, in Bedouin society, do not 'cry' but sometimes weep silently. They embrace one another and often have to be torn from each others' arms. They advise their bereaved relatives to control themselves and console them by referring to the will and mercy of God. There is an interesting exception made for men to 'cry' in the ritual laments performed by descendants of local saints during the annual festivals at the tombs of saints or holy men: 'Men of the saintly lineage sing "poems" about their forefathers in a quivering voice as they move from tent to tent, blessing those who have come to pay their respects and cursing those who cross them. People describe this singing as "crying" over the saint.'[23] It is interesting that Bedouin men cry in a ceremonial context, and seem to be embarrassed by crying when it is not incorporated into a ritual performance.

It is worth remembering here that many of the major religions established in the Middle East are based on ritual lament. All of these lamenting religious cults focus on the unjust or untimely death of a young man or a god. In one group of cults a beautiful young man is mourned by his goddess-lover: Adonis is lamented by Aphrodite, the Babylonian Tammuz by Ishtar, Phrygian Attis by Cybele, Egyptian Osiris by his wife Isis. As might be expected in such cults, women play a prominent part, often leading the ceremonial weeping for the dead god. In the later religions of Christianity and Shiite Muhammadanism, the dead Christ and the prophet Husain are mourned not only by women relatives but by a group of disciples. The unjust death of these martyrs and their ritual laments re-enacted by the faithful become the central 'passion' of each religion, and in both, men have become the dominant mourners. Elias Canetti, whose interest in laments centres on the violent behaviour of what he terms the 'lamenting pack', cites the Muharram Festival of the Shiites as a terrifying example of the violent frenzy such a crowd engenders.[24] Canetti's observations are based on eye-witness accounts of the passion plays organized during the festivals and of the 'Day of Blood' in the streets of Teheran. The action of the passion play was preceded by a lament, begun by a Dervish accompanied by the audience, who beat their breasts in regular rhythm. Others joined the singing until the action of the play began. In a sequence of scenes, the suffering and death of Husain and his followers was re-enacted. During the performance the audience wept and groaned, beating themselves on the head or breast. But the real violence of the crowd took place in the city of Teheran at the feast of Ashura, when half a million people took to the streets. The faithful dressed in white shirts that would be covered in blood by evening as they mutilated themselves with swords. As their frenzy became more intense, many of the participants were fatally injured either by themselves or other members of the crowd who joined in the mayhem. Television coverage of the funeral of the Ayatollah Khomeini has made us familiar with the behaviour of the 'lamenting pack' in Iranian culture. While women were among the mourning crowd at the Ayatollah's funeral, the ritual was dominated by men and its violent moments were their preserve. It seems that such expressions of violent grief by men, when they form part of a culturally determined ritual, may be another instance of 'deep play', one which is difficult to control because

the border between spectator and observer is ill-defined. Martyrdom re-enacted creates new martyrs.

It is difficult to generalize on the basis of a limited number of
lament studies and to come to any conclusions as to why men
and women express grief differently. The largest comparative
study of lament to date (Rosenblatt, Walsh and Jackson 1976)
dealt with seventy-eight cultures, and found that while it was
not always possible to observe a gender difference in mourning,
in the majority of cultures women expressed grief more often
and in a different form from men. The researchers suggest that
one reason why women express their grief more frequently and
openly than men is that they experience loss more deeply
because their emotional ties are stronger. A second explanation
they offer is that weeping can be interpreted as a cry for help
and that women are thought to be more disposed to ask for help
in the crisis engendered by bereavement. Lastly, they suggest
that the manifestations of grief: weeping, tearing one's hair and
clothes and so on, may reflect women's lower social status.
Women are thought to be free to express their grief openly,
whereas it is regarded as not fitting for men, or presumably
women of a higher social standing, to do so.

The evidence from the Homeric poems and from the early
medieval poetry in western Europe suggests that, even in
western cultures, men may have once expressed grief at least as
openly and extravagantly as women, the explanations that
Rosenblatt *et al.* put forward for a common pattern of gender-
specific grieving seem to me to beg more questions than they
answer. It is impossible to come to any conclusions about
which sex feels grief more, and it seems naïve, particularly in
the light of more searching studies like that of Feld or Alexiou,
to interpret women's reflective and carefully structured laments
as cries for help. As for the relationship between social status
and grief, there may be some truth in the perceived relationship
between expressions of mourning and social status in some
societies, but it is difficult to sort out which came first. Is it
because women are of lower social status that they are free to
mourn the dead in an obvious fashion, or is it that they are
perceived as lower in status because they indulge in loud
lamentation? There are suggestions that women in cultures
where lament is still considered an art actually enjoy a certain
status *because* of their skill in lament. Studies of the Ingrians of

Finland and Russia[25] and in rural Greece[26] stress the anomalies between the social position of women in the cultures they describe and the powerful role they play as lamenters. Caraveli-Chaves goes as far as to say that lament establishes a bridge not only between the living and the dead but between 'the powerful and the oppressed, women and men. ... it is the oppressed woman of the "patriarchal" Greek village world who is the manipulator of the magical language of the lament, which can draw bridges across these disparate realms, transforming lamentation into equipment for living'.[27] Similarly, Nenola-Kallio concludes that: 'Women whose living conditions make them from time to time wish for their own death or that of their child make themselves vulnerable by offering themselves as preservers of the cosmic order in a social crisis caused by death. By expressing their grief and loss they at the same time seek in culture a solution to the conflict of life and death which, because of their outlook on the world and their biological role, is always latent in them.'[28]

Strong evidence against any explanation of the gender specificity of lament based on the helplessness or low social status of women seems to be the legislation or official imprecations directed against women's lament from the sixth century BC onwards in Greece. I will discuss that legislation in detail in chapter 3, but it hardly supports a notion of lament as the expression of the helpless and downtrodden. Rather, it would suggest a belief in women's laments or lamenting women as a force to be reckoned with. Plutarch's remarks about mourning as 'something feminine, weak and ignoble; women are more inclined to it than men, barbarians more than Hellenes, commoners more than aristocrats',[29] are indicative of the rhetoric used to justify the suppression of female mourning. They may typify the sentiments of the aristocracy of his day, but by lumping together mourning, women and barbarians, Plutarch reveals more about Greek chauvinism than about the essential nature of lament.

If we accept that women are the ones who, in most societies, turn tears of grief into structured laments, we can view the discrediting of lament as merely an extension of male chauvinism in a patriarchal society, but I think that there is more to it than that. The male/female opposition displayed in attempts to suppress lament is based, it would seem, on a recognition of women's traditional control of the community's relationship with its dead, and of the authority conferred by such control. There is undoubtedly a strong element of fear involved in the legislation against lament, a fear based on the association of laments not only with the dead, but with possession, madness and violence.

LAMENT AND MADNESS

As Foucault has demonstrated, madness, as western man defines it, is an invention of his own imagination, one that takes different forms in different ages.[30] The Ship of Fools or *Narrenschiff* was the Renaissance's answer to the medieval spectre of leprosy as a symbol of the macabre. The symbolic Dance of Death that horridly preoccupies the medieval imagination is supplanted, during the Renaissance, by a more benign image – the Dance of Fools. Mockery of madness replaces the solemnity of death and fear turns inwards towards irony.[31] If Foucault has demonstrated that madness and death can succeed one another, from one age to another, as central preoccupations of western imagination, we should not be surprised that the rituals of death can also be confused with or appear to be identical to the manifestations of madness. The witch and the shaman, the medium and the wailing woman are all seen, at some historical moment or in some particular culture, as being possessed by dangerous powers, but the lamenter, in her ritual dialogue with death, may be viewed as linking madness to death in a unique equivalence. Like the witch, who inverts the basic premise of society through her occult powers and becomes sexually ambiguous with her symbol of domesticity protruding aggressively from between her legs,[32] so the lamenter turns the patriarchal society upside down by her authority over the rituals of death.

In rural Ireland the connection between lamenting or 'keening' women and madness is explicit in the traditional folk culture. The women who sang, until recently, the long improvised laments called *caoineadh*[33] were sometimes semi-professionals, otherwise relatives of the dead. Called *bean chointe*, they were traditionally portrayed with dishevelled hair, their clothes awry and their feet bare. Rather than following roads or paths they were said to travel 'over the mountain', leaping in the air on hearing of their loved one's death and drinking the blood of the deceased upon finding him.[34] In an interesting parallel with Greek folk lament, the Virgin is portrayed in Irish tradition as a typical wailing woman with loosened hair and bare feet who leaps and even drinks blood. The motifs used to depict mourning women, motifs extended to the lamenting Virgin Mary, also characterize the behaviour of *geilt* or madmen. Following the example of Padraig O'Riain,[35] Partridge tries to explain the connection between mourning women and madmen in the Irish tradition in terms of van Gennep's rites of passage theory. According to such a theory, the mourning person is in a state of transition, a liminal state which involves a withdrawal from society. During this period the individual may be encouraged to act or choose to act in a way that is the opposite of his or her normal, culturally defined status.

The self-mutilation which is a common feature of mourning in numerous cultures, the obvious connection with possession in the mourner's dialogue with the dead, and the inversion of common male/female roles in ritual mourning may all contribute to the perception of lamenting women as both mad and dangerous. In the carnival-like atmosphere induced by death, the world is turned upside-down. Social organization is temporarily disrupted and new relationships must be formed so that the fabric of society can be reknit. But just as there is a liminal period for the bereaved, so there is a period of readjustment between the old social order that included the deceased, and the new, in which his absence will be the occasion for a restatement of relationships. In this liminal phase, the Dance of Death and the Dance of Fools may become indistinguishable. Death provides women with the licence to express themselves that is denied them in normal life, but lest they consolidate their temporary power, and the world remain topsy-turvy, it may be seen, at least in retrospect, as aberration, even as madness.[36]

Despite the association of lamenting women with madness in some cultures, there is evidence from a number of studies of lament that the poetic expression of grief is perceived by the lamenters themselves not only as an emotional outburst but as a means of mediating that emotion and thereby avoiding the excesses of madness that death might otherwise provoke. In the modern Greek context it is not generally the bereaved relatives themselves who sing laments; they are regarded as being in too great distress to articulate their grief at the time of death. Rather, it is a group of women who have usually experienced bereavement themselves and can recreate their emotional responses at one remove. Bereaved women who express their grief in a wild or unrestrained fashion may be reprimanded by other women and told to join in the singing.[37] Danforth found that in the village he calls 'Potamia', 'The women ... generally agree that the singing of laments is preferable to wild shouting and wailing as a means of expressing grief at death rituals. Many women believe that such shouting is physically harmful and may cause illness. It is also likely that during this period of uncontrolled shouting the bereaved relative of the deceased may say something inappropriate or embarrassing.'[38] A series of photographs taken by Mary Vouras at the *Epitaphios* ceremony in a Greek village supports Danforth's observations. We see the ceremony suddenly interrupted by a woman who has recently lost several of her relatives. She screams and cries out in what appears to be a mixture of grief and rage at her loss. The women in the church immediately surround her and encourage her to sing a lament while the priest ignores her outburst, continuing to intone the liturgy. As the women join the bereaved, singing their own laments, she gradually calms herself. What began as a despairing wail has been channelled by a tradition of participation in one another's grief, into a structured lament.[39]

LAMENT AND EMOTION

The observations of Danforth and Vouras are not unique. It has been widely observed that laments are perceived by those who perform them as fulfilling an emotionally necessary, even a satisfying, function both for the lamenter and the bereaved. This therapeutic aspect of lament is related but not identical to the liminal aspect of lament, to lament as a bridge between the living and the dead. The apparent contradiction between the identification of lamenting women with insanity or wildness and a perception of lament as calming and controlling violent emotion may be partly a difference of viewpoint between participant and observer. Women who lament are more likely to see their role as therapeutic than men who observe them; although there is evidence in rural Greece, for example, that men regard women's laments as both beneficial and desirable.

To die 'unwept' by one's female relatives, is still a serious misfortune. Cultural differences between attitudes to laments, and divergent attitudes to lament within a particular culture are also related to the broader question of how a particular society views emotion.

Emotion is a difficult subject to discuss even in one's own society, let alone in comparative terms. It is one thing to observe that weeping and laments are almost universal phenomena, quite another to come to any conclusions about how they relate to any given culture's construction of emotion. And yet if we accept that laments are a universal response to bereavement, any discussion of lament is meaningless unless we make some attempt to understand how the emotional response to death is expressed, even controlled through wept songs. To understand, however imperfectly, how emotion and lament are related in Greece or any other culture also involves understanding the particular cultural assumptions of our own view of emotion.

It may be commonplace to assert that women are thought to be more emotional than men in western societies, but it is one of the few undisputed assumptions in a long and often contradictory discourse about emotion that begins with Plato and continues through the early Christian fathers to the modern age. In an attempt to understand what she calls 'the Euroamerican construction of emotion', and to see how it functions as an ideology within the broader power relations of our society, Catherine Lutz identifies a number of key assumptions about emotion which are widely held if not necessarily compatible.[40]

A primary western notion is that emotion stands in contrast both to thought and to estrangement. The first is the more common opposition, and although Lutz claims that it has a long genealogy, the dichotomy has never gone unchallenged. It was by no means clear in ancient Greece and can probably be traced, in western philosophy, no further back than Hume.[41] The contrast frequently drawn between 'affect' and 'cognition', 'passion' and 'reason', 'feeling' and 'thinking' is linked, as Lutz points out, to a wider series of paired concepts such as irrational/rational, vulnerable/controlled, chaos/order, physical/mental, female/male. While these paired oppositions frequently devalue emotion, emotion is positively ranged against estrangement or alienation as part of another series of paired concepts that include life/death, community/individualism, natural/cultural, authentic/contrived. This positive view of emotion, prominent during the Romantic period, has continued to influence our own popular culture, in which the stereotype of the alien who possesses superior intelligence but lacks emotion is not uncommon.

The contradictions inherent in the concepts of emotion vs. rationality and emotion vs. alienation may be viewed as symptomatic of the contradictions of modern western society, or as allowing for ambivalence. They are strongly tied, as Lutz demonstrates, to the social practices of Euroamerican life. In situations where emotion is devalued, it is frequently associated with chaos. Modern thinkers may credit the emotionally chaotic part of the human brain as a necessary underpinning for rationality and social organization (cf. Freud's unconscious and Durkheim's 'collective effervescence'), but the energy of disorderly emotions is perceived as dangerous to others and weakening to those experiencing them. Conversely, the irrationality of emotions may be viewed as mysterious and as an attractive alternative to the coolly rational.

If, as Lutz claims, modern western society has focused on rationality as a measure of the mature and sensible man, confining emotion to the category of irrational, then 'all those occasions and individuals in which emotion is identified can be dismissed ... [and] it becomes sensible to label "emotional" those who would be discounted'.[42] It is worth keeping in mind that critiques of reason have always arisen simultaneously with defences of reason in western philosophy from Xenophon to Nietszche and Hume, and that feminist critiques are original in their focus on gender difference, rather than their opposition to what is perceived as the contemporary bias in favour of reason.[43] While some feminists are loathe to perpetuate the divisions of gender by describing women's thinking as intuitive or emotional, others allow for the possibility of a different type of rationality, not necessarily innately female, but culturally conditioned over many centuries, that gives value to women's ways of knowing and caring.[44] However the debate is resolved, and however women categorize themselves, there is general agreement in feminist scholarship that western society has taken the 'emotional' nature of women as a given, a quality that places them in a category of irrational and unreliable beings like children, and even, more recently, like terrorists. The connection between emotion and perceived threats to authority has to do with the concept of emotion as wild and disorderly. Emotional outbursts are not only a threat to law and order; they can lead to physical violence.

The notion that emotions are biological imperatives, that they just happen, lies behind the traditional leniency towards 'crimes of passion'. Such an attitude presupposes that the emotions 'blind' us or 'carry us away', and that the person who is under the sway of strong emotions is potentially both vulnerable and dangerous. In a society which sees the emotional as weak, those who have no power are defined as more emotional, often excessively emotional. In ancient Greece, the connection between emotionality, women and barbarians is made explicit by Plutarch. Emotional beings are also thought to be more physical. Psychological theories of emotion frequently view it as synonymous with its physical symptoms, or as originating in the body as distinct from the mind. Lévi-Strauss defines emotions as being 'always *results* either of the power of the body or the impotence of the mind'.[45] Despite recent attempts to develop cognitive theories of emotion, the common perception of emotions in our society is still one that defines emotion as physical and 'natural' as opposed to cultural. This creates a problem for cultural anthropologists who try to describe the emotional aspects of culture. How are we to account for differences in apparent emotional responses in diverse cultures if emotions are 'natural'? Some anthropologists have claimed that it is culturalization that masks or disguises the real emotions, that emotions are 'precultural facts'. What concerns them is the relationship between these facts and cultural facts such as common beliefs and social institutions.

Perhaps the most commonly held belief about emotion in the west is that women have more of it than men. Both in popular culture and in academic and clinical communities, women have consistently been portrayed as more 'naturally' emotional and more emotionally expressive than men.[46] The expression of emotional pain, such as that induced by death, is considered especially the preserve of women. Women in cultures as diverse as those of Finland, the New Guinea highlands and Greece are regarded as having a superior ability to express such pain in laments. The reasons given for their greater capacity vary from their physical experience of childbirth to the timbre of their voices, but in many cultures it is clearly considered to be innate.

Anger, according to Lutz, is the only emotion where men are generally thought to exceed women in the depth of their response, but their anger is usually considered a justifiable response to a particular stimulus, whereas women's anger is seen as more diffuse and irrational. This may be true of modern Euroamerican culture, but it is not so in cultures where the law of vendetta prevails, or where there has been a history of political repression such as Ireland or the Israeli-occupied territories. Nor does it reflect the portrayal of women in Greek tragedy. In the southern Peloponnese, where blood feuds were common at least until the 1950s, women's laments for the dead were frequently an inspiration for revenge. The anger of the mother or sister of a murdered man, expressed in the form of a lengthy narrative dirge, seems to have spurred male relatives to retaliatory murder, sometimes shaming the tardy or acting as a sort of ritual preparation.

Even if it is not biologically but rather socially determined, arising from women's greater engagement in interpersonal relationships, women's capacity to feel and express emotions, particularly through tears, is still thought to be 'natural'. Men's disengagement, in this context, is seen as unnatural and culture bound. It is by association, in our society, with nature rather than culture, with the subjective rather than the objective, that emotion swings uncertainly between two poles in the domain of ethics and morality. Viewed as the moral centre of our being – the heart as opposed to the head – our emotions can be a reliable guide to moral action. If our heart is in the right place, we are liable to try, at least, to do good. On the other hand, the whole intellectual framework of our society is one which views dispassionate observation of the factual as essential for the advancement of knowledge. Morality as a guide to public ethics cannot, within such a scheme, be allowed to depend on the subjective perception of the emotions, but must be arrived at by attempting to eliminate emotion from any considerations of at least public morality. As Lutz points out, 'morality ... bears a contradictory relation to the concept of emotion.'[47]

If it is clear that the attitude of western culture towards emotion is ambivalent, there is no reason to suppose that any other culture has an unequivocal response to it. There may be circumstances in any culture when to feel deeply and respond visibly are considered appropriate. Death is an occasion where one would expect a universal approbation of strong emotional reaction and response, yet even towards death there is wide variation in attitudes to the outward expression of grief. Wailing and laments, which are the commonest responses we know of to death, are no longer common in the modern western world, and in the cultures where they are found they may be valued, despised or feared, often simultaneously. As a form of emotional expression, usually practised by women, the ambivalence can be comprehended as part of the broader question of a particular culture's response to emotion and the differing expressions of feeling expected of men and women in that society.

Since emotion, and expressions of emotion are, in western society, frequently considered in opposition to the rational, one would not expect laments to be regarded as expressions of thought. They may be seen in the same way as unstructured crying is frequently seen, as serving some useful communal function. They may also be viewed as a moving, aesthetic response to death or separation, but they have not been generally associated with complex ideas. And yet what emerges from recent studies of laments as practised in a number of cultures, from the highlands of New Guinea to the villages of rural Greece, is that laments can be at once emotional and deeply thoughtful. They seem to be a means of exploring the pain of grief and loss in a form of communal expression that is both communicative and structured. Within the traditional metres and melodic formulas a particular culture or subculture uses for lament, additional text will be added to fit the particular occasion of an individual's death. The pre-existent structures into which laments are fitted may themselves help to structure or control grief, turning 'thoughtless' weeping into a thoughtful emotional response, but it is the individual lamenter who adds to the traditional stock of music and text formulas in order to heighten and channel emotional response. In this sense performers of lament are creators, folk poets. It is tempting to speculate that the individual creators of laments are the fore-runners of all 'tragic' poetry, but since we can no more establish the veracity of such a hypothesis than we can the notion of ancient matriarchal societies preceding patriarchies, we run the risk of damaging the credibility of a much more verifiable thesis. It can be established by analysis of texts that literary genres have drawn heavily on folk laments as a source of inspiration. In later chapters I will be examining how and why two literary genres of fifth-century BC Athens appropriated the function and forms of lament as they engaged in a dialogue with death, and how the poets of modern Greece have continued that dialogue. Before that, another element of lament needs to be examined.

LAMENT AND MEMORY

Besides expressing and channelling emotion, lamenters are also responsible for inscribing or, perhaps one could more accurately say, keeping the memory of the deceased alive. The expression is an interesting one. In formal English the imagery of committing something to memory is firmly linked to the processes of writing – inscribe, imprint, engrave, impress – whereas the informal expressions – keep, hold, carry, bear in mind – suggest a different attitude to memory as a weighty substance, a load to carry or preserve in the storehouse of the mind. This imagery is reinforced, in laments from many cultures, by the common practice of amassing proper names. The separation and loss that dislocate the life of the individual and interrupt normal social intercourse demand not only an emotional expression of pain, but the restoration of a sense of permanence. The careful preservation of the memory of the deceased, not only through praise of individual attributes but frequently by the construction of a complex map of the social and physical landscape the individual inhabited, seems to fulfil a need not only in the bereaved but in the community. Bruce Chatwin, in his book, *The Songlines*, demonstrates the importance of topographical names to the Australian Aboriginals. By naming every tree, rocky outcrop or creek in song, the Aboriginal is singing the world into existence. Each individual, according to Chatwin's sources, has his own songline which may be linked or criss-crossed by many others. Consequently, the whole of Australia can be read as a sort of musical score.[48] Among such nomadic cultures, where people and landscape are linked in a complex organic relationship, the naming process may be in part a mnemonic device for survival, but the prevalence of toponyms in laments suggests another relationship between naming and memory. In the narrative laments from Mani, as in the laments

from the New Guinea highlands, proper names and place names
that locate the dead person firmly in memory may be a device
for anchoring the nebulous dead in the concrete surroundings of
the survivor. By the repeated naming of proper names, the
lamenter also makes personal what may otherwise be a conventional formula of mourning. In the following lament from
Mani, composed by the mother of Sravrianis Doureka at her
funeral in 1932, the lamenter lists the villages where her
daughter was admired:

'Ε ζηλεμένη Σταβριανή,
οπού ζε προζηλεύασι
προσηλιακά κι αποσκιερά
κι από τη χώρα του Παχύ
κι από τη Δρυαλί κι απ'Αργιλιά
κι από τα Κολοκυθιανά.[49]

Eh, beloved Stavriani,
wherever they set their gaze on you
the sunlit and the shady slopes
from Hora of Pahi
from Driali and from Argilia
and from Kolokythiana.

Similarly in the well-known Maniot lament 'Tis Ligorous' or
'Tou Vetoula' (1828–30?), the sister of Vetoulas, after hearing
of his murder, does not answer but goes to sit in the natural
amphitheatre of the old stone quarry where her sister-in-law
finds her:

Στα Αλικα που έφτασε
στη Λατομά που πέρασε
στα Αλικα στη Λατομά
στο παταράκι τ'Αγιαντριάς
Χάμου στη ρούγα εκάθοντα
δεν εχαιρέτα πούπετα.[50]

At Alika where she arrived
at Latoma where she passed by
at Alika at Latoma
in the little amphitheatre of St Andreas,
she sat down in the rocky yard
and greeted no one.

In this case it is the bereaved who is firmly placed in a landscape whose every feature she names as she remembers her own pain. Similarly, in a Kululi lament recorded by Feld, there is a reiteration of both proper names and place names that forms 'a map of shared experiences' and gives the lament a quality of 'hardness' that the Kululi admire:[51]

Cross-cousin, you and I were together at the bank of Sago creek,
Cross-cousin, we were together by the dead trunk of a *we* tree there, cross-cousin, cross-cousin,
Cross-cousin, Cross cousin, I'm wondering if you've gone to Olabia, cross-cousin,
Cross-cousin, I'm wondering if you've gone to Duda's father's place, cross cousin,
Cross-cousin, I'm wondering if you've gone to Gania's husband's place, cross-cousin, cross-cousin.

In Feld's elaborate analysis of this lament, completed after seven months of discussion, playing back of his recording to the performers and other members of the community, walking over the landscape to observe the features named in the text, and transcribing the music, he concluded that the text was itself like a song because its images formed a logical pattern. He also became aware that it was full of hidden meanings encoded into it by the careful sequence of names that gave it an angry edge (another dimension of the hardness that was admired?). In the next chapter, where I analyse some of the revenge laments from Mani, it will be seen that the Maniot *moirologhístra* develops a similar structure in her text by the ordered sequence of names that map a social and physical landscape.[52]

MUSICAL FEATURES OF LAMENT

What is remarkable about a performance such as the wept lament recorded by Feld is that it occurs spontaneously, as an immediate response to grief, and yet it is admired for its careful crafting. The other thing the Kululi praised about this particular performance of lament was that it was 'really like an *iyeu* bird' (ornate fruitdove). In a society where the dead are believed to 'go' as birds, the song of this dove is found particularly moving:

> Weeping is the sound form most directly associated with becoming a bird, which is to say, the sound form most closely associated with death and loss. While seemingly more complex, song is less direct and never a truly improvised and spontaneous embodiment of sadness ...[The lament] is constructed as a modality of melodic weeping with a specific pitch code that turns it into a melodic-sung-texted-weeping in contexts of death and loss. . . . Moving from spontaneous and improvised to compositionally crafted weeping creates an aesthetic tension demanding the response that, like the deceased, the weeper, too, has become a bird.[53]

The question of the relationship of voice quality and pitch to emotional expression, specifically to the grief and anger induced by death, is something that has been very little considered in studies of Greek lament. In ancient Greece there is considerable literary evidence to suggest that birds were classified in an elaborate symbolic system comparable with the one Feld examined among the Kululi, but the precise relationship between bird call and human sound or song in antiquity is something we can only guess at. Regarding the pitch, timbre and tuning of instruments, we have limited knowledge, but that these musical elements were associated with certain emotions we know from various sources, including Plato. Modern Greek studies of lament have concentrated largely on the texts of laments to the exclusion of musical considerations.[54] My own reading of modern Greek folk laments in the chapter that follows will focus largely on textual analysis, but I hope to show that it is impossible to ignore the non-verbal qualities of lament even in the absence of a recording or score. We must at least be aware that the reaction of a contemporary audience to any lament, including those we find in classical tragedy, were as much conditioned by their musical structure, the timbre and pitch of the lead lamenter's individual voice, her sobs, moans, shrieks and sighs and by the polyphonic texture of the women's voices, as they were by the text.

CONCLUSION

It should be clear from the discussion so far that any attempt to understand how laments function and why they should be regarded as potentially harmful in a society like that of ancient Greece will involve much broader issues involving societal attitudes to life and death, to emotion and memory, to women and to music.

In the following chapters I will try to make some contribution to our understanding of the nature of Greek folk laments by analysing the texts of a group of laments from various regions of Greece. In chapter 3, I will focus on the revenge laments of Inner Mani not only because these long, narrative texts suggest the potential for violent revenge inherent in such a genre, but because they fly in the face of many of our western preconceptions about the nature of women, death and grieving. In my analysis, I will make the assumption, based on Margaret Alexiou's classic study, that these laments are related, through a continuous oral tradition dating back at least as far as the Homeric period, to the laments of ancient Greece. What we know of traditional women's laments in other cultures, but particularly those of modern Greece, is, I believe, as relevant to our understanding of the laws of Solon, as it is to our reading of tragedy. It is not my concern to point to other possible continuities between ancient and modern Greece, but rather to extend the discussion of lament begun by Alexiou. It is worth keeping in mind, perhaps, that in the twentieth century, as in the fifth century BC, there has been a shift in Greece from a largely oral tradition to a literary one, and that women's traditional laments are, for reasons that may not be wholly unrelated to their demise in antiquity, now devalued and disappearing in most areas of the country. The absence of laments, as I hope to demonstrate, not only impoverishes society by depriving it of a structured emotional response to death. It takes from women and places in the mouths of institutional and public figures what women have always been perceived as doing better than men: expressing the inexpressible pain and separation of death.

Chapter 2

The painful art: women's laments for the dead in rural Greece

I'm a real Maniot woman
and a hard rock of the Morea.
(Maniot lament)

SINGING ONE'S OWN FATE

The most extensive examination of laments in Greece remains Margaret Alexiou's *The Ritual Lament in Greek Tradition* (1974). In her study of laments from Homer and the classical period to the present day, Alexiou established that there was a continuous tradition linking various popular and learned forms of the lament in Greece. The modern Greek word for lament, μοιρολόγι (*moirolói*), as she pointed out, was, despite some attempts to argue otherwise, almost certainly composed of the two ancient elements, *moira* (fate) and *logos* (speech, word).[1] As it first appears in the *Life of Alexander*, attributed to Pseudo-Kallisthenes (*c*.300 BC), the word is used as a verb, *moirologō*, meaning just what one would imagine it to mean: I foretell my own fate or doom.[2] The connection of foretelling one's own fate to lament, Alexiou suggests, is familiar from tragedy, where, among others, Antigone, Cassandra, Oedipus, Jocasta, Medea and Phaedra all lament their own fate (*moira* or *tyche*). The notion of *moira* as man's allotted fate is a common one in funeral inscriptions and most literary genres in ancient Greece. This sense of the word survived through the popular Greek literature of the Alexandrian, Roman and Byzantine periods. The modern Greek folk tradition of the *moirolói* as a ritual lament, especially one for the dead, is connected not to the personification of *moira* or *tyche* as the spinner or writer of one's fate, but rather to the belief in the three weaving women or *moirai* who determine one's fate at birth by 'writing' their marks on the face of children.[3] There has probably always been some overlap in the two senses of the word *moirolói*. In any case it is useful to keep the etymology of the word in mind, because, as we will see, the women who lament the dead in the Greek folk tradition are frequently more concerned with lamenting their own fate than with that of the deceased.

No one would dispute that the common word for a lament in modern Greece is *moirolói*, but when it comes to classifying the various types of *moirológhia*, and determining how they differ from other types of song, or from ritual wailing, we find ourselves in the sort of murky confusion that inhibits all attempts at strict taxonomy of a living tradition. In an article published in 1981,[4] Michael Herzfeld warns against the dangers of absolute generic distinctions in classifying such genres as τραγούδια (songs) and μοιρολόγια (laments). Herzfeld points out the limitations of Simos Menardos' attempt to distinguish the two genres in terms of their ritual context. Menardos, he claims, fails to see that wedding songs (τραγούδια) and funeral laments conform to the same pattern in a number of respects.[5] As I have pointed out in chapter 1, this similarity between wedding songs and laments is common to many cultures and may be explained partially by the fact that weddings in cultures like rural Greece, most of which is virilocal, involve the departure of the bride from her parents' home, and often from her village. It is frequently the mother and other female relatives of the bride who sing these wedding laments, mourning her prospective absence in much the same way as they mourn a son or husband who emigrates to another country to work.[6] The Greek folk saying: 'Δεν υπάρχει γάμος άκλαυτος και νεκρός αγέλαστος' (There's no such thing as a wedding unwept-over or a death without laughter), suggests that there is a popular recognition of the ambiguous relationship between these two rites of passage.

Recognizing the ambivalence in the conceptual relationship between the wedding song (or wedding lament) and the funeral lament, Herzfeld proceeds to demonstrate ambiguities in the lexical configuration of these terms. He allows that a lament is and is not a song, but he maintains the complementary opposition of *tragoúdhi* and *moirolói* in terms of their respective emotive character. 'Any description of graveside laments as *traghudhia*,' according to Herzfeld, 'must be metaphorical, nonsensical, or ironic.'[7] I would be more cautious than Herzfeld in stating just what a *moirolói* is and is not. In the region of southern Mani called Inner Mani, a region especially noted for its laments by Greeks themselves, the term *moirolói* is used for a much wider variety of material than in other regions. The Maniot writer and folklorist, Kassis, goes as far as to say that: 'The *moirolói* is *tragoúdhi*, the demotic song of Mani.'[8] It is true that, apart from what are called 'dancing songs', heard at weddings or celebrations, laments have become the most common form of song in Mani. It is still common for men to sing laments as 'table songs' in the same way as Klephtic and Akritic ballads would be performed in other regions. There is even, as in Crete, a whole class of satiric Maniot *moirológhia* that ridicule the most solemn of dirges while remaining nominally within the same category. In Thessaly and Epirus, instrumental pieces for clarinet, played outside the context of funerals, are designated *moirológhia*, although I have not found a musician able to articulate why they are so termed.[9] It may be, as Herzfeld suggests, that we need more holistic studies of lament, such as those of Anna Caraveli-Chaves, Nadia Seremetakis or Loring Danforth, in order to arrive at an understanding of how *moirológhia* are differentiated from and related to other genres of song and speech. On the other hand, there is a danger, in narrowing one's focus to the compass of a particular village and to a discrete time period, of missing important elements that a broader, comparative study allows. Keeping in mind that paradoxes abound in Greek folk culture, I propose to accept the designation given to the laments for the dead by the performers themselves, rather than adopt those of a particular researcher. This will mean that, in my analysis of *moirológhia*, I include the long narrative laments of Mani, some of which have passed into the general repertoire of songs sung by men and women on occasions other than funerals.

SOURCES: MANIOT LAMENTS

The first recordings I made of *moirológhia* were in 1979. Vasiliki Tsakanika was from the village of Veltsista near Iannina, in Epirus, and was known for her performances of various types of song, especially laments. Her grandson asked me to record her singing before she died, and I took the opportunity of one of her visits to Athens to invite her to my house. She was already in frail health and I expected her to sing three or four laments. Once she began, though, there was no stopping her. For nearly two hours she sang, sometimes breaking down and weeping or commenting on her own performance, but unwilling to rest until she had completed her repertoire. Talking to Kyria Vasso and to other women who are regarded as fine *moirologhístres*, or performers of lament, gave me some idea about how lamenting women see themselves, while my discussions with Greek women and men about laments has helped me form some generalizations about how lamenting women are viewed. My other sources of recorded laments, apart from those that are commercially available, come from the singer Mariza Koch, who has been a performer of and collector of laments for many years, and from the ethnomusicologist Sotiris Chianis, who allowed me to make use of his field recordings made in Arcadia in 1956. Published collections of lament texts and studies of lament by other researchers have supplied the remainder of my data, and it is on a particular collection of laments made by a Greek who is not a professional ethnographer that I intend to focus my attention in this study. Kyriakos Kassis's collection of laments of Inner Mani is the most extensive anthology of this genre to date and although the texts are not accompanied by musical notation, the multiple versions from various sources are transcribed from field recordings made over a period of twenty years.[10] The texts are accompanied by historical commentary and recorded interviews with performers. Kassis, himself a native of Inner Mani and from a family that includes a number of well-known lamenters, collected information and laments from 138 sources and made recordings of hundreds of laments. The broad scope of Kassis's anthology, together with its narrow geographical focus, makes it possible to trace diachronic changes in the laments as well as synchronic variation.

One reason why I have focused on the Maniot laments is because many of them are concerned not only with the pain of loss, but with revenge and retribution. The infamous blood feuds of Inner Mani, which began, as far as can be determined, as early as the fourteenth century and were still being fought at

least as late as the Second World War, have been the subject of
a great deal of commentary.[11] In lengthy narrative laments,
women whose male relatives had been killed by members of a
rival family sang the dead man's tale and called for the death of
his murderers, often threatening to kill the guilty parties themselves. These are unusual laments for modern Greece, where
blood feuding is not a common practice, but they may shed
some light on why laments came into bad repute in the Athens
of Solon's day, during a period when blood feuds still existed,
and why they occupy such an important place in tragedy.

It has been the custom, among Greek ethnographers, to
divide laments proper from eschatological songs (so-called
'Τραγούδια του Κάτου Κόσμου') that deal with the common
Greek folk portrayal of a dark Hades ruled by Charos and his
wife. But such a division is hard to maintain when so many
laments contain references to the underworld, and songs about
the underworld are frequently performed in the ritual context of
a funeral. Another distinction that is sometimes made is between
the composed or generalized laments that are part of a standard
repertoire in a given region, and that may be used by lamenters
regardless of the particular circumstances of death, and the
personalized lament addressed by a female relative to the
deceased. It is to this category that the majority of laments of
Inner Mani belong. These spare, unadorned narratives are not
the most immediately appealing laments of Greece. Indeed, they
do not always follow the conventions of imagery, theme and
structure found in other regions of the country. In their stark
confrontation with death Maniot laments seem to be hewn from
the same unforgiving material as the landscape that nurtures
their creators. As the mother of Yiorgos Kossonakos described
herself in the lament she composed for her son known as 'Του
Κορφιωτακη' (Korfiotakis' Lament):

I'm a real Maniot woman
and hard rock of the Morea.

I have already indicated that the term *moirolói* seems to be
applied by the Maniots more broadly than it is in other parts of
Greece. *Moirológhia* are even performed as work songs, and it
was while working in an olive press in 1968 that Kassis made a
number of his recordings of fellow workers. The oldest of
laments that have become part of the general repertoire of

occasional song may have been added to or altered by men or women as they were passed down from one generation to the next, but no one disputes that they are women's songs originally composed and performed either at a funeral or at one of the memorial services that take place after three, nine, forty days, six months and a year following a death. The lamenter herself may forget exactly what she sang at the time of her grief, but there are always members of her audience who are careful followers of lament (according to Kassis, in Mani these *aficionados* are more often men than women). If her lament is skilled, the *moirologhístra*'s creation will be admired and appropriated into the repertoire of what might be termed lament-as-song. If not, it is likely to be satirized for its metrical faults and lack of sequence.[12]

GENDER AND LAMENT IN MANI AND OTHER REGIONS OF GREECE

Men may sing laments but women are almost always the makers of lament in Greece. Why is it specifically a woman's role to lament the dead in this culture? Is there anything gender-specific about the way Greek women confront death or orchestrate the reaction of the community to a death through their laments? Do women hear or 'read' laments differently from men? And what of the reaction of Greek men to lament? Where it is negative, is it so because lament is clearly a woman's art?

Recent studies by anthropologists Anna Caraveli-Chaves and Nadia Seremetakis have attempted to answer some of these questions. Seremetakis argues for antiphony as the dominant organizational principle of the laments of Mani. In her view the antiphony of performance, expressed in the interchange between soloist and chorus, underscores a broader relationship of small female lament group to the community, and of women to men. The interchange becomes 'a formal procedure for the production and reception of jural discourse and for the cultural construction of truth . . . .[as well as] a political strategy that organises the relationship of women to male-dominated institutions'.[13] Seremetakis contends that the antiphonic 'construction' of pain not only lies at the heart of lament performance but is consciously used by women as a means of social manipulation.

As one would expect, according to such a model, women jealously guard their right to lament. At the wake, when females related through male kin to the deceased surround the coffin, squabbles may break out over both singing and sitting positions (1990: 487). Claims to precedence are made on the basis of 'shared histories of material and emotional reciprocity between the performer and the dead'. The women demonstrate their closeness to the deceased not only through position in song or spoken testimony, but by direct physical contact, touching and caressing the hair or head of the corpse or holding the forehead (488). When the male relatives enter to pay their respects to the dead, their behaviour is strikingly different. They remain in small groups on the margin of the ceremony, or wait at the entrances of the church or house:

> In contrast to the linguistic, emotional and tactile intimacies of the women, men (including the priest) maintain a purely visual relation to the dead. . . . This visual distancing is also directed to the female mourners by men. Women are fully aware of the gender division of space in the ritual and of the value connotation of spatial intimacy and spatial distance in relation to the corpse. The mourner, while improvising a lament standing or sitting by the corpse, will ironically call to particular men to come close or to vocally respond. The men do not cross the boundary set by gender and by death. In contrast, when lament singers name other female participants and ask them to respond or draw closer, the latter react by bursting into tears and entering into mourning themselves.
>
> (488–9)

Given the unlikeliness of acceptance, the appeal to a male member of the community to 'come close' or even join in the lament is, in Seremetakis' view, a deliberate device to attract attention and make the man 'bear witness' to the truth of the lamenter's narrative. The chorus of women may also be appealed to as witnesses, an especially important function when the lament is concerned with revenge or disputed property. This public hearing aspect of the lament is regarded as essential by the Maniot women. Without it, death is not only silent and unmarked for the deceased, but marks the 'social death of the mourner without witness'.

As a social institution, the *kláma*, or group of lamenting

women, stands in contrast to the *yerondikí*, the all-male council that has traditionally been the source of public decision making in the isolated, lawless world of Inner Mani. The same issues of revenge or land disputes were raised in both fora, and conflicts between them are seen by Seremetakis as expressive of tensions between the maximal lineage of the male council and the minimal household unit of the other (504–6). The evidence from the revenge laments themselves suggests that Seremetakis may not be wholly correct in her view that women support the 'minimal unit'. Women's loyalty, in many of these laments, seems to lie with the male kin, especially brothers, rather than with husbands or even children. Also, the insistence on antiphony as a dominant structural and organizational device leads Seremetakis to overemphasize conflict and opposition in lament performance. The fact that men take pleasure in singing these laments and admire the creative art of their authors suggests a somewhat more ambivalent and fluid relationship between the two 'choruses' of the Maniot village.

Anna Caraveli-Chaves' work on lament is centred on the village of Dzermiades in Crete.[14] On the question of men's reaction to women's laments, she found that their attitude was ambivalent, 'ranging from outright hostility to uneasy mocking of the tradition and, in some cases, to thinly-disguised admiration'.[15] She also found that there was 'an underlying fear of laments as magic songs, songs which open up perilous channels of communication between the living and the dead'.[16] Analysing laments within the social context of the village, Caraveli-Chaves saw them as a communally sanctioned outlet for emotional expression, one which, as an element of women's domination over the rituals of the life cycle, particularly the rites of passage, provided them with a compensating sphere of power to the more obvious social dominance of the village men. The conventions of lament texts as well as their transmission and performance, according to Caraveli-Chaves, act as a bond and communicative device between the women of the village, cementing ties between them. In the same way laments 'bridge and mediate between vital realms of experience. . . . The lamenter becomes the medium through whom the dead speaks to the living, the shaman who leads the living to the underworld and back, thus effecting a communal confrontation with death and, through it, a catharsis.'[17]

Analysing versions of a lament sung by two women in the village of Dzermiades, Caraveli-Chaves concludes that the text itself emphasizes aspects of the dead woman's life that are 'intrinsically linked to her role as a woman in her society' and that 'the subject matter of a lament can be used to affirm bonding among the female participants – bonding through shared suffering being the most potent type'.[18] In fact the notion of 'female suffering' in Caraveli-Chaves' experience exists beyond the conventions of lament as a 'code in female communication'. Not only do they share a belief that they have a harder lot to bear in life, but 'women's position within the cycle of life is recognised as one which affords them an uneven share of suffering as well as privileged understanding. . . . It is a woman's capacity for reproduction that also gives her firsthand access to the realm of the dead, as she becomes more vulnerable to pain and loss than men.'[19]

This notion that women have a superior knowledge of pain through the experience of childbirth and rearing children is not an uncommon one. In 1968 I spent a month in the gynaecological ward of one of the poorest public hospitals in Athens. There were twenty-six women in the ward, and the doctors, who were exclusively male, treated us as if we were small children, giving us little information about our condition, and upbraiding those who asked questions or complained about their treatment. While the women used a formal mode of address to speak to the doctors, the doctors frequently called them by their first names. During the doctors' rounds, the women were usually docile and submissive unless they were in pain. Morphine was administered sparingly and the women often screamed for hours before they were given any medication. Having been brought up in a stoical culture I restrained my expression of pain to groans and grunts. The doctors confided in me that Greek women, unlike foreigners, were cowards and 'animals' because they screamed in pain. At night, after the doctors and nurses had left, the women would discuss the doctors' behaviour and their own suffering with a certain amount of pride: 'If only doctors knew what it was like to bear children they wouldn't behave like that. They wouldn't be doing it if they didn't want to put their hands up your legs. It's we women who know about pain; the men know nothing.' Such a combination of shared pain, female chauvinism and satisfaction taken from superior insight is expressed in a number of lament texts, including one by a daughter for her mother transcribed by Caraveli-Chaves:

> There is no one else who knows your sorrows, the plight of your life.
> I, alone, am left here, mother, to stand up by your side.

It is not only women's biological role as childbearer that gives her, as it were, a handle on suffering. In a lament recorded by Sotirios Chianis in Kandila, Arkardia, in 1959, the *moiro-loghístra* suggests that a lifetime's experience of suffering gives her the right to lament:

Οποιος δεν ξέρει θάνατο, δεν κλαίει πεθαμένους, Βάσιω, Βάσιω μου
Κι'όποιος δεν ξέρει ξενητειά, δεν κλαίει ξενητεμένους, Βασιλικούλα μου
Ο κι όποιος δεν ξέρει απ'αρρώστια, δεν κλαίει τους αρρώστους, Βάσιω, Βάσιω μου
Αχ! εγώ ξέρω από θάνατο, και κλαίω τους πεθαμένους, Βασιλικούλα μου
Αχ! εγώ ξέρω και ξενιτειά, κλαίω ξενετεμένους, Βάσιω, Βάσιω μου
Αχ! εγώ ξέρω απ' αρρώστια, και κλαίω τους αρρώστους, Βάσιω, Βάσιω μου.[20]

> Who doesn't know death, doesn't cry for the dead, my Vasso
> And who doesn't know foreign lands doesn't cry for those abroad, my little Vasso
> And who doesn't know about sickness, doesn't cry for the sick, Vasso, my Vasso
> Ah! I know about death and I cry for the dead, my little Vasso,
> Ah! I know foreign lands and cry for those abroad, Vasso, my Vasso,
> Ah! I know about sickness and cry for the sick, Vasso, my Vasso.

In the extraordinarily bleak picture of female suffering delineated in the nineteenth-century folk laments of the Ingrian-speaking peoples of Finland and Russia, the lamenter frequently expresses a longing for death in preference to life as a woman, particularly an orphaned or widowed one:

Why did you give birth to me, my bearer-in-your-womb/
bring me into this world, my rocker-in-the-world?/ Why did
you not choke me, benumbed/ and smother me, distressed/
against your own breasts/ my bringer?/ I have already wept
over my birth day, much bewailing/ and cursed the moment
of my conception, forsaken/ so hard have turned for me,
unhappy/ those orphan's days of mine, unhappy/ and the
hired girl's days, faded.[21]

Similarly in Greece, the loss of a husband or male relative who
acts as protector and bread-winner, or the loss of a child,
particularly a male child, leaves a woman not only in emotional
distress, but robs her of status in the community. In the
Thessalian village where Loring Danforth did his research, he
concluded that although women were marginalized, the fact
that they represented family ties gave them a kind of status.[22] A
mother's lament from Gortinia makes it clear how death
deprives women of this status:

Οποιά χασε τον άντρα της, έχασε την τιμή της
κι'οποιά χασε τη μάνα της, έχασε τη κουβέντα,
κι' οποιά χασε τον αδερφό, έχασε τα φτερά της,
κι'οποιά χασε την αδερφή, έχασε το σιριάνι,
κι'οποιά χασε μικρά παιδιά, έχασε την καρδιά της.

(Politis:200)[23]

Whoever lost her husband lost her respect
and whoever lost her mother lost her conversation
and whoever lost her brother lost her wings
and whoever lost her sister lost her walks
and whoever lost small children lost her heart.

The description of the dependence of Greek women on family
ties for status and freedom of movement in this lament is as
succinct as it is poignant. Caraveli-Chaves points out that
widowhood, like emigration, is used as a metaphorical extension of death in the Greek folk tradition. There are many bitter
laments composed by widows about their status, not only
because it leaves them socially isolated, but it encourages village
men to mock them, often imputing to them a voracious sexual
appetite. In Mani a number of the so-called 'satirical laments'
are preoccupied with the theme of widows and old maids. The
example here is one of a number first published by Pasayianis:

Λάλησ' ο κούκος στα βουνά
και φεύγει ο μαγαζάτορας
κι'ο έμπορας του μαγαζιού
κι'εγώ καθούλα κι αμαρού
(που εταίριαζε κι απάνταρε)
να κάθομαι στο μαγαζί
να πίνου το γλυκό κρασί
να κάνου χρόνου και παιδί.
–Ελα κοντά μου, Κωσταντή,
κι εγώ σου δώνου το κλειδί
του μαγαζιού και του σπιτιού
κι αν δεν το θέεις του μαγαγιού
εγώ το δώνου του Ντινιού.²³

The cuckoo sings in the mountains
and the shopkeeper leaves
and the salesman and I,
lay-about and lazy
(who have no mate nor husband)
sit in the shop
to drink sweet wine
to spend time and have a child.
– Come close Constandis,
and I'll give you the key
to the shop and the house
and if you don't want the shop
I'll give it to Dinios.

However bad a marriage may be, the death of a husband is seen as a disaster, especially if a woman has children to raise. The widow Stavriani Linara, known as Kakoulonifis, used the occasion of a funeral to compose a lament for her own fate. Her mother died when she was a child and her father before he could provide her with a dowry. She was forced to marry a poor young man who died a few months after the wedding, leaving her pregnant. To raise her son, she was obliged to remarry an older man, a widower who was also very poor and had children of his own. Widowed a second time, she recited the hardships of her long life, particularly what she suffered at the hands of relatives and in-laws, in a lament for one of her male relatives:

Μ'έφαε η κακούργα γρηά,
του Φώτο η μάνα κι η κυρά
και του Φωτάκο η πεθερά.
Κι ο Φυτιλιάνικος γαμπρός
με κρέμασε στον αγκρεμό
με σπάγγο μίας δεκαράς
στη μ Πούντα κα στη Μακρυνά
που τρώει καραβόσκιουνα.
Να τρώου τη γ ξεροφελιά
να πίνου την αρμαλακιά.[24]

The old bitch used me up
Fotos' mother and grandma
and Fotakos' mother-in-law.
And half-brother Fitilianikos
hung me over the cliff
by a length of cheap string
at Pounta on Makryna shore
that cuts the boat ropes up.
He left me to eat dry weeds
and drink the brackish water.

The widows' songs support the findings of Danforth and Caraveli-Chaves concerning women's dependence on family ties, particularly male family ties, for status, but I have some reservations about Danforth's use of the term 'marginalisation'. It presumes there is some centre field, occupied by men, on the periphery of which women live their lives. This spatial metaphor, so often used by feminists and literary critics concerned with the canon of great works, depends very much on where you are standing. As a western observer, entering a Greek village, it certainly seems an apt one. The central village square, with its *cafeneía* and *tavérnes* is the focus of interest for the visitor and it is predominantly a man's world where men's concerns are voiced. If, on the other hand, you wander into the back streets where people live most of their lives, the picture changes. The common Greek folk metonyms for home, *tzáki* (kitchen hearth) and *avlí* (courtyard) designate important spaces that women control. In some sense it is Greek men who occupy the margin rather than the centre of the village as a place to live one's life, or as a haven to return to after exile or emigration. Anthropologists studying Greek village life have considered the two spheres of male and female dominance in terms of public and private, home and outside the home,[25] but there is at least one *public* space that women dominate – the graveyard – and if their voice is restrained outside the house on other occasions, in the face of death it is heard by the whole community.

The fact that while men may generally claim to disapprove of women's laments, they frequently admire, learn and perform laments composed by women suggests that there is a recognition of women's creative ability that extends beyond the strictly domestic sphere. The observations of those who have studied women's laments from diverse areas of Greece indicate that not only are women perceived as having a natural authority over the rituals of death, but that gifted lamenters may use the opportunity of the public prominence to voice their broader concerns and to rouse others to action, particularly to avenge an unnatural death. It may be the exceptional intrusion of women into the public sphere and the possibility of using the opportunity of their dominion over death to extend their control of life that cause men to have an uneasy and ambivalent relationship towards the *moirologhístres*. It may also be that what was once an accepted part of village life is now seen by a younger generation, particularly by the men who have travelled to urban centres or gone abroad to work, as an anachronism in a rapidly changing society.

NARRATIVE LAMENTS OF INNER MANI: TEMPERING OF PAIN

As I have already noted, the laments of Inner Mani are, in a number of respects, untypical of the rest of Greece. They are composed in iambic eight-syllable verse, with an irregular alternation of masculine and feminine endings rather than in the usual Greek folk metre of fifteen-syllable lines. The long narrative laments display few of the usual structural devices of laments and songs from other regions. Refrains and appeals to the dead, as well as the use of dialogue and stichomythia common to laments from most regions of Greece are found in some Maniot laments, but the 'antiphonal structure and antithetical thought' that Margaret Alexiou traces as continuous features of laments in the Greek tradition are not common in Inner Mani.[26] The wealth of symbolic allusion found in laments from other parts of Greece is missing too. At first hearing, the unadorned narrative laments seem to be rather flat in tone except for the occasional emotional appeals to the dead. To appreciate the contrast between these laments and the more generalized laments sung in Outer Mani or the adjacent areas of the Peloponnese, one must place them side by side.

The lament 'I had a little bird' is popular all over the Peloponnese. The text is from a recording made by Sotirios Chianis in the Arcadian mountain village of Kandila in 1959. An indication of the adaptability of such well-known laments is that the *moiologhístra*, Evangelia Fotopoulou, said that although it was obviously composed originally as a lament for a son, she sang it on the occasion of the death of her own mother for whom she was still in mourning:

Πούλακι είχα στο κλουβί και το είχα ημερομένα, μωρ' μανούλα μου,
Το τάιζα τη ζάχαρη, το πότιζα το μόσχο, μωρ' μανούλα μου
Το τάιζα τη ζάχαρη, το πότιζα το μόσχο, μώρ' μανούλα μου
Κι' από τον μόσχο τον πολλή, κι' από τη μυρουδιά του, μανουλίτσα μου
Μου σκανταλίστει το κλουβί και μόφυγε τ' αηδόνι, μωρ' μανούλα μου
Κι ο πουλολόγος παέι κοντά με το κλουβί στα χέρια, μωρ' μανούλα μου
–Ελα χρύσο πουλάκι μου, έλα στο μαθημά σου, μωρ' μανούλα μου
–Ελα χρύσο πουλάκι μου, έλα στο μαθημά σου, μωρ' μανουλα μου
–Το τι καλό να θυμηθώ, πίσο γιά να γυρίσω, μωρ' μανούλα μου
Πο' σύ 'τρωγες καλό ψωμί, και 'γώ 'τρωγα κριθάρι, μωρ' μανούλα μου
Πο' σύ 'τρωγες καλό ψωμί, και 'γώ 'τρωγα κριθάρι, μωρ' μανούλα μου
Πο' σύ 'πινες γλυκό κρασί, και 'γώ 'πινα το ξύδι, μωρ' μανούλα μου.[27]

I had a little bird in a cage and it was tame, oh mother,
I fed it on sugar, gave it balm to drink, oh my mother,
I fed it on sugar, gave it balm to drink, oh my mother

And from so much balm and from its sweet smell, little
   mother,
It fled its cage and left me, the nightingale, my mother,
And the birdman comes close with the cage in his hands, oh
   mother
– Come golden bird, come for your lesson, oh my mother
– Come golden bird, come for your lesson, oh my mother
– How good to remember how to come back, oh mother
Where you once ate fine bread and I ate barley, oh mother,
Where you once ate fine bread and I ate barley, oh mother,
Where you once drank sweet wine and I drank vinegar, oh
   mother.

Here we see a number of the conventional formulas of folk
lament. There is the contrast between the idyllic past and the
tragic present, found in both the folk tradition and in laments
throughout the Greek tradition.[28] The direct dialogue with the
dead is also a common device as is the metaphor of the bird
(nightingales are common, but eagles and hawks are frequently
used to symbolize young men). The distinctly sinister image of
the birdman enticing the child to a lesson is, as far as I know, an
unusual one, but the image of death as a journey, either on foot,
on Charos's black horse or by boat to a strange land from
which the dead strive to return, is found in numerous laments.[29]
   The language of folk laments from most of the regions of
Greece is largely composed of striking metaphors that address
the fact of death by indirect allusion, substituting imagery for
direct description. What make such standard laments personal
are the variations between performances. These may consist of
direct appeals to the dead by name, subtle variations in the text,
the emotional intensity of the performer and musical qualities
such as pitch and timbre of the voice. One lamenter Sotiris
Chianis recorded chose to sing a particular lament at a pitch
considerably higher than the others she performed. When she
was asked why, she could not or would not explain, except to
say that that was the way she always sang the particular lament.
At some stage a particular *moirologhístra* must have composed
a lament that has become part of the common repertoire, but
the use of symbolic language allows it to be used for a number
of occasions, including those that seem quite unsuited to the
text. Even the narrative laments addressed to a particular

individual can be reused for others, or sung outside the ritual context of a funeral or memorial service, but they remain firmly connected to the memory of a particular person who died and to the woman who composed them.

One such lament is the long narrative ballad known as 'Tou Vetoula' or 'Ti Ligorous'. It is interesting that many of the laments are known by the name of the lamenter who originally composed them, as well as by the name of the male subject of the narrative. 'Vetoulas', meaning a young male goat, was the nickname of Dimitris Liakakos, who was involved in a feud with a family called Liopoulos and was ambushed and shot by Petros Liopoulos. His sister, Ligourou, who must have composed the original version of the lament between 1828 and 1830, was responsible for inciting her younger brother and other relatives to avenge his death. The lamenter speaks of herself in the third person, a device known as speaking *sta indiánika*:[30]

Ενα Σαββάτο από βραδύς
οπό ξεμέρουνε Λαμπρή
στο γ κόσμο και του Χριστιανούς
εσυγγυρίστη η Ληγορού
Βάνει κουλούρια στη μποιδιά
κόκκινα αβγά στη ζουναιριά
και πάει στουν αλλουνούνε της
από τη Κοίτα στ'Αλικα.
Στο δρόμο που επάαινε
επέρασε απ' αψηλά
από τα Σπηλιωτιάνικα.
Επέρασε στου Μπουλαριούς
και ρούγα ηύρε τους οχτρούς
κι έκαμε πέτρινιη καρδιά
κανένας δεν εμίλησε
κι όλους τους χαιρέτησε.
Ο Πέτρος ο Λιόπουλος
απάνου εξεσηκώθηκε
Είπε '–καλώς τη Λιγορού
καλώς τη καλωσώρισες
Μωρή, α μπάεις στ'Αλικα
να μπεις στουν αλωνούνε ζου
πες τους να κάμομε καλά

κι'εμείς τους το πλιερώνομε
το γίδι που σκοτώσαμε
νη πέντε γρόχια νη εφτά
στο φόρτσο δώνομε κι εννηά
Κι α δεν το θέτε κι έτσαδα
ας τονε φάει αρμαλακιά
κάτου στα Γιάλια χαμπηλά
στη ζγούρνα του Κεραμιδά.'
Δεν αποκρίθη η Λιγορού
βάνει στη στράτα στα μπροστά
μοιρολογιώντα κλαίοντα.
Στα Αλικα που έφτασε
στα Αλικα στη Λατομά
δεν εχαιρέτα πουθενά.[31]

One Saturday evening
before Easter day dawned
for all the world and Christian folk
Ligorou prepared herself
put round rusks in her apron
red eggs tied in her sash
and went to visit her brothers
from Kitta to Alika.
On the road as she went along
she went around from higher up
passing by Spiliotianika.
She passed where the Bouliarous lived
and found her enemies in the lane
and made her heart like stone.
No one said a word to her
and she greeted every one.
Petros Liopoulos stood up
saying 'Welcome Ligorou
welcome and good day to you
Wench, if you go to Alika
tell your brothers this:
tell them if they behave themselves
we'll pay them for
the nanny goat we killed
either five or six groschen
at a pinch we'll give them nine.

And if you don't want it that way
let the local policemen have him
down at Yialia, way down
at the hollow of Keramidha.'
Ligorou didn't answer
She went along the street
lamenting and crying.
When she arrived at Alika
at Alika at Latoma
she greeted no one.

In the verses that follow, Ligorou's brother-in-law, understanding from her strange behaviour that something is amiss, asks her for an explanation. She repeats word for word what she was told by the murderer of her brother. Then comes her cry for revenge, one that, by calling Yiannis' honour into question, gives him little choice but to act:

Κι' έσκουξ η Ληγορή φωνή
ο τόπος ν'ανατριαλιστέι:
—Δεν είχε ο Βέτουλας καφό,
δεν είχε πρωτοχάδερφο;
Εχάθη νάμαι σερνικός
και να φορού βρακί και γώ!
Ν'άχου στον ώμου το σαρμά
να κυνηγήσου το φονιά!

And Ligorou let out a shrill cry
that made the place shudder all around
– Did Vetoulas have no brother,
did he have no first cousin?
If only I'd been a male
and could wear pants myself!
To have shouldered the gun myself
and chased the murderer!

Yiannis is maddened (literally 'possessed by an evil spirit') and goes to the widow of Vetoulas to fetch a gun. She is reluctant at first but eventually gives him the weapon and as he is on his way a young billy-goat bleats. He addresses the goat saying: 'Come close Satan, come close Vetoulas.' The goat bleats again, and again he calls it Satan, asking it to: 'Come close and finish off this work.' He arrives at the village and finds the outer door of

Petros Liopoulos' house open. In the inner room, Petros is eating his evening porridge with a child in his arms. Yiannis fires and 'the porridge was full of brains'. Having avenged the murder he flees, leaving the gun behind. In some versions he kills the child as well, in others not, but the details of the child in Petros's arms, the brains in the porridge (*hiló* is a milky pap often eaten by the peasants of Mani as an evening meal) and the gun being left behind are found in other versions. In a number of longer, but less commonly sung versions, Yiannis, after fleeing from village to village and being hidden by relatives who are on his side in the feud, arrives at his mother's house where he asks for his reward for bringing her the good news that he has avenged Vetoulas. She tells him to walk proudly to Alika where he will come into an inheritance. He passes the door of the man he has murdered like a hero and meets the proud Ligorou who shares his triumph.

THE NAMING OF NAMES

At first hearing this is a strange lament. Some would argue that it is no longer strictly a lament, rather that it has become part of the popular repertoire of Maniot folk songs, but it is still sung by *moirologhístres* in a ritual context, and it contains many of the typical features of the more recently composed laments from the region. The opening lines that set it in time, then name the leading characters and place them firmly in the landscape are characteristic. Other laments begin with the words 'Early one Monday morning', 'On a holiday, a Sunday', 'One Saturday at nine, I was coming from Panghia', 'One night right at midnight', etc. In the well-known lament 'Tou Nikolou Sassari', the wife of the pirate hero of the lament begs him not to leave for Turkish waters but he pays no heed. In the introduction, where we learn of her pleas to her husband, there is no mention of time, but when we come to the day when she learns of her husband's death, having seen his boat return with black sails set, we are given precise details of the day (a Sunday and a public holiday), of how she was dressed and how she sat combing her daughter's hair as she trained her binoculars on the sea. The necessity of fixing a death precisely in time seems to be common to laments from other cultures. In Lorca's famous 'Lament for Ignacio Sánchez Mejías', a poem based on a folk tradition of laments for the dead, the hour of the bullfighter's death, *las cinco de la tarde* is repeated thirty times until it mesmerizes the reader.

What effect or function does this insistence on the day, the hour of death have? I suspect it has to do with the way laments deal with pain, and with the desire of the bereaved to hammer such details into a hard metallic shape that they can keep in their memory. Lorca said of Spain that it was a country 'where what matters most has the ultimate metallic quality of death'.[32] There is a similar insistence on the hard metal, in this case on precious metal in a Greek lament of a mother for her dead child, where the lamenter says she wants to keep the pain she feels and will 'go to a goldsmith to have it [her pain] gold-plated'.[33] Kassis quotes a well-known lamenter from Mani speaking of her art as composed in 'η σκληραγώγιο που φέρνει ο πόνος' (the tempering/inuring that pain brings).[34] In other Maniot laments the lamenter 'turns her heart to stone' or describes herself as a 'hard rock'. Steven Feld notes that 'hardness' is a quality admired by the Kululi in laments. To say death is metallic or hard may be to say that we desire to make it so in memory and so avoid its frightful nebulousness. There also seems to be an admiration, in these societies, for control of emotional tone, for understatement rather than excess.

Besides the precise definition of time, the profusion of proper names and place names in 'Tou Vetoula' are common to almost all Maniot laments. Place names are often recounted during a walk through the landscape, either by the dead or the lamenter. It is as if, like the Kululi lamenters of New Guinea, the lamenter is deliberately staking out the territory of memory, marking it, like a map, with names of the familiar features of the landscape the deceased knew and which knew him. Similarly, the names of those who were either related to or in any way close to the dead are often listed by the lamenter. In 'Tou Korfiotaki', composed by the mother of a young man implicated in the murder of a government minister as a lament for the dead man and a defence of her son, place and proper names not only connect the murdered politician, who died in Athens, to his place of birth but to other outstanding sons of Mani:

Στου Κορφιωτάκι το λοντά
η Κοσσόνυφη η γριά
κάθεται και μοιρολογά

και τήνε τριγυρίζουσι
όλα τη Μάνης τα χωϊριά
το Σταυροπήγι κι ο Ζυγός
Και ο Νίκλος ο πολεμικός
και του Ζερβόμπεη ο γιός
ο χαϊδεμένο της γαμπρός.
Σκούζει χουγιάζει δυνατά
από ψυχή κι από καϊρδιά:
– Ανάθεμα στη γ κουμπουϊριά
πώπεσε στη μ πρωτεύουσα
Και σκότωσε τον υπουργό
του Κορφιωτάκι τον υγιό.³⁵

In Korfiotakis' courtyard
Old Mrs Kosonakos
sits and laments
and all around her
are the villages of Mani
Stavropighi and Zygos
and Niklos the fighting land
and the son of Zervobey
her beloved brother-in-law.
She shrieks, she calls out loud
from her heart and soul:
– A curse on the shot
that was fired in the capital
and killed the minister
the son of Korfiotakis.

In laments from all regions of Greece, to die in exile from one's own home territory is regarded as an additional tragedy. Here the lamenter places blame for the young man's death on an anonymous gunshot in Athens, stressing that 'among the people of Laconia/ he had honour and respect'. To have honour or *timí*, as outside observers have noted and Greeks themselves will tell you, is of overriding importance to the Greek male in life and death and it can only be had in one's own territory.³⁶ The laments of one's female relatives are an essential part of that honour, making death in their absence even more bitter. In this case the lamenter is not immediate kin, but she gives her credentials for lamenting him as she switches from third to first person

Εγώ το κλαίου 'λικρινά
μες απ' τα φύλλα τη καιρδιάς
τ'είμαι Μανιάτα φυσικιά
κι αντάνια πέτρα του Μωρηά.[37]

I lament him truly
from the bottom of my heart
I'm a real Maniot woman
and a hard stone of the Morea.

The shift of focus from the dead man to the person of the lamenter herself is again typical of these laments. Whether she recounts the story in the third- or first-person, the lamenter, rather than the deceased, occupies the centre of the narrative.

Whereas in the laments of most regions, the deceased is praised in a series of metaphors – a cypress tree, a light, a bird, a flower, a pillar that supports the house – in the laments of Inner Mani the sparing use of such metaphors in the narrative laments is striking. Instead, the dead man or woman is addressed by name, often together with the profession a man held, especially if it is one to be proud of (lawyer, teacher, doctor).

Another feature peculiar to the Maniot laments is the absence of the usual Greek folk imagery of death. In the laments common to most regions of Greece the dead lie in darkness in the 'black earth' under a 'spidery slab'. Christian imagery is often mixed with pagan, but generally it is Charos, the sinister rider on a black horse, who carries the dead to his underworld kingdom of *Adis* (Hades) where he and his wife Charondissa often eat a grisly meal of the tender flesh of young children. In the narrative laments of Mani, the underworld is rarely mentioned, and when it is, like the place names that fix us in the countryside of Mani, Hades and the underworld become toponyms in an imaginary landscape:

Αγροίκα το, μπαρμπα-παπά,
φεύγε και αλλού να λειτουργάς
κι αν έχει ο Αδης διάβατα
κι η Κάτου Γης περάσματα
φεύγε να βρεις τον ψάρτη σου,
τον ψευτο Λογοθέτακα,
το γιό του να καλιναρχά
και το δικό μου το παιδί
το θυμιατό να ζε κρατεί.[38]

Listen old priest
go away and preach somewhere else
and if there's a crossing to Hades
and a way to the Underworld
go and find your cantor
the false Logothetakas
let his son accompany him
and let my own son
be your censor-bearer.

The concern of the Maniot laments seems less with death itself than with the manner and place of death. A death in exile from Mani, a death before the realization of a young man's potential or a young woman's marriage, above all, a death by enemies that goes unavenged – these are the focus of the Maniot lamenters, for they affect the living and often transform the pain of loss into anger which has the potential for action. The harsh code of honour that demands a death for a death is fuelled by female anger, female pain. It is to the revenge laments that I will turn in the next chapter seeking to find in them more direct motivation behind the legislation against laments and female mourning in ancient Greece, but before I do I would like to examine how two Maniot laments deal with pain when there is no question of revenge.

KOUNDOUNARA'S LAMENT

The lament for Dikaios Yiatrakos was composed by his mother, the famous Maniot lamenter known as 'Koundounara' or 'Koundounifi'. The story of her marriage is an important proem to the lament.[39] Koundounara's husband came from the village of Layia. He took his bride by force and shut her up in his house. She soon became pregnant and gave birth to a son. The child was born a little before Easter, the time of the *Epitaphios* ceremony in which women play a major part. Koundounara's husband said to himself, 'Since she's given birth she won't leave me.' So he let her go to the church, to help the other women with the preparations for the ceremony, but she took the opportunity to escape to her father's house, abandoning her child. When her husband went to fetch her back

Koundounara refused to go with him saying: 'If you want me to come back to your house and remain your wife, you'll have to bring back a heifer with a bell on it and you'll come through this door on your knees.' Her husband found the heifer, put a bell around its neck and went to fetch his wife. She came back to him as she had promised, but to avenge himself he poured scalding oil over her, burning her badly. When her husband died Koundounara sat at the wake with her relatives. Suddenly she took a small lamp, lifted her skirt and stood astride his coffin reciting this little verse: 'Look Dimitri/ at the little plaything [the word λαλό, meaning a child's toy or game is used here to refer to her own vagina] you scalded/ once upon a time./ Dimitri I straddle you/ and may my plaything make you jealous.'

Koundounara's son was a medical student and engaged to be married when he was killed in the Greco-Turkish war of 1897. Her lament for him is considered by other *moirologhístres* to be one of the finest in the repertoire:

Τ'αντρόγενο όντας σμείξουσι
θα κρυφοκουβεντιάσουσι
καλά παιϊδιά να κάμουσι
και πράμα να προσκάμουσι.
Οντες που σμείξαμε και μεις
ο ξεσουωτός κι η βρωμερή
βάζαμε τα κεφάλια μας
σ'ένα στενό προσκέφαλο
και κρυφο κουβεϊντιάσαμε
καλά παιδιά να κάμομε
και πράμα να προσκάμομε.
Εκάμαμε καλό παιδί
το βάλαμε και στο σπουδή
το βγάλαμε και φοιτητή.
Μ'άλλος δεν φταίει τίποτα
όλα τα φταίει ο βασιλιάς
πόβγαλε τη διαταγή
και μάζεψε στρατό πολύ
και πήρε τη λεβεντουϊριά
γιά να νικήσει τη Τουρκιά.
Και τόνε παίρνει κληρωτό
και τόνε βάνει μπροστινό

στη Λάρισα στο Δημοκό.
Κει είπασι τ'εσκοτώθηκε
και μένα ο Δικήο μου
ο τίμιό μου φοιτητής.
Ε, κόρακά μου που πετάς
με τα κατάμαυρα φτερά
και πλεεις στα ουρανιά
μην είϊδιες το Δικήο μου
τα φύλλα τη καρδιά μου
νη να μην έφερες εσύ
καμμιά του φανέρουση
νη πόδι του νη χέρι του
νη το λειρό του δάχτυλο
πούχε το ασημόβεργα.
Νη να μη ζούπε τίποτα
να 'ρθεις να πεις στη μάννα του
γιά να του βράζει τα σπερνά
να δώνει του παπά βλογιά.
Τι δεν πιστεύει τη μάννα του
τ' έναι καημένη και ψητή
από τα νύχια ως τη γ κορφή
γιά δεν εστόλησε γαμπρό
ούτε ψερό ούτε ζωντανό.
Στη πόρτα θε να καρτερέι
ώστα υπάρχει και ώστα ζει
για να ξανοίξει και να ιδεί
μη έρχεται από το στρατί
ο γελαστό της φοιτητής.[40]

When man and wife are one
they talk to each other in secret
of how they'll make good children
and how they'll make their fortune.
We did the same when we joined up
the dried-up husband and the dirty wife
we put our heads together
on a narrow pillow
and talked to each other in secret
of how we'd make good children
and how we'd make our fortune.
We made a good child

and turned him into a student.
No one else is to blame
it's all the fault of the king
it was he who gave the order
and collected lots of soldiers
and took away the bright young lads
so as to defeat the Turks.
He took them as conscripts
put them in the front line
at Larissa, at Dimoko.
And my Dikio went there and got killed
my honoured student.
Hey, my crow that flies
with your jet-black wings
sailing through the sky
if you by chance see my Dikio
my heart of hearts
could you bring me some sign
either his foot or hand
or his smallest finger
where he wore the silver ring.
Or if he said nothing to you
come and tell his mother
so she can boil the funeral wheat
and the priest can give a blessing.
For his mother doesn't believe it
she is burnt and roasted
from her nails to the top of her head
because she didn't dress a bridegroom
either dead or alive.
She wants to wait at her door
as long as she exists and lives
in case he comes home from the army
her laughing student son.

The circumstances of Dikios' death are particularly painful for
the bereaved mother. Her son died in exile, fighting a war
neither he nor his mother believed in. There are no remains for
her to bury and the mother is left with the tormenting doubt
that her son may still be alive. Koundounara's hopes for the
future as well as her own prestige were vested in her son who

had achieved high social status as a medical student. Moreover, he was engaged but not yet married (in which case it would be customary to bury him dressed as a bridegroom).

THE HEART OF STONE: SELF-CONTROL AND THE STRUCTURING OF PAIN

I will not attempt to deal with the non-verbal elements of this lament – with voice quality, melodic and rhythmic elements, gesture, etc., but simply with a text as it appears in transcription. It is important to keep in mind that laments are, by general agreement, not usually composed immediately on the occasion of a death and often not performed by the immediate kin at the funeral of the deceased but may be worked at slowly over a period of days or even months before they are performed in public.

The most obvious feature of the language of the introductory lines of Koundounara's lament is its dry, impersonal tone, its apparent lack of emotion. In the first fourteen lines there is only one hint of what is being kept under control, an outburst of disgust at her husband and herself: 'The dried up husband and the dirty wife.' The narrative continues in lines that are bereft of figures of speech and the elaborate code of symbols used to praise the dead in laments from other regions. Blame for the son's death is then laid not on the enemy he went to fight, but squarely on the king who conscripted him against his will. And although the mother has probably never seen the place of her son's death, two toponyms are given – at one of these Koundounara's son must have fallen. This is the central section of the lament, and nine lines are devoted to indicting the king. Anger against herself has been transferred, by the lamenter, to the figure of authority she considers responsible for her son's death. There is no hint of nationalism here, no sense that the young man died in a good cause. As we shall see, the expression of anger against authority in any form: the police, the state, even the doctors considered responsible for a death is a common feature of the Maniot laments.

When the narrative is interrupted by the address to a crow, the style of the lament changes. The appearance of birds who bring messages from the dead is a common device in heroic ballads and laments from all over Greece, but whereas male characters tend to ignore bird omens, women are more inclined to take them seriously.[41] In this version of the lament the introduction of the crow is accompanied by a generalized figure of speech (it sails through the skies) but in other versions the crow's flight is over 'the mountains of Thessaly' or 'by Larissa and Dimoko'. The crow is only partly symbolic in this context. The one thing that interests the lamenter is that the crow may have seen her dead son and be able to bring not a message, or even some token – the silver ring – but a tangible sign, a piece of his body, the finger that wore the ring. Flesh (uncooked) is the only proof, it seems, that will satisfy the mother and allow her to cook the funeral food and request the priest's blessing for the dead. The lament ends with the customary focus of attention on the pain of the lamenter. Instead of boiling the funeral wheat, the mother herself is being cooked (it can be argued that *kaiméni*, literally burnt, is such a common word for 'unfortunate' that it has lost its literal meaning. Melting and burning are frequent metaphors for pain in laments but in combination with *psití*, meaning roasted or baked, and applied to the mother's whole body, the metaphor is appropriate as the negative of proper or ideal cooking, i.e. the boiling of the funeral food). It is an irresistible Lévi-Straussian cluster of oppositions and mediations, especially in conjunction with the lines that follow, where the mother states as the principal reason for her distress the fact that she was unable to dress her son as a bridegroom either alive or dead. The usual metaphor of death-as-wedding mediating the finality of death is, like the cooking metaphor, an expression of the impotent mother's need for the busy-ness of the funeral, for action. The finger she specifically asks the crow for is the one that wore the engagement ring. The mother has achieved her ambition of having a good son, a medical student, but her work is left half-finished; she has not yet married him and ensured the continuity of her line. It is the sense of uncompleted business, in life and in death, that torments Koundounara as much as anything else.

Why is Koundounara's lament still popular in Mani? What does it *do* for the lamenter or her listeners? Is it therapeutic? Does it offer a structural and semantic formula for transforming the unbearable into the tolerable? Is it threatening to the social order? Does it tell us anything about attitudes to death, particularly women's attitudes to death in the Mani? Can we generalize from it to other Greek laments, modern or ancient? Does it have a deeper meaning hidden beneath the surface of its text that the intuitive listener can reveal?

CRIES THAT SHAKE THE WORLD

These are all difficult questions and it would be disingenuous to suggest I had not already considered them and drawn some conclusions. To begin at the end, I think that laments like Koundounara's are not guileful. They say what they have to say in the same way as these village women confront death, i.e. with a gaze as hard as rock, a pain that has already been tempered before it is transformed into song. At the same time this tough exterior that is a structure for expressing pain and a structuring of pain itself, is fissured. Whether by design or by irresistible pressure, cries of anger and pain escape through a crack in the even surface of the narrative like jets of molten lava. Sometimes the outburst is addressed to the dead, sometimes to the *moirologhístra* herself (the dried-up husband and the dirty wife), even, as in Koundounara's lament for her son, to a crow, and inevitably, to the real or imaginary cause of death, in this case the king. These cries are often literal ones, points in the performance where the lamenter will raise pitch and volume to emphasize the dramatic break in her narrative. The lamenter herself is quite conscious of the impact such cries have on a listener:

Στην Ανω Πούλα θ'ανεβού
να ιδού τα αστέρια τ'ουρανού
να σκούξω απ'άγρια φωνή
ο κόσμος ν'ανακουνηθή[42]

I'll climb up to High Poula
to see the stars in the sky
to shriek in a fierce voice
and shake up all the world.

Similarly, Ligorou's outburst in the lament for Vetoulas has a cosmic impact:

Κι'έσκουξ' η Λιγορού φωνή
ο τόπος ν'ανατριαλιστεί

And Ligorou let out a shrill cry
that made the place shudder all around.

It is clear that these women know the power of their own cries. In the revenge laments, they are put to immediate use, but even when there is no possibility for translating anger into action, the outbursts in the controlled body of a narrative are so persistent a feature of the Maniot laments, their position within the text sufficiently regular (almost always preceded by a calm introduction, frequently in mid-position followed by a return to practical detail) to suggest that they are a conscious device of the lamenter, one long established, perhaps in the oral tradition, but open to considerable variation and manipulated for effect.[43]

BREATH, SIGHS AND SOBS

Like the cries that puncture the text, so sobs, sighs and sudden intakes of breath are integral to the performance of lament. Singers of dramatic or plaintive songs from opera to blues will use their breath for heightened emotional effect. Since soul and breath are synonymous in Greek culture (being out of breath, dying and losing one's soul are all conveyed by the single word *xepsyhisménos*), manipulations of breath in laments may carry additional emotional weight, although the associations of breath with soul or spirit are common to most cultures.[44] It may be the perceived connection of breath leaving the body with death that has led to the widespread use of wind instruments, particularly the flute, in the context of funerals. The ancient Greek double-pipe or *aulos* was associated with the elegy and the expression of grief.[45] Its mythical origins linked the *aulos* with the pain of loss in the legend of Pan and Syrinx. Double-pipes were played by the Phoenicians in the rites for the dead Adonis. Both instruments may derive from an Egyptian wind instrument associated with mourning and the god of the dead, Osiris. It is also interesting that in medieval plainsong and Byzantine hymns the word 'neume', a corruption of *pneuma* (breath), was used for the signs that indicated pitch, i.e. the earliest musical notation. In the middle Byzantine period (1100–1450), when pitch notation was refined to differentiate between a stepwise progression of notes and sudden leaps of pitch, the neumes for adjacent movement were called *sōmata* (bodies), while those indicating wider intervals were called *pneumata*. Whether or not there was an element of humour in the naming of these sprightly intervals, it suggests that breathing and singing, like weeping and singing have always been so intimately associated that it may be difficult to determine where a sigh ends and a song begins. While musical and textual transcriptions usually omit such extra musical features as sighs and sobs, they are as much a part of laments as the rhythmic sway of the body or the beating of clenched fists on the mourner's chest.

THE COMMUNAL ART

The popularity of a lament like Koundounara's for her son has to do with the way she manipulates traditional structures to make her private pain and anger a generalized or communal reflection on death. If that is as naïve as saying that *Hamlet* or *Oedipus the King* have remained popular because they seem to universalize the tragedy of the human condition, then I can respond only that, to the Maniots who know laments well, Koundounara's art is respected as a great one. Perhaps the best account of how the lamenter's skill is viewed as an art comes from the lamenter herself. In a Maniot lament composed in about 1920, Vassiliki Petrongona pays tribute to a great lamenter who was her teacher:

Σφάλισο το δευτέρι ζου
οπού κρατάς στο χέρι ζου
κι απόθησό το καταγής
να ντ' αναγνώσομε μαζί
ο δάσκαλος και ο μαθητής.
Ε παλαιά μου Χαλιμά
και σύνοψη δεσποτικιά
π'οχεις γραμμένα τ' άσωτα
και να χαρείς ο τι αγαπάς
κι απο τα δυό σου πλευρά.[46]

Make sure of your account
where you hold hands
and lay it on the ground
so that we can read it together

the teacher and the pupil
Eh, my Halima
my breviary of high authority
where you write down the profligate
and enjoy what you love
on either side of you.

The metaphors used in this long introductory tribute are arresting, especially if we consider that this is an oral tradition. The women who 'pass' the lament from one to another frequently hold hands. In this case the older and more experienced lamenter, known as the *koriféa* or soloist, has led off, and the younger lamenter 'insures' her 'account', i.e. her lament, by basing it firmly on the account of her predecessor. The metaphor of a ledger, a book of accounts, is maintained in line four, where the lamenter says teacher and pupil will 'read it' together. Up to this point the lamenter has been addressing herself. Now she addresses her teacher directly and the metaphor changes. She calls her 'my old Halima' (the enchanting Arabian tale-teller of *The Thousand and One Nights*) and a *sýnopsis despotikiá*. The phrase may denote either an archbishop's breviary or a brief account and both as an ecclesiastical or secular metaphor the idea of an authoritative record is maintained. The mistress of lament has 'written' the profligate into this brief account book. Are we to think of her as a judge? Or should we consider the word *ásota* in its sense of limitless, eternal? In either case her authority is proudly asserted. The last two lines of this introduction, which have nothing to do with the lament proper, invite the older lamenter to take pleasure in what she loves, i.e. her shared art of lament, and the women on either side who are presumably friends as well as fellow lamenters.

THE BOOK OF FATE

None of the metaphors used to praise the woman lamenter comes from the world of women's activities nor from the world of oral folklore except for the 'Halima' metaphor, which comes from a foreign tradition known in Greece through the written word. The connection between writing, weaving and fate, or the Three Fates, has already been mentioned.[47] In the folk tradition of Greece, the decrees of fate may be written in a book, or on paper, as well as on the skull, in the form of marks that are 'read', usually by old women skilled in such things. The metaphor of writing is extended, in the lament, to accounting, the enchantment of wonder tales and to a holy or authoritative book in which the profligate are inscribed. It might be argued that the lamenter herself has become both an instrument of fate and Fate herself. Her song is certainly enchanting, but it is also practical. There is something more businesslike than threatening about the opening lines of this lament. Like a baroque motet improvised by a gifted pupil on the ground bass of a master composer, it is an ordered creation, shared and enjoyed for its own sake, but keeping a greater purpose always in mind.

THE ORDERING OF PAIN

The question of how or whether such a lament has therapeutic value is probably unanswerable. Within the community it is felt to be therapeutic within the context of mourning the dead, and pleasurable outside that context. As another Maniot lamenter declares: 'κάλλιο έχω να μοιρολογώ/ παρά να φάω και να πιώ.' (I would rather lament/ than eat or drink). The structuring of pain into a song is itself an externalization of suffering. It may be that the shared activity of singing about another's pain shifts the locus of pain from the individual to the group in the same way as the assignment of blame for a death shifts pain to anger, and anger frequently to a prescription for action. In both cases there is a movement from the inner world of private suffering to the outer, from one's own body (Koundounara's burning body) to the object of one's hatred, from private tears to shrill cries that affect the landscape all around. There may also be a similar movement at work in the naming of names, the toponyms and proper names that inscribe the deceased in a social and geographic register or account book. Naming, blaming, fixing in a landscape: these are all gestures of order and control. For those who sing them, laments may be the reordering of one's inner emotional reactions to death into a tangible outward expression. Koundounara's need for the physical remains of her son reflects the same need for reordering her life through ritual as her lament. By performing the traditional rites for her son's body she would have been able to shift her pain onto the concrete, to externalize and so resolve her inner torment.

Order and control may be associated with lament in the small communities of Inner Mani or in remote villages in many parts of the world, but laments have also been associated with exactly the opposite: with chaos and disorder. The capacity of laments to externalize pain and transform it into anger and reciprocal violence, and the failure of women lamenters to respect any authority over death but their own, combined with the need of larger social units for a form of order that conflicts with these tendencies may be among the reasons why laments have fallen into disrepute in modern Greece as they did in the early city-states of antiquity.

Chapter 3

The politics of revenge in the laments of Inner Mani: duty, honour and poisoned eggs

BLAMING AND NAMING: THE SETTLING OF ACCOUNTS

As we have seen, one of the features of the laments of Mani is that the calm, hard surface of the narrative is inevitably broken at one or two places by a cry. The emotional outburst some-times takes the form of a direct address to the dead; at other times it may be an address to oneself or to a third person supposed responsible for the death. The agent of death may not be obvious, but there still seems to be a need to assign blame to someone specific. Koundounara, in her lament for her son, blamed the king who had conscripted him into the army. In the lament for Yiorgos Kossonakos, a permanent officer in the Greek army who was drowned when the Turks sank the Greek vessel *Arkady* carrying Cretan refugees to the mainland in 1867, the widow curses the state, the sub-prefect of the district and representative for Mani in the parliament, for sending Maniot troops to support the Cretan cause.[1] When the cause of death is a natural one, God himself may be named as the enemy. In a lament for a twelve-year-old boy, the only son of a widowed mother, who died of a fever between the two world wars, his mother says that God is wicked for killing an orphan. She is warned by her relatives and the other villagers not to curse God because it is sinful and evil, but she answers them back in her lament, saying:

– This thing God did
on the Saviour's holy day
when he killed the orphan –
isn't it sinful and evil?[2]

Similarly, in the lament of Yiorgakainas for her drowned son, which begins with a straightforward account of how the young man embarked on his last voyage, the mother suddenly cries out in anger, addressing Saint Dimitri directly:

Αγιε Δημήτρη, αφέντη μου
ποτέ μου δεν ζε δόξασα
και δεν ζε φωτολόησα,
ποτέ δεν ζ'άναψα κερί;
Δεν ζού 'φερα στη μνήμη ζου
δύο ασημοκάντηλα
και μανουάλια τέσσερα;
Για δεν εβοήθησες κι εσύ,
μες στου Τσιρίγου το νησί,
πού 'καμε τον Ντελή Βοριά
κι αναβουρκώθη η θάλασσα
κι έσκασε κύματα πλαϊτά;
Γέμισ' η θάλασσα πανιά
κι οι βράχοι αγγελικά κοϊρά.[3]

St Dimitri, my master,
didn't I always praise you
and honour you with light?
Did I fail to light a candle?
Didn't I bring two silver
candles on your memorial
day and four candelabra?
Why didn't you help as well
leeward of Tsirigou island
when the north wind blew
and the sea brimmed over
and broke in crooked waves?
The sea filled with sails
and the rocks with angelic bodies.

As we have seen in other laments, even if anger is directed towards God or a saint, the anguished mother shifts her pain outwards, away from herself. Despite the drama of the outburst, it is controlled and practical. The metaphor of lament as reckoning, familiar from Petrongona's lament, is elaborated here in the mother's complaints to the saint who has not kept his side of the bargain. She has 'esteemed' (literally calculated) the saint in light, and she carefully enumerates the expensive candles she has burned for him. Honour is at stake here, and although there can be no redress except to withdraw future gifts, the lament is the medium used to express outrage at the saint's dishonourable behaviour.

When the author of death is a human enemy, redress is not only possible but necessary to preserve one's honour. The same metaphor of calculation and accountability reappears in one of the most popular revenge narratives of Mani, the lament of Kalopothos Sakkakos. This lament, dating from the mid-nineteenth century, was composed by Kalopothos' sister, Paraski, not only to express grief at the death of her only brother, but to explain in detail how she avenged it. It is a long narrative, of which there are many variations, and it begins, with customary exactitude and flatness of tone, on the morning of Easter Sunday when Paraski is preparing the traditional Easter foods. As soon as she begins cooking she notices something is amiss:

Μια σκόλη και μια κυριακή
οπό ξημέρουνε Λαμπρή
έβανα και έψησα ψωμί.
Εψηνα δεν εψήνοτα
μόνε κομμάϊτια εγήνοτα,
έψηνα τι τυρόπιττες,
έφηνα δεν εψήνοντα
μπουκιές και αρμίιδια εγίνοντα.
Εβαφα κόκκινα τ'αυγά
και κείνα δε με βάφοντα
μόνε με γίνοντα μουντά.
Αμέσος το κατάλαβα
τ'ετούτο έναι γιά κακό.[4]

One holiday and one Sunday,
the dawn of Easter day
I set the bread to bake
I baked but it didn't bake
it only came to pieces.
I baked cheese pies as well
I baked but they didn't bake
they turned to little crumbs.
I dyed the eggs red

and they refused to dye
but only turned out dark.
I understood straight away
that this was an evil sign.

Paraski consults her 13-year-old daughter (in other versions her father) as to the meaning of the evil omen and is told not to delay but to go to her only brother who is up in the mountains looking after the animals. She sets off to find him, but on her way she meets her husband, her brother-in-law and her 'taciturn' father-in-law. She asks them what her brother is doing. They tell them that when they left him in the barn he was milking the sheep to make cheese. When Paraski reaches the sheepfold the sheep are bleating and the dogs bark savagely, leaping up at her. She is surprised that the dogs don't recognize her and says to them: 'Aren't I the housewife who used to feed you bread and give you water to drink?' Paraski throws an Easter rusk to the older dog and a red egg to the puppy, and they calm down and let her enter the sheepfold. The suspense has been carefully orchestrated through the interchange with the dogs, and it continues to build as she looks for her brother in the semi-darkness of the sheepfold. Then comes the awful climax:

Ηύρεκα μιά παλιοραχιά
ολόβουτη στα αίματα,
τήνε κατρανακύλησα.
Ηύρα το γ Καλοπόθοζ μου
πεσμένο ήτα τα μπούμουτρα
χουσμένο μες' στα αίματα
συδιπλωμένο στη ραχιά.
Το γύρισα το φίλησα
και είχε σαράντα μαχαιριές
και δυο διπλοχατζαϊριές
μες' τις αγιάτρεφτες μεϊριές.
Κι είχε και μία μαχαιϊριά
μες' στην αριστερή μειριά
στο κεφαλάρι τη καρδιάς.

I found an old cape
all bathed in blood.
I turned it over,
found my Kalopothos

fallen face down
smothered in blood
his back doubled.
I turned him over, kissed him
and he had forty knife-wounds
and two double dagger-wounds
in places that can't be cured
and one other wound
on the left-hand side
at the top part of his heart.

The careful examination of the body and enumeration of wounds are as methodical as an accountant's. We are spared no horrid detail, but grief is already being measured by the implacable calculation of revenge. Paraski asks her dead brother who his murderer was. The answer, which indicts the three members of her family she met on the road, comes from 'Satan', who 'helped a little too, so that you would have misfortune', We recall the lament of Vetoulas, where the bleating ram is recognized as Satan by the brother on his way to avenge the murder. It might seem, from the association of Satan with the prompting of violent revenge, that such motivation is recognized as inconsistent with Christian teaching, but there is no sense of a struggle by the avenger with her conscience; on the contrary, Paraski sets about her task as if obeying the dictates of a higher moral duty.

Leaving her brother's body in the sheepfold, the sister sets out for her patrial village. She shrieks and cries out as she fetches a mule to bring the body back, but her relatives initially suspect her of complicity in the murder of her own brother and send her away. Paraski goes to a neighbouring village to buy poison. At one shop she doesn't find any, but at the second, a grocery owned by Petros the saddler, she finds what she needs. The shopkeeper is suspicious at first and asks her why she wants the poison. She claims she has a problem with rats. Again there is a steady building up of suspense as the details of her purchase are carefully disclosed, one following the next in an orderly sequence.

When she arrives home she shows no sign of distress. Her brother-in-law and father-in-law ask her to prepare a local dish, a type of omelette. She breaks twenty-five eggs to make the dish, adds some pork fat and dribbles in the poison. When it is ready, she goes out into the courtyard to fetch the three murderers of her brother. 'Come,' she says, 'I've fixed the food and it'll get cold.' The men sit together to have their meal; she at some distance. 'Hey, sister-in-law, come and sit with us; we'll all eat together,' says her brother-in-law, but Paraski claims to have eaten while she cooked. 'Eat your fill,' she says to them as they begin eating, 'But I want you to pay for the Virgin's candle.'

'Sister-in-law, the omelette's bitter.'

'The flour mustn't have been good; it must have been stale. Take another spoonful and finish off the job.'

Immediately following this interchange comes the second climax of the lament, as horrible in its detail as the first. The eyes of the poisoned victims roll wildly. They drop their spoons and their arms and legs stiffen. The taciturn father-in-law realizes what has happened and groans: 'You bitch, you've poisoned us!' Her reply is a triumphant balancing of accounts:

> – Τόσο δα δεν το ξέρατε
> δεν το καταλαβαίνατε
> όντα τον εσκοτώνατε
> μένα το γ Καλοπόθος μου
> το μοναχόνε μου καφό
> που ήτα ντελίνι και στοιχειό;
> Στα χέρια δεν το πχιάνετε
> και δεν το καταφέρνατε.
> Το φάτε στα κλεφτά-κλεφτά
> μα τόνε δίκηωσα καλά
> με κριάρι με παχύ σφαχτό
> κι όχι με παλιοζύγουρο.
> Εκαμα ότι εκάματε
> κι' εκτέλεσα το χρέο μου
> με τόκο και κεφάλαιο.
>
> Το κάματε με τεχνικό
> να φάτε κληρονομικό
> Μα τώρα εκέρδισα εγώ.

All this time didn't you know
didn't you all realize
at the time you were killing

my Kalopothos, my only brother
who was strong and stoutly built?
You couldn't get a hold of him
and you didn't manage to grab him.
Secretly you ate him up
but I avenged him well
with a ram, with a fat slaughter
and didn't weigh him short
I did just what you did
and carried out my duty
with interest and capital besides.

You did your deed by guile –
to make sure of your inheritance,
but now I've won it all.

Having finished her speech, Paraski goes back to her parents
again and first tells her mother what she has done. 'You did
well,' says her mother. 'May you eat and drink [your in-
heritance] with the new husband you'll find.' To her father she
says, 'We have taken our rights and a little more besides.' 'If
you're telling the truth,' her father replies, 'I'll make you a glass
cage to sing in so that your enemies will never find you.'

The lament ends with a brief address to the dead brother,
telling him his gloomy sister has avenged him 'with two or
three', and a cry for herself in the third person, the only real
outburst of the lament: 'Alas, the wretched one! What other
Christian has buried, on the same Easter Sunday, at dawn and
at evening, her brother and her husband!'

The story Paraski tells in her lament seems too dramatic, too
carefully manipulated towards its macabre climax, to be spontaneous. The coincidence of the murder with Easter is also
improbably appropriate, but however much it may have been
embroidered over the years, the lament is accepted as a true
account of Paraski's revenge. Dramatic it may be, but it is
neither morbid nor extravagant. In the aftermath of death,
anger and violence, the 'hard rock of Mani' uses the familiar
metaphors of accounting combined with sacrifice to immortalize
her revenge. Her brother was 'strong and stout', and the three
who killed him 'ate him slyly'. She has 'avenged him well/ with
a ram, with a fat slaughter/ and didn't weigh him short/ I ...
carried out my duty with interest and capital'. The pride in these

lines is fierce. According to the strange code of honour that prevails in the blood feuds of Mani, it is important to warn your victim in advance, not take him by surprise. A dishonourable death has been avenged by the implacable bookkeeper, Paraski, who has paid dearly for it in every sense, killing three for one, and killing her own husband, source of her social status and wealth. Since most feuds concern property, disputed land or animals, the metaphors of the ram and the fat animals are understandable, but the word *sfaktó* has, even in modern Greek, the ring of sacrifice to it. In the lines that follow, Paraski expresses the hope that her daughter will be well, a good housekeeper, and that she will 'eat' their portion. Eating is a common metaphor for using up or wasting, but in combination with *merdhikó* (share, portion), it extends the metaphor of food and eating which is immediately repeated in reference to the inheritance the murderers had hoped for.

FOOD AND COOKING

As in the lament of Koundounara for her son, the proper cooking of ritual foods and its opposite, the failure to cook things correctly, taken together with the metaphors of eating and the fatal meal itself, form a cluster of signs that are woven through Paraski's narrative. The lament begins with an attempt at ritual cooking: the baking of the Easter breads and the dyeing of the eggs. The failure of the bread and cheese pies to bake, and of the eggs to take the red dye are recognized as omens, but their significance must be spelled out by a young girl, the daughter apparently having some skill at reading such signs.[5] Paraski addresses her daughter as *mavrisméni Kyriakí*, literally 'blackened Sunday'. She will use the same adjective for herself in the final lines of the lament, but here it seems premature, unless the prophet-daughter is already tinged by the deed her mother will perform on her nameday. Leaving for the sheepfold, Paraski takes Easter rusks and red eggs in her apron and sash to give to her brother. When she asks the three murderers about her brother, they give her an elaborate answer, again concerned with the preparation of food. The brother is 'milking, to make cheese/ to eat it and have a good time/ because he wasn't feeling so well/ To eat milk and cheese and fresh *mezithra*' (a type of soft cheese). There is a deliberate irony in their words, especially considering this is Easter Sunday, not a day one would expect to eat cheese, but rather lamb. To enter the sheepfold guarded by the crazed dogs, Paraski at first tells the animals she was the housewife who used to feed them, and then, as a diversion, throws them the traditional Easter foods intended for her brother, so that she can enter the darkened hut. The classical symbolism of the gesture is impossible to ignore, and like many other features of the lament, suggests some artful reworking. To complete and confuse the symbolic picture, Paraski finds her brother slaughtered in a sheepfold on the one day of the year when even the poorest Greek family would normally slaughter a sheep for the traditional Easter meal.

With the discovery of the murdered brother, the first section of the lament ends. Traditional foods have failed to cook and have led Paraski to her slaughtered brother who has replaced the paschal lamb as innocent victim and desirable food. Now the sister will prepare food again, this time deliberately mis-cooking eggs in the fatal omelette. The cooking is carefully described: twenty-five eggs are broken to make a 'fat' dish. The dialogue at the table has the masterly irony of a born dramatist. The men are called to the table in case the food gets cold. The brother-in-law invites Paraski to sit at the table with them and eat. She refuses, saying she has eaten while she was cooking it, and that she is only interested in 'the last mouthful'. As she enjoins them to eat, she even allows herself the luxury of a hint of the reckoning she has planned, by suggesting they 'pay the Virgin's candle', at the same time coolly averting their suspicion at the bitter taste of the omelette by claiming that the flour is stale.

When the three men realize they have been poisoned, Paraski's rhetoric changes abruptly. Slaughter and sacrifice become her metaphors as she uses the adjective *stichió* (both fat and strong), to describe her brother. She proudly declares she has avenged him by the killing of the ram and by a 'fat' slaughter. This killing is not an empty ritual but a squaring of accounts, 'with interest and capital'. Since she has lost both brother and husband and will be a fugitive, as her father indicates, from the avenging relatives of the men she has slain, Paraski would seem to have gained a dubious victory, but avenging her brother's murder has given her honour, and by singing the song of her own fate, she has gained immortality among the Mani.

ANCIENT PARALLELS

The parallels between this lament and ancient tragedy have been noted by Greek ethnographers.[6] Not only is the superior claim of *fára* over *gámos*, of the ancient *genos* or *philē* over ties acquired through marriage passionately affirmed by Paraski's lament, reminding us inevitably of Antigone's hierarchical sense of loyalties, but the calculated revenge executed by a nineteenth-century Maniot woman suggests the cycle of violence perpetuated, according to mythical and tragic accounts, in the ancient House of Atreus that once lay a hundred miles to the north. Lament is the medium through which revenge is promoted, and it is a woman's medium. It is more common for men than women to execute revenge, but Paraski's case is not unique. In a lament that underlines both the continued loyalty of a married woman to her patrial clan and the necessity to protect its honour, another Maniot woman of the same name takes up arms.

THE AVENGING SISTER: WOMAN, BECOME A MAN

Petros Mariolis, a young professor, was from a family involved in a feud with the Patsourakis family from Nomias. He had a 'tower' (the traditional stone houses of Mani were built like fortresses during the period of the blood feuds) in the village of Dri to which the rival family laid claim. Warned by a bird of evil omen (the *gióni* or nightjar) that the castle has fallen, his sister tells her husband she will go and find out whether the bird told her the truth. The husband accompanies her to the tower but they find it closed. A neighbour tells them that the brother has been severely wounded by his enemies and taken by friends to a doctor in the town of Kalamata. Paraski asks her husband what they should do. He suggests following the brother to Kalamata to find out how he is,

– Να φύγομε, ε Παρασκή
να φτάσομε αποβραδίς
στη γ Καλαμάτα στο γιατρό
να ιδούμε αν έναι ζωντανός.
– Εσύ να φύγεις Παντελή
και όπου θέεις να ιδιαβείς.
Εγώ στο μ πύργο θ'ανεβού
και δε θα κρόου τους οχτρούς.

Οσο θε νάμαι ζωντανή
ο πύργος δε θα πατηθεί.
Το κάστρο θα ξαρματωθεί
άμα χαθεί κι η Παρασκή.[7]

– Let's leave now, Paraski,
and reach the doctor in Kalamata
by evening to see if he's alive.
– You leave now, Pantelis,
and travel wherever you please.
I'll go up in the tower
to fire on the enemies below.
As long as I am alive
no one will set foot in the tower.
The fortress will only fall
when Paraski herself is lost.

Another case of a sister avenging her brother's death is preserved in a mother's lament for her daughter, Vyeniki. The lament begins with a description of how the brother, Ligoris, was taken to Kalamata after being seriously wounded by his enemies. On his return he was treated to a feast by his *koumbári*.[8] Asked if he wanted an escort for protection against his enemies, the young man was insulted and went out into the street alone. He ran into his enemies who greeted him in a friendly way and told him not to be afraid of them, but as he turned his back to go, they shot him. They cut out his viscera, and passing by his house, offered them to his sister saying: 'Health and joy to you, Vyeniki!/ A message from your Ligoris/ and a basket of giblets/to eat and enjoy.'

As the lament begins, Vyeniki is still ignorant of the murder. When she learns what has happened, her mother encourages her to avenge him saying:

– Ετώρα, μαυρο Βγενική,
γυναίκα, άντρας να γενείς.
Ζούστικο κι αρματόθηκο
και πάρε το γ καλό σαρμά
και να ζουστείς τη ζουναϊριά
οπ' όχει το φοσύγγια
και τρέχα στα Γυρίσματα
να κυνηγήσεις το φονιά
να δικηωθεί ο Ληγόρη μας.[9]

– Now, black Vyeniki
woman, become a man.
Buckle up and arm yourself
and take the good rifle
and tighten up the belt
where you keep your cartridges
run quickly to Yirismata
to chase after the murderer
so our Ligoris will be avenged.

When she encounters the enemies of her brother, they greet her as they did her brother, in a friendly way, but she draws her weapon and kills two of them. The mother's fortitude wavers as she considers the danger her daughter is in: 'Ah, where are you, black-Vyeniki/ you're a female child/ and you want to go to jail?' But the daughter is undaunted: 'Don't worry, mother, don't worry/ I won't go to jail/ but you go quickly to Tzimova/ and bring some ammunition./ We'll sit in the tower/ where the enemies pass by/ and the murderer will be with them.' Again the mother reminds her daughter that she is a female child, and again her daughter ignores her. The mother brings her daughter ammunition and the two women climb up to the terrace of the tower. When the enemies pass by they try to talk Vyeniki into a truce, but she scorns them and opens fire again, killing the murderer and three of his cousins but losing her own life in the process. As her mother says: 'By the time she had said her *díkia* (here, the announcement of her just revenge) her soul had left her.'

Vyeniki's mother has sung both the lament for her son and for her daughter, but as is common in these revenge narratives, the greater part of the lament is taken up with a detailed account of how just revenge was achieved. The case of Vyeniki was unusual but not unique. Men were generally expected to exact revenge, but when there was no adult male member of the family women either took vengeance into their own hands or waited until their sons were old enough to perform their expected duty.

WOMEN AS INSTIGATORS OF REVENGE

One of the oldest laments still popular in Mani is that of Pavlos Koutalidis.[10] The widow who recounts the story has waited eighteen years since the death of her husband so that her sons could grow up and avenge the death of their father who was killed 'unjustly and without good reason'. One Easter morning she sets seven plates on table instead of six. When a son notices and asks her why, she says that it is for their father who is still unavenged. Now that they are old enough, she tells them to take their rifles and hunt down the enemies of her husband, in particular one Pavlos Koutalidis:

> Αλλιώς και δεν το κάμετε
> χαίρι να μην έχετε
> κι η μαύρη η κατάρα μου
> να σας ακολουθά παντού!

> If you do otherwise
> may you have no joy
> and may my black curse
> follow you everywhere!

The boys ask their mother's blessing and assure her they will avenge their father immediately on this Easter holiday. They set off with their guns and kill Pavlos immediately but are forced to fight a day-long battle with his followers. When they return home they announce their success in words that echo Paraski's:

> – Μάννα τα συχαρίκια μας
> το πήραμε το δίκηο μας
> με το κασέμι το παχύ,
> τον Κουταλίδη τον τρανό
> που ήτα στο ντόπο φόβητρο.

> Mother, your blessings on us
> we took our just revenge
> on the fat ram himself
> old Koutalidis who was feared
> all round these parts.

Kissing her sons on both cheeks, the mother replies:

– Δόξα στην τύχη κι είχη τα!
Τώρα είμαι μάννα με παιδιά
και δεν είμαι πεντάκληρη!

Praise to fortune and joy to me!
Now I'm a mother with sons
and not disinherited five-fold.

Not only are women frequently the initiators of revenge, but they are merciless to men who fail to take up arms. In the lament of Yiorgadza Nikolinakos, his wife mocks him for allowing himself to be duped and disarmed by his powerful *koumbáros*. He pleads with her to have patience, that he will eventually pay back the insult, but she gives him no quarter:

– Γιαννούλα, λάβε υπομονή
το δίκαννο θα πλιερωθεί
μ' ένανε νη με δυό-τρεις.
– Ξαρμαματωμένε Γιωργατζά
το σπίτι μας δε ζε χουρά.[11]

– Yiannoula, have patience
the rifle will be paid back
with one, two or three.
– Disarmed Yiorgatza
there's no room for you in our house.

The authority of women in the revenge laments goes unchallenged. They are neither innocent bystanders in a violent game of honour nor the bloodthirsty instigators of gratuitous murder. They are, however, as involved in the cycle of revenge as their men, and as concerned with questions of honour. It has been said by anthropologists that it is the men in rural Greece who must preserve their *timí* (honour) and that the women's honour is achieved by modesty that avoids *dhropí* (shame).[12] In the Maniot laments it is clear that traditional modesty can be suspended in the service of family honour, and that for a woman to act like a man is not necessarily shameful.[13] The fact that these laments have passed into the repertoire of male singers indicates more than a degree of admiration for the fierce female defence of family honour that transcends all quotidian gender roles.

CONFLICTING AUTHORITIES

While Inner Mani remained an isolated, virtually autonomous area of Greece, the concept of family loyalty revealed in the laments was tenable. The fact that it ran counter to the teaching of the Orthodox Church did not seem to have perturbed the women of Mani; in fact there are suggestions of some conflation of Christian motifs with revenge narratives. Easter seems a popular time to execute revenge and the failure of Easter foods to cook in Paraski's lament is the ominous sign that her brother has been murdered like a lamb among his sheep. The apparent inconsistency of Christian motifs combined with pagan metaphors of sacrifice is typical not only of the laments of other regions of Greece but of most Greek songs and folk-tales.

It was only when Inner Mani became slowly integrated into the Greek state that the blood feuds and the laments that chronicle and promote them posed any conceivable threat to authority. It is a lawcourt of the early Greek state under its first king, Otto of Bavaria, that forms the setting for a lament in which a widow whose only son has been killed by his enemies threatens to take the law into her own hands. The killers of Old Brettis's son were tried in Mistra and the widow was taken to the trial by the people of her village. In the courtroom she pulled out a long knife and said:

– κύριε πρόεδρε,
α δεν τούσε δικάσετε
νη θάνατο νη πίζωη
λέπεις ετούτο το σπαθή;
θα πάου στο μ πάνο μαχαλά
κι α δε μπορού μεγάλονε
θα πχιάσου ένα μικρό παιδί
και θα ντο σφάξου σαν αρνί
γατί 'χα μοναχό παιδί
και μου το καμμαϊτιάσασι.[14]

– Mr President,
if you don't condemn them
to death or a life sentence
you see this dagger?
I'll go to the upper quarter
and if I can't find a grown-up

I'll grab a small child
and I'll slay him like a lamb
for mine was an only child
and they cut him to pieces.

Here is a clear case of a lament that provokes the authority of
the state. From the late nineteenth century on, such laments are
common, not simply blaming the government or the king for the
death of a son, but taking sides in local political struggles, and
supporting fugitives of the state against the authorities. The
lament for Mayor Dai, composed in 1866(?) is one of many
such laments. The mayor of the village of Stefania, who
originated from Pambaka in Mani, belonged to the so-called
'democratic' camp. Just before the elections he had come to
an agreement with Maniot fugitives to grant them amnesty
if he were elected. The public prosecutor for the area of
Laconia, Voidis Mavromikhailis, seeing that he had great
popular support, murdered him just before the elections. A
group of fugitives waited to avenge the murder at the Evrota
bridge, but the plot was discovered and government troops were
sent to kill the rebels. Two were killed, one escaped and another
managed to blockade himself in a nearby ruined church. The
lament was sung by a cousin of the mayor's:

Ε μαύρο δήμαρχε Νταή
και Μιχαλάκη Μόφορη
που ζας εσκότως' ο Βοϊδής
στου Λέημονα στου Ντούρ-Αλή,
τι ήτα το πέρασμα στενό.
Σκοτώθη ο μαύρο Δημιανός
λαβώθηκε κι ο Μόφορης
κι ο χοντροκούκης ο ραγιάς
επήδησε στη θάλασσα
κι έμειν' ο δόλιος Σταυριανός
στο ρημοκλήσι μοναχός.[15]

Eh, black Mayor Dai
and Mihalaki Mofori
who were killed by Voidis
at Leimona at Dour-Ali
where the crossing was narrow.
Black Dimianos was killed

and Moforis was wounded
and Hondrokoukos the bondsman
leapt into the sea
and poor Stavrianos was left
in the ruined church alone.

During the German occupation of Greece some Maniots joined the left-wing resistance, others the right, and the laments of this period became, for a short time, vehicles for the expression of nationalist sentiment. Costantina Dimaronga, who was only a teenage girl when the war broke out, composed a lament for the left-wing resistance organization EAM which has remained popular. In it she praises the bravery of the Greeks in the Albanian War and criticizes the king for abandoning the Greeks to their fate when the Germans invaded. She describes how the leaders of the partisan army recruited the young Maniots to their cause and when the old men expressed their doubts about the wisdom of opposing the Germans, a youth responded:

– Το δέντρο της ελευτεριάς
με αίμα τη παλληκαϊριάς
πρέπει να το ποτίσομε
γιά να ντην αποχτήσομε.[16]

– If we are to win it,
the tree of freedom
must be watered
with the blood of bravery.

LAMENTS OF PARTISAN POLITICS

The Second World War was a very different kind of conflict for Greece, one that made itself felt even in remote areas like the Mani. Whereas women had once cursed the government or the king for involving their sons in foreign wars, they now cursed them for failure to confront the foreign powers that occupied their lands and killed their men. Laments became expressions of hatred for the Germans and women not only supported their menfolk who resisted the occupation, but joined in the resistance themselves. Costantina Dimaronga joined the partisans in the mountains when she was only 18 years old. In an act of daring that was repeated in villages all over Greece during the

German occupation, she and two other women risked execution
by burying their cousin and a group of fellow resistance fighters
killed in the battle of Verga-Armyrou. Turned back on their
way to buy food, the three women ignored warnings that they
would be shot if they approached the site of the battle. They
found the Greek partisans 'slaughtered like lambs/ with their
brains scattered'. Among the dead was their cousin, Lias
Kananakis, for whom the lament was composed. They decided
to bury him, but were stopped by the Germans at gunpoint.
Returning to the village, they found an old man, a crippled shopkeeper, who gave them a pick and a shovel and agreed to help
them bury the dead. The three women buried their cousin near
the church and put a stone cross on the grave. Then they
proceeded to bury another twelve men in simple graves, and the
resistance leaders sent a priest to perform a burial service. The
lament, composed by Dimaronga for her cousin, was improvised
when the female relatives of the dead wept together on hearing
the news. The dead cousin is referred to almost as a detail in
Dimaronga's narrative of her own daring. She tells her tale with
pride, but there is bitterness against those who refused to help
her bury the dead, and anger against those Greeks who actively
collaborated with the Germans:

Εχόρεψε ο Σατανάς
μεσ' στη μ πατρίδα την Ελλάς
για να χωρίσει ο λαός:
άλλος να μείνει Ελληνικός
ν' αγωνιστεί από το βουνό
κι άλλος να πάει με τους οχτρούς
με Ιταλούς, με Γερμανούς
και χιούνεται σαν το νερό
το αίμα το Ελληνικό.[17]

Satan danced in
the fatherland, Greece,
to divide the people:
one to remain Greek
and fight from the mountains
the other going with the enemies
the Italians, the Germans
and Greek blood
flows like water.

Dimaronga's lament is more than an Antigone-like demonstration of the strength of familial obligation to the dead. The combination of nationalist and partisan sentiments expressed in the lament indicate that she is both politically aware and committed to a cause that extends beyond her immediate family. Before the Second World War and the German occupation, there is little evidence of a sense of nationalism in the laments. Whoever is responsible for causing a death, be it the government or the king, is generally regarded as an enemy. There are occasional exceptions. During the Balkan War of 1912–13, a young Maniot soldier was killed in the battle of Tzoumayia. After he and other members of the family who had died or been wounded in the war had been lamented by the younger women, an 80-year-old aunt of the dead man joined in the lament. Despite the fact that the younger women had praised the young men's heroism, the blind old aunt berated them for weeping over their dead and for criticizing the king and Venizelos:

τον τόπο μας βρωμίσατε
τους άντρες σας προσβάλλετε
τον τόπο μας ντροπιάζετε
και τα παιδιά που κάνετε
θε να ντα κάμετε δειλούς
να σκιάζονται το μ πόλεμο!
Τι παραπαιτενίζεστε,
βγάνετε τα μαλλιά ζας;[18]

You've dirtied our country
and shamed your men
and you seek to make
your children cowards
to be afraid of war.
Why do you cry so much,
pulling out your hair?

Although she has lost her young relatives in the war, the lamenter says not only were the young men's deaths given freely for their country but that in criticizing Venizelos for provoking the war her fellow lamenters display their ignorance. 'Why don't you learn your letters?' she upbraids them. 'May a snake eat your tongues/ for confusing our leader/ Venizelos with the reason/ why the war happened.' She then proceeds to give the women a long lesson in the true history of the causes of the war and ends by praising the king and Venizelos for bringing glory to their country. Her final piece of advice to the women is that they not marry but raise the orphans of the war and leave off weeping.

The burst of nationalist sentiment that accompanied the irredentist 'Megali Idea' movement and ended with the defeat of the Greek forces at Smyrna may have been briefly reflected in the laments of the period, but the deep division between Royalists and Venizelists that began in the period of the First World War was to leave a permanent mark, even in the villages of Inner Mani. The Second World War initially united Greeks in another nationalist struggle, but almost as soon as the resistance against the Germans began, it was split between the popular left-wing resistance organization, EAM, and rival organizations that were either loyal to the king or opposed to the communist-led resistance. In the Civil War that followed the Second World War, the division Dimaronga likens, in her lament, to the 'dance of Satan' between left-wing ex-resistance fighters and right-wing supporters of the government, many of them former collaborators, erupted into bitter fighting. The Civil War eclipsed, for a time, the violence of old family feuds. What is interesting is that in this period when the traditional family and local loyalties are temporarily replaced by partisan politics, women's laments frequently express both their political loyalties and their opposition to the violence of the period.

In her lament for the schoolteacher Thomas Leotsakos, his widow admires her husband's courage and leadership as an officer in the resistance, but underlines the suffering that his loyalty to EAM brought on his family:

τ'όχετε βρει από παλιά
να είσαστε όλο μπροστά,
Θε μου, γιά την Ελευτεριά.
Γι'αυτό, Θωμά πολεμιστή,
τίποτε δεν εδίστασες
και όλους μας αρνήθηκες,
γυναίκα σου και τα παιδιά
και τους γονείς σου χωριστά.
Και τραβήξαμε πολλά. . . .[19]

You lads had got used
to being always in the lead
my God, for Freedom.
That's why, fighter Thomas,
you shrank from nothing
and denied all of us
your wife and your children
and especially your parents.
And we suffered a lot.

A young cousin of Thomas Leotsakis' was just out of high
school when he joined the resistance. He was executed in 1948
during the Civil War. At the forty-day memorial service of his
death, his sister sang a long lament for her brother. She began
by summarizing the struggle the family had had to educate the
boy through high school so that he would have a good life and
the family would have prestige. But Yiannis gave up all this to
join the resistance. To persuade his reluctant mother to give him
her blessing he appealed to her pride:

– Ελα, μαννούλα μου χρυσή,
να μάσε δώσεις την ευχή
Σπαρτιάτισσα γιά να γενείς
και γιά το 'ταν 'πιτάν' να πείς![20]

Come, mother dearest,
give us your blessing
and you'll be like a Spartan
mother urging on her son.

The mother asks what will become of her if her son is killed,
and he tells her that she should be glad if he dies fighting for the
freedom of her other children. The lament describes how the
mother gave her blessing and how, after fighting in a number of
battles, Yiannis was seriously wounded. The sister followed her
brother to the mountains where he lay in a makeshift field
hospital. Warned that the Germans had discovered their where-
abouts and were about to arrive, his comrades hid Yiannis in a
cave. Eventually he made his way home. No sooner had he
arrived than the Germans came looking for him and again he
was forced to hide in the mountains. Risking her own life, the
sister carried food to him, and as soon as he had enough

strength he rejoined the resistance. When the Germans retreated the young man resumed his studies in Piraeus, but he was quickly betrayed as a former member of EAM and arrested. He went before a firing squad but was only wounded. The second time he went before his executioners he was given a chance to save his life by renouncing his political allegiance but he refused. The sister's account of his heroic death expresses that mixture of admiration and regret which is typical of the wartime laments. She addresses her brother directly, calling him both her 'brave lad' and an 'egoist' for refusing to save his own life. She ends by describing him defying his executioners with a cry of 'Long live Freedom'. But she reminds him, as if in a last admonition, that: 'You were a fresh young shoot/ only twenty years old.'

MODERN MANIOT LAMENTS

With the end of the Civil War and the beginnings of mass emigration in the 1950s, the villages of Inner Mani ceased to be riven by political and personal violence. Most laments of the modern period are for people who have died a natural death, but into the laments for the older generation of Mani, *moirologhístres* will still weave narratives of former conflicts, and in their accounts they continue to apportion blame wherever they can. An old ex-EAM fighter I know in a village near the border of Inner Mani has already chosen the *moirologhístres* he wishes to sing at his funeral, women he can rely on to present his side of the political picture and deride his enemies.

In the quarters of Piraeus where many Maniot families now live, there are a number of well-known lamenters who continue the tradition. Among these women, the old revenge laments are popular, but newly composed laments seem to have lost their angry edge and become calmly fatalistic. In a 1975 lament for a young girl killed on her honeymoon in an automobile accident, her great aunt, Marthoula Kalkatzakou-Kassi, gives a long account of all the male relatives she has lost, but concludes that her niece's death was 'written on the papers' (i.e. by fate). 'Eh, my preened partridge,' the old woman addresses her niece, 'You'll never come back/ your fate was written.'[21]

CONCLUSION

Having looked at how laments function in a number of traditional societies, particularly in modern Greece, it is time to reconsider the question of why attempts were made to restrict lament in the classical city-states. It may be argued that the comparison is invalid, that nothing we know of modern laments can explain how laments functioned and were regarded in antiquity. But in a culture where a continuous tradition of lament has been established, I believe we are bound to take the evidence of the modern laments into consideration. The issue of banning laments is not a minor one, involving, as it does, issues that have affected the status of women in western society ever since. If we understand some common features of the tradition we are in a better position to know not simply why laments were banned, but how they were appropriated and turned against the lamenter, and what was lost as a result. Among these common features, at least in Mani are (1) that laments are conscious artistic narratives created and performed by women, some of whom are regarded as having superior ability in composing them; (2) that they are, or were, highly regarded by the community as a whole; (3) that they are considered therapeutic and even pleasurable; (4) that they assist memory by fixing the dead in a precise landscape; (5) that they are usually centred on the pain of the bereaved and rarely take the form of an encomium; (6) that it is common for the lamenter to shift pain outwards by blaming the agent of death; (7) that vengeance is frequently instigated and exacted by women; (8) that loyalty to brother generally exceeds loyalty to husband and that family loyalty is privileged over loyalty to the state; and (9) that they structure pain in an elaborate symbolic language that seems to be a way of mediating the separation and finality of death.

Chapter 4

Mourning in a man's world: the *Epitaphios Logos* and the banning of laments in fifth-century Athens

For no good comes of cold laments.
> (Homer, *Iliad*, XXIV, 524)

We surely say that a decent man will believe that . . . being dead is not a terrible thing. . . . There is no further need of wailing and lamentations. . . . They are useless to women who are to be decent, let alone for men.
> (Plato, *Republic*, III, 398)

Then we should be quite right to cut out from our poetry, lamentations by famous men. We can give them to the less reputable women characters or to the bad men, so that those whom we say we are bringing up as guardians of our state will be ashamed to imitate them.
> (Plato, *Republic*, III, 387 ff.)

Mourning is something feminine, weak, ignoble: women are more inclined to it than men, barbarians more than Greeks, commoners more than aristocrats.
> (Plutarch, *Letter to Apollonius*)

What's this? An outburst of female lust?
That beating of drums and shouting 'Sevazios!'
Is that the wailing to Adonis from roof
to roof I once heard in the assembly?
That wretched Demostratos was busy
proposing a naval expedition to Sicily
while his wife danced on the rooftops
shouting, 'Woe for Adonis!' Demostratos
suggested drafting Zakynthian hoplites
and his wife, still on the roof and tipsy
wailed: 'Beat your breasts for Adonis!'

and the son of a bitch pushed his plan through –
that's what you get from women: moral chaos!
(Aristophanes, Lysistrata, 387–97)

Like some flat-footed policeman trying to restore order at
Woodstock, the officious *proboulos*, or commissioner of public
safety, in Aristophanes' *Lysistrata*, bumbles onto the Acro-
polis, where the women have taken over the Athenian treasury in
an attempt to stop the Peloponnesian War. The curious thing
about the *Lysistrata* passage is that, as a civic official, the
proboulos is merely reflecting the attitude of the state. Solon
had passed a law in Athens that 'regulated women's appear-
ances in public, as well as their festivals, and put an end to wild
and disorderly behaviour . . . he abolished the practice of lacerating the flesh at funerals, of reciting set dirges, and of lamenting
a person at the funeral ceremonies of another.'[1] Those who
disobeyed Solon's laws were to be punished by 'the board of
censors for women for weak and unmanly behaviour, and for
carrying their mourning to extravagant lengths'.[2]

An extraordinary notion, surely, to be punished as a woman
for being unmanly! What lies behind this strange law that lumps
together women's festivals and funerals, and censors female
lament in classical Athens? Is it unique to Athens? Is there any
basis for associating women mourners with wild or disorderly
behaviour? Could such behaviour threaten, in any way, the
society at large? Before we look at mourning at funerals, it is
worth digressing, for a moment, to the question of women's
festivals, particularly the *Adonia*, in order to see what connection the Athenian state could possibly make between such
apparently disparate occasions.[3]

The subject of the *Adonia*, or festival for Adonis has been
addressed at length by Margaret Alexiou, by Marcel Detienne
and more recently by John Winkler.[4] As Winkler suggests, the
limited sources we have (one passage from Plato, two from
comedy) do not support Detienne's conclusion that the *Adonia*
were celebrated mainly by courtesans or that they were, in fact,
lascivious occasions.[5] That women celebrated them in the
absence of men, and that they lamented the dead Adonis,
laughed and drank wine together during the period in which
they cultivated quick-growing roof-top gardens of green plants
that they forced to fruition and then allowed to wither, is about

all we know of the *Adonia*. Winkler's originality is to attempt to see the festival from a female perspective and to ask what the women were laughing and wailing about as they cultivated their airy gardens. Noticing an apparent fondness in Sappho for tales of powerful goddesses like Eos who seduce young lovers, use them for their pleasure and are faced with the embarrassing problem of ageing mortality, Winkler concludes that the reference to Aphrodite depositing Adonis in a lettuce patch, mentioned in a number of sources, symbolizes his lost virility, the plant being well known for its anti-aphrodisiac qualities.[6] Like the lettuce that grows limp in the noonday sun, the fast-wilting gardens of the festival seem an appropriate if misandric metaphor for the male contribution to fertility. If, as Plato states, the festival lasted exactly eight days, it suggests a deliberate contrast to the eight months of agriculture needed to produce Demeter's grain.[7] Demeter's festivals – the *Thesmophoria, Haloa, Stenia* – were, despite their exclusively female nature, supported by the state, since they were thought to promote the generation of crops and children. While women's role both in preparing flour and carrying children is clearly linked to the nurturing of the seed, men's role in the process of generation can be compared to that of Adonis, Aphrodite's brief lover. 'What the gardens, with their quickly rising and quickly wilting sprouts symbolize,' according to Winkler, 'is the marginal or subordinate role that men play in both agriculture (vis-à-vis the earth) and human generation (vis-à-vis wives and mothers).'[8] If we follow Winkler's argument through, the famous cry of 'Woe for Adonis!' becomes a ribald joke, a reflection on the short-lived virility of the male god in contrast to the steady fertility of the female.

Winkler's is an ingenious, attractive theory, although his sources are few and not without prejudice. If we were to take the comic poets and Plato as our guides, say, to the tragedies of Euripides, we might arrive at an amusing but diminished view of his plays. Trying to imagine how women saw their own role in a society like that of ancient Greece by reading male sources is as difficult an exercise as peeling the drapery from a marble image of Aphrodite. What Winkler and an increasing number of classicists have realized is that anthropological studies of contemporary Mediterranean society may provide at least a suggestive supplement to ancient source material.[9] While accounts of women written by men may portray them as passive or ideally subservient and women may themselves tacitly co-operate with such an ideology, anthropological studies indicate women are well aware of their dominant role in the life cycle. As Winkler observes, 'Women's double consciousness about their own existence and about men's representations of it is connected with their encompassing activities – birth, nurturance and the care of the dead – activities in which they manage and control the fundamental course of life.'[10] The paradoxical nature of modern Greek laments, where anything from ribaldry to political satire can be woven into a dirge, where women may sing and dance while their husbands lie dying or sing the same song at a wedding or funeral, remind us that Eros and Thanatos, like tears and laughter, were intimately associated in antiquity. Their conjunction in the *Adonia* does not mean that the ritual wailing performed for the dead god was in any sense a parody. At the wakes of Greek gypsies, women break off lamenting at sunset and spend the hours of darkness telling wonder tales.[11] It is quite possible that the women who wailed for the dead Adonis were similarly capable of switching from one mode of behaviour to the other with no sense of incongruity.

The paradoxes that characterize the funerals and folklore of modern Greece may help us understand why Solon's laws were directed at women's behaviour in two superficially contrasting situations: festivals and funerals. It is significant that in the major festivals in which women took the leading roles – the *Thesmophoria*, the *Anthesteria*, the Eleusinian mystery rites, the *Adonia* – there is a direct connection between the rites performed for the god or goddess and mourning for the dead. The Eleusinian mysteries, linking Dionysos to Demeter and her lost daughter, dramatize the relationship between fertility and death. Adonis was not only Aphrodite's eager young lover; he was also, in his Syrian form of Tammuz, a son whose worshippers joined his lover/mother in lamenting his death. The greater *Dionysia*, held in Athens in mid-winter, connected Dionysos to the dead. In the passage from the *Lysistrata*, women's behaviour as celebrants of Dionysios/Sevazios and of Adonis is linked as if it were identical, making obvious the connection between possession, in the Dionysian sense, and laments for the dead god.

Dionysos, the god associated with madness and possession, adds a darker dimension to the ribald carousing on Athenian roof-tops. We begin to see the connection being drawn by Solon and other legislators from the sixth century onwards between women's 'excessive' behaviour at festivals and funerals; between women's traditional laments for the dead and the madness induced in them by carrying their grief for the dead god to extremes. We may presume that one reason an attempt was made to control women's behaviour was because it was traditional for them to be unrestrained on such occasions as the *Adonia*, whether they were weeping, laughing or doing a bit of both. Just how 'wild and disorderly' they became is hard to deduce from our meagre, perhaps unreliable, literary sources,[12] but that they were traditionally in charge both of festivals related to mourning and of the lamenting at funerals and that they made a good deal of noise at both, seems undeniable. That the *polis* found it necessary, almost from its inception, to legislate against what seems to have been the traditional behaviour of women in these situations suggests that there are deeper issues involved than bawdy nights on the tiles of Athens or banshee-like wailing over the dead bodies of men and gods.

Abrupt changes in a society's attitude to death occur rarely, but at certain points in the history of western Europe, as Philippe Ariès has demonstrated, there have been marked changes in the way our society, or at least its upper echelons, has regarded death and mourning.[13] Ariès does not address the issue of how such changes in western Europe relate to shifts in social attitudes to women as traditional tenders of the corpse and lamenters of the dead. In the case of the newly emerging city-states of classical Greece, it is impossible to ignore the close relationship between changing attitudes to death, expressed in legislation, literature and philosophy, and the role of women mourners. I will argue that the change in attitude that appears to have taken place towards mourning the dead in late sixth- and fifth-century Athens was intimately connected to establishment of the *polis*. As a political and social unit, the *polis* was always an uneasy alliance *of* family groups, united for the purposes of waging war. As J.-P. Vernant has argued, while war and marriage were complementary in Greek religious thought and in the institutional practices associated with private vengeance, they cease to be so in the context of the city-state.[14] Instead of matrimonial exchange being a means of solving disputes or sowing further strife, marriage was generally arranged between members of the same *polis*. Family units were regrouped in a large community and war became an affair of state. During the archaic period a number of matrimonial practices seem to have co-existed in harmony since they fulfilled different ends. Marriage, as it came to be established in the classical period, was, according to Vernant, an attempt 'to ensure, through strict rules governing marriage, the permanence of the city itself through constant reproduction'. [15] No longer a commodity of exchange between powerful families or warring factions, women lost their value as precious objects and their ability to influence the course of conflict. The *polis*'s attempt to curtail women's role in the public spectacles of festivals and funerals must be viewed in the context of a broader disenfranchisement of women. By drawing sharp lines between the public and private spheres of life, and assigning women's role strictly to the latter, the new democratic institutions effectively negated women's participation even in the traditional rituals they once controlled. [16]

THE RITUAL NATURE OF ANCIENT LAMENT

There was nothing spontaneous about the ancient Greek lament. [17] From Homeric times, it was linked with burial as a necessary part of the *geras thanontōn*, the privileges of the dead. To leave someone *aklauton athapton* (unwept and unburied), as Elpenor reminded Odysseus on his visit to the underworld, was not only to deprive the dead person of his rights as a human being, but to offend the gods and thereby to turn the dead into a threat to the living, a 'reminder of the gods'. [18] Lamenting a person before his death was also an offence in antiquity as it is in modern Greece. [19] Only at the *prothesis*, or wake, after the proper sacrifices had been made, and offerings of food and drink presented to the dead, were laments sung as part of the elaborate rituals of mourning and burial. Evidence for the nature of such ritual behaviour and for the differing behaviour of men and women during the *prothesis* and at the tomb comes from a limited but persuasive combination of archaeological and literary sources. In vase paintings, men are rarely depicted close to the body, but appear in formal procession with right arms raised in a conventional gesture of mourning. Around the bier of the dead man, whose head is clasped by the chief mourner, the women stand, their arms raised, sometimes beating their heads, or pulling out their hair in what Alexiou refers to as 'wild ecstasy'.[20]

Extravagant in their gesture, the women must also have made a good deal of noise. Alexiou concludes that 'lamentation involved movement as well as wailing and singing. Since each movement was determined by a pattern of ritual, frequently accompanied by the shrill music of the *aulos* (reed-pipe), the scene must have resembled a dance, sometimes slow and solemn, sometimes wild and ecstatic.'[21] The restrictive legislation, not only at Athens, but at Gambreion and Delphi, insists on silence during the funeral procession, suggesting that it had been traditional for the women to lament at this stage.[22] At the tomb itself, where animals were sacrificed and traditional offerings of a lock of hair, wine, oil and food were made to the dead, the women relatives of the deceased lamented again. The elaborate offerings and prayers of the burial service may have involved a combination of fear that the dead might return to harm the living, and the hope of renewed fertility from Mother Earth.[23] The traditional appeals to the earth, documented in fifth-century and later inscriptions, link the funeral to other women's rituals involving fertility. At each stage of the funeral ceremony, it seems it was customary for women to play not only a leading role as performers of laments, but one that was closely related to their participation in other festivals involving death and fertility. In fact it may have been hard for the outside observer to draw the line between funeral and festival, although it would be a mistake to suggest that the chief performers in the drama of the funeral were confused as to the proper ritual response to death.

Perhaps the first thing that is new, in the funerals of the *polis*, the first clue to a change in attitude, is the presence of this outside observer: the funerals of a state, like its festivals, are controlled public spectacles in which there is always a didactic element. In traditional communities, festivals and funerals may be open to all or restricted by sex or age, but there is no division of interest between actor and audience. It is taken for granted that such ceremonies are performed by the community for its own benefit. Now, in the larger unit of social organization called the *polis*, someone – using the flat-footed *proboulos* and his like as policemen – is taking it upon himself to observe and censor what has gone unquestioned for as long as people can remember. Before we look at the motivation behind and the consequences of such controlled observation, it is important to summarize what we know of the pre-classical attitude to death and mourning. Our main literary sources are the Homeric poems.

DEATH AND LAMENT IN THE PRE-CLASSICAL PERIOD

Courtly poems about the death of heroes may not teach us very much about a society at large, but in the absence of other literary evidence, the Homeric poems must be used, as Ariès used *La chanson de Roland* or *Le morte d'Arthur*, to suggest how the aristocratic warriors of medieval France or pre-classical Troy and their consorts mourned their dead. We may expect, since these poems are intended for an aristocratic audience, that they will not reflect heretical attitudes, at least on the surface, but present their listeners with an acceptable picture of courtly behaviour.

The poems of the early Middle Ages from which Ariès derives his view of the 'tame' death and 'wild' mourning are, like the *Iliad*, chronicles of heroes at war, most of them removed from their wives and families. Under these circumstances, mourning seems to have been extravagantly displayed. Seeing his friend Oliver is dead, Roland faints and 'against his breast he clasps him tightly in his arms'.[24] Similarly Charlemagne, coming upon his nephew lying dead on the battlefield at Roncevaux, 'trembles with grief' and 'falls senseless on [the body], so great is his anguish'.[25] The young man's uncle is not alone in his prostration: 'In front of the whole army, in front of 100,000 Frenchmen of whom "there is not one who does not weep violently", or "fall unconscious to the ground", the emperor pulls his white beard and tears his hair with both hands.'[26] King Arthur and Gawain are similarly afflicted. After saying a lament for his brothers, Gawain 'went to them, and as he clasped them in his arms, he fainted so many times in rapid succession that in the end the barons were alarmed and feared that he would expire before their eyes'.[27]

Achilles' grief for Patrocles, as described in book XVIII of the *Iliad* is marked by gestures strikingly similar to those of the medieval knight:

He spoke, and the black cloud of sorrow covered Achilles.
In both hands he caught up the sooty dust, pouring it
all over his head, disfiguring his beautiful face
and the black ashes were scattered over his scented tunic.
And he himself, great in his greatness, lay full length
in the dust and tore out his hair with his own hands and
defiled it.[28]

Like Charlemagne, Achilles is not alone in his gestures of grief.
Not only do the female slaves that he and Patrocles have taken
prisoner weep and 'beat their breast', but Antilochos weeps
beside him, holding his hands lest he do himself harm. This
gesture of restraint is also common to the medieval narratives.
'It was up to the entourage,' as Ariès notes, 'to check the
transports of the chief mourner: "Sire Emperor," says Geoffroi
d'Anjou to Charlemagne, "do not abandon yourself so wholly to
this grief." "Sire," the barons say to King Arthur, "we think he
should be taken from this place and laid in some room away
from people, until his brothers have been buried, for if he
remains near them, he will surely die of grief." '[29] Biblical
parallels also suggest themselves. Men wail and rend their
garments in their grief (Genesis, 37:34, Esther, 4:1, Job, 1:20)
but they are comforted and offered bread and wine by their
companions (Job, 2:13, II Samuel, 3:35, Jeremiah, 16:3). Similarly, in the epic of Gilgamesh, after the hero has wept and torn
his hair for a long period, and has begun to search for his lost
companion in the other world, Siduri, the goddess of wine,
reprimands him. 'As for you, Gilgamesh,' she says, 'fill your
belly with good things; day and night, night and day, dance and
be merry, feast and rejoice. Let your clothes be fresh, bathe
yourself in water, cherish the little child that holds your hand,
and make your wife happy in your embrace; for this too is the
lot of man.' [30] Achilles will, in his turn, check the weeping of
Priam after they have wept so loudly that their groans sounded
throughout the house:

After Achilles had taken full satisfaction in lament
and the passion for it had left his heart and limbs, then
he rose from his chair and, taking his hand, pulled the old
    man
to his feet, pitying the grey head, the grey beard
and spoke, addressing him in winged words: Unlucky

man, how many evils you have had to endure in your heart!
How did you dare to come alone to the Achaian ships
and stand before the eyes of one who killed so many
of your brave sons? Your heart must be made of iron.
Come, sit on this chair and we'll let our sorrows lie
despite our grief. For no good comes of cold laments.[31]

Giving way to loud and uncontrolled weeping is not only
normal, it seems, in the world of the knightly heroes, but gives a
certain pleasure. On the other hand it is not to be indulged in
alone or too long, lest it become dangerous or morbid. In the heat
of passionate grief, a man may indulge himself in lament almost
to the brink of death without incurring shame, but he relies on
his comrades to pull him back to himself. 'No good comes of *cold*
laments', Achilles tells Priam. Should we conclude that laments
wailed 'in the heat of the moment' serve their purpose? The
evidence suggests so. No one mourned more extravagantly than
Achilles for Patrocles, but he insists several times on the useless-
ness of mourning (*Iliad* XXIV 523–4, 549–50, 560, 600–20) at
first becoming angry, then reminding the old king that it is time
for supper and that even Niobe, after she had wept for all her
dead children, remembered to eat. The old man will take his
son's body back to Troy and then, as Achilles reminds him, in the
proper context of the funeral ritual he will be 'much wept-over'.
Priam obeys and the two men sit down to a hearty meal. There is
no suggestion of tears and wailing over the dead as being
unmanly, provided the circumstances are appropriate.[32] In fact
the quintessential mourning mother, Niobe, is a model for
appropriate grief. On the other hand, as Hélène Monsacré has
observed in an elaborate study of weeping in the *Iliad*, men's
tears are differentiated from women's by their force and spontaneity.[33] The source of the warrior's tears is in a dark spring (IX
13–15, XVI 2–4), the colour denoting death and misery. Male
weeping begins with the same shuddering or trembling of the
body that is the manifestation of fear, or with a pricking in
the nostrils. Tears are fecund, burning – even the horses of
Achilles shed burning tears. When the context is dramatic,
men may utter sharp cries.[34] Only out of combat do men dissolve
in tears like women, losing their substance as they weep.
Elsewhere, Monsacré insists, tears are an essentially virile
attribute, one appropriated from the feminine but recast in a

male mode that redoubles the hero's energy. She notes that at the core of the hero's virility are elements drawn from the feminine; by first assuming, then surpassing this feminine side of his personality, the hero assumes his true character.[35] According to Monsacré's theory, women (and she is forced to refer to the *Odyssey* for her best example (XIX 204)) have no comparable outlet for their grief in storms of tears. Instead tears 'dissolve' or 'melt' them, consuming their life; their laments are controlled by narrowly proscribed feminine ritual.[36] Monsacré's observation of the difference between men's and women's weeping seems to me valuable, but her conclusion in is danger of slipping into the same reductionism that Winkler notes in Detienne's analysis of the *Adonia*, except that this time the perspective is a feminist one. The women of the *Iliad*, as we shall see, are neither consumed nor helpless in their laments, and it is the men, rather than the women, who must be enjoined to stop weeping lest they become morbid or dangerous.

WOMEN'S LAMENTS IN HOMER

As we have seen, men who live in the unnatural world of the battlefield indulge in transports of weeping. Achilles makes so much noise weeping for Patrocles that his cries reach the ears of his mother in the depths of the sea and she and her sisters, the sea-goddesses, begin a lament of their own. Thetis may be a goddess, but her instinctive reaction to her son's distress is that of a human mother. The passage (*Iliad* XVII, 1, 35–64) is an interesting one. First the nymphs and sisters of Thetis are listed carefully until, after naming thirty-three of them, the poet seems to tire of his catalogue and conclude: 'and the rest who, in the depths of the sea were Nereids'. Not till the whole company are gathered and all 'beating their breasts' does Thetis 'lead off the lament'. At this point the Nereids know nothing, except that their sister is distressed. The beating of their breasts is a mere formality. Thetis' lament centres on her own misfortune but reminds us that it is she who has controlled her son's life from the moment of his conception:

> Listen, sister Nereids, and know, all of you
> the sorrow I have in my heart, how wretched I am
> to have borne the best of sons, blameless, mighty
> among heroes. Like a tall tree I nurtured him, fruit

of my orchard. I sent him away in the curved ships
to fight at Troy; Now I shall never welcome him
home, returning to the house of Peleus. And yet
while he lives and looks on the sun he suffers, and though
by going I can do nothing to help I'll go to look
on my lovely son and hear with my own ears
what sadness he suffers as he stays far from the fighting.
(*Iliad* XVII, 52–64)

Thetis' immortality may excuse her ill-omened lament for her
son – he is, after all, not dead yet – but her grief is both genuine
and fully controlled. The imagery of the lament, like its focus on
the suffering of the bereaved, is strikingly close to many of the
folk laments in which a young man is compared to a tall tree,
often a cypress, and the mother complains that she will never
welcome him in her home.[37] In almost every line Thetis reminds
us that she has ordered the cycle of her son's life, and though
powerless to prevent his death, she will help him achieve his
final *kleos*. Understanding her son's need for vengeance, she
orders from Hephaestos the magnificent armour she knows will
bring him immortality. It is Thetis, too, who puts a stop to her
son's lamenting saying, in words Achilles will echo to the
weeping Priam, 'My son, we must let this man lie dead despite/
our grief, since the gods willed his death' (*Iliad* XIX, 8–9). It is
hard to imagine any less helpless or restricted lament than
Thetis' *goos* for her son.

Achilles' grief for Patrocles has been expressed in inarticulate
gesture and cry. It is Briseis, the slave girl, who begins the first
true lament for Patrocles. She addresses him directly, in the
manner of most traditional laments, and predictably she focuses
on her own plight. She speaks of how she saw her family
murdered, her city sacked, and had it not been for Patrocles, her
fate would have been to live in sadness forever. But Patrocles
pitied her and promised to wed her to 'godlike Achilles'. Briseis
is expected to lament and she, like the other women captives,
finds reason enough in her own condition: 'I weep for you
ceaselessly, for you were always kind./ So she spoke, weeping,
and the women around her moaned/ Speaking outwardly for
Patrocles, but each with her own sorrows' (*Iliad* XIX, 300–2).
There is a strong suggestion here of the professional. In the
Greek folk tradition, *moirologhístres* who lament at the funeral

of someone not close to them will deliberately focus on some private suffering to acquire the necessary *ponos* for a performance. When Achilles joins the lament, he echoes the style of Briseis, weeping for his own loss of Patrocles who used to 'set a delicious supper before me/ quickly and efficiently'. Urged by his fellow commanders to eat, Achilles cannot touch his food because of his longing for Patrocles (food and his beloved seem inextricably joined in his memory); but no sooner does he mention his suffering than his thoughts turn from his companion to his father and his son, both of whom will be deprived by his own death.

At Patrocles' elaborate funeral ceremony, Achilles, as the chief mourner, takes the place usually occupied by the nearest woman relative, holding the head of the corpse. Cutting a lock of his hair and placing it in Patrocles' hands, 'he stirred up a desire for lamenting' in the Achaians (XXIII, 151–2). It is Achilles, though, who also puts an end to the lament, saying to Agamemnon: 'Even in lament, there can be enough' (157). There is no suggestion of a composed lament here. The men are weeping, and they continue to weep as they prepare the funeral pyre and Achilles sacrifices Trojan captives and beasts, renewing his promises of vengeance.

The battlefield is an unnatural place to live and die. Whatever can be learned about pre-classical Greek or western European early medieval attitudes to death and mourning from the narratives of battle is inevitably biased by the almost exclusively male society of war. The Trojans, though, are fighting on their own territory, and their female relatives are at home when they lament their dead. This may be one reason why Homer devotes his most elaborate and moving treatment of lament to the funeral of Hector, but the position of the laments in the narrative suggests that they fulfil an artistic purpose of greater importance than the dramatic representation of female mourning. The last words of the poem, as of life itself, belong to the women, and their laments are a vehicle for summarizing the artistic and philosophical themes of the narrative. The ostensible theme of the book is the anger of Achilles, but Achilles' anger has two phases: the first an impotent, childish rage of jealousy directed against Agamemnon, the second the anger of grief that turns to active revenge and ultimate glory. The women of the *Iliad* may have no outlet for their grief and anger in action, but the elaborate rituals of the funeral give them a forum for the controlled expression of their pain that is normally denied to men. To the men's *kleos* is opposed the women's (and perhaps the poet's?) *goos*.[38]

The initial reaction of the women to Hector's death is similar to the men's. His mother tears her hair, throws off her veil and raises a loud wail (XXII, 45–6), his wife runs raving out of the house, falls gasping to the ground, and also throws off her veil and headdress. Her servants fear for her life, but she revives and breaks into an informal lament, immediately linking her own misfortune with her husband's. Both, she declares, are ill-fated, and their destiny mutually gloomy; Hector will go to the house of Hades, and she will be left a widow in his house. Her infant son, raised in luxury, will suffer unaccustomed hardship without his father's protection. Worst of all, Hector's body, that she should have dressed in fine clothes, will be left to the dogs and worms to eat (XXII, 477–515).

It is only at Hector's *prothesis* that the formal laments begin. The scene tells us a great deal about the structure of lament as well as its origins.[39] The word Homer uses most commonly for lamentation is *goos*. In fact there are only two occasions on which Homer uses the word *thrēnos*, a term that appears to be interchangeable with *goos* in many classical texts. In the *Odyssey*, at the *prothesis* of Achilles, the wailing (*olophyromenai*) of the Nereids who are Achilles' kinswomen, is contrasted with the lovely laments (*thrēneon*) of the nine muses, responding to one another. The high, clear tones of the muses' lament, moreover, stir the Argives to weeping. (*Odyssey* XXIV, 58–62). The second use of the word *thrēnos* occurs at Hector's *prothesis*. Here 'they brought in singers/ leaders of laments who sang mournfully./ While they lamented, the women wailed./ White-armed Andromache led their lament' (*Iliad* XXIV, 720–3). Although only the laments of the kinswomen – Andromache, Hecuba and Helen – are given in full, there are clearly two groups of mourners present, the professional singers of the *thrēnos* and the kinswomen, whose laments are apparently sung in response to the verses of the professionals.[40] Alexiou notes that the *gooi*, as they occur in Homer, have two features in common: 'first, that they are improvisations inspired by the grief of the occasion, and second, that they are sung by the dead man's relatives or close friends.'[41] The women 'lead off' the lament in turn. Andromache is the first, beginning her lament with a direct address to her husband, full of reproach and bitterness for the perilous situation in which he has left her and her son. Next follows Hecuba, again addressing her son directly, but almost impersonally, as the dearest of her sons and a man dear to the gods. Finally, and surprisingly, comes Helen, the indirect cause of Hector's death and of the city's destruction.

The three-part form of these laments – address to the dead, narrative and renewed address [42] may be more regular than that of the folk laments of modern Greece, but there are clear parallels between the two traditions. Both the address to the dead and the alternation of narrative with direct appeal have already been noted in a number of folk laments. Even more striking than the parallels in form are the similarities in content. Andromache's sadness, as Charles Segal has noted,[43] is a motif that runs through the *Iliad* from one end to the other, but for all her pain, she utters no word of praise for her husband. Instead she realistically elaborates her plight as a widow who will be forced into slavery, just as her son, as the heir of Hector, must inevitably suffer. Knowing that vengeance is inevitable, she even predicts her son's death, telling the boy directly that many Greeks met their death at Hector's hands and that his father was 'not merciful in the misery of war'(XXIV, 739). There is an element, familar from the folk laments, of blame as Andromache addresses herself again to her dead husband, reminding him that he has left his parents to suffer and lament and abandoned his wife and child. Her bitterness and pain surpass that of his parents, because Hector did not die in bed, stretching out his arms and giving her some some last word of wisdom to remember him by (743–4). Andromache's sorrow both at the unnatural manner of Hector's death, and at the absence of a parting word accords well with Ariès' notion of the 'tame' or 'traditional' death.[44] Until the late Middle Ages, in western European sources, an essential characteristic of death is advance warning.[45] The dying man, aware that his last hour is drawing near, lies down in his bed, recollects the people he loved, farewells them if they are present and commends his soul to God. Failure to complete these essential last rites is thought to be a terrible misfortune, both for the dying and for those he leaves behind. It is the manner of Hector's death, as much as the death itself, which makes it tragic for his wife and family.

Unlike Andromache, Hecuba does not accuse the 'son who was dearest to me in spirit' of forsaking her but nor does she praise him, except to note his physical beauty. There is a note of hopeless resignation in her voice as Hecuba mentions, without naming them, the other sons Achilles has sold into slavery.

It is left to Helen, whose final solo closes the kinswomen's lament, to praise the dead man for his personal qualities. Monsacré claims that Helen's lament is different from the other women's because she is on the margin of conventional femininity – her tears are not due to helplessness but to guilt and shame.[46] The only female character in the epic to express such autonomous feelings, she 'transcends the traditional limits reserved for women' and weeps for the human condition.[47] It is worth noting that Helen is, at this point, as unsure of her own destiny as the other women. Like them, she has lost the spouse of her choice and is as likely to be ill-used by her ex-husband as they by their new ones. She has also, it appears, been an unwelcome guest in the Trojan court, a fact she underlines when she, like Briseis, notes the dead hero's exceptional kindness to her as an exile. It is precisely because women's laments are traditionally a means of summing up not only a single life, but life itself, that they occupy this position in the narrative, and that Helen, who has been the ostensible cause of all this suffering, should be the last to lament seems appropriate artistic licence. It is interesting, too, that not one of the women praises Hector as a hero in battle. He dies. His womenfolk and companions weep. A grand funeral is held and it is followed, as befits the occasion, by a grand feast.

THE HOMERIC VIEW OF MOURNING

If Homer can be relied on as a guide to the way men and women mourned and lamented their dead in the pre-classical period, we might say that the picture he gives us corresponds, in a number of respects, to Ariès' concept of the 'tame' or 'traditional' death as well as to the descriptions anthropologists and folklorists have given of death rituals and lament in a number of non-western cultures. Some of the more obvious characteristics of Homeric mourning are: (1) Extravagant, out-of-control behaviour, including loud wailing, tearing the hair and lacerating one's face. This is a common initial response to death, especially by men but also by women. It is a public response and one's companions generally rescue one from seriously harming oneself. (2) Indulgence in such behaviour seems to give satisfaction, and is acceptable for a time, after which it is proper to remind the mourner that too much mourning is a bad thing. Ideally the mourner should now pay attention to his own needs and have a good meal.[48](3) Women are the ones who are in charge of the formal laments. There are two groups involved, kinswomen and professional mourners, who may be forced to lament under duress, or be hired as skilled performers. (4) The women kinsfolk sing one after the other, their laments spontaneous although composed in a predictable ternary form and followed by a choral response. What the professional mourners sing is not known. (5) The kinswomen's laments for their menfolk killed in battle are not filled with praise of their heroic feats, but generally focus on the plight of the bereaved. (6) Their laments form an integral part of the elaborate rites for the dead.

CHANGE AND RESTRICTIONS IN THE CLASSICAL PERIOD

There is nothing to suggest that the Homeric depiction of death and mourning did not represent the general attitude of the Greeks before the classical period. As Alexiou remarks, 'Archaeology, epigraphy and literature all bear witness to the importance attached to funeral ritual in the societies of prehistoric and archaic Greece.'[49] Vermeule adds that the ceremonies of mourning and farewell to the dead 'were probably the oldest and least-changing art-form in Greece'.[50] Suddenly, though, in the sixth century BC, a change as dramatic as the one noted by Ariès between the early and late Middle Ages in the north and west of Europe comes about in Greece. There is no change in the sequence of ceremonies, and little change in their representation on vases. The change is one that appears to reflect a change of attitude towards mourning the dead. Legislation is passed, first by Solon at Athens, later in Ioulis on the island of Keos, then at Delphi towards the end of the fifth century, at Gambreion in Asia Minor in the third century and at a number of other places in the Greek world.[51] The legislation varies from place to place, but the similarities are remarkable. In all cases, women are especially singled out by the restrictions. At Athens, the emphasis is on the banning of offerings at the grave and the limitation of the right to mourn to kinswomen, but the extension of the laws to other women's activities, which has already been remarked on, and the comments of later Greek theorists,[52] suggest that women were the special target of the legislation. At Keos, the provisions of the law are similar. Grave offerings are limited, the *ekforá* is to take place in silence, and, as at Athens, the women are ordered to stand behind the men. Only the immediate kinswomen and five additional female relatives are permitted to attend the ceremony. The inevitable assumption is that it had been customary for large numbers of female relatives to take part in the most public part of the funeral, the procession, and that their participation had been prominent and vocal.

The restrictions on funeral practices at Delphi are found in the social and religious laws of the priestly clan of the Labyadai. The late fifth-century legislation, which seems to be a revision of earlier laws, limits the value of grave offerings and again tightly restricts the behaviour of mourners.[53] The corpse had to be veiled and carried in silence during the *ekforá*. Nor was it permitted to lay down the bier and wail at 'turnings in the road' or outside the houses of others. Mourners, except for the immediate relatives, were not permitted to remain at the graveside and even close relatives were not to lament for 'those long dead'. Wailing and set laments were also forbidden on the customary days after burial and on the anniversary of the death.

Evidence from later inscriptions and literary sources confirms the general trend of the legislation passed at Athens, Keos and Delphi.[54] The curbing of extravagance in all the laws suggests that they were aimed not at the poor but the rich. The limiting of the right to mourn to immediate family, Alexiou conjectures, may have been related to a change of emphasis from clan to family. The fact that women are singled out by the legislation and that they are forbidden to lament during the part of the funeral ritual where they are most likely to draw attention to themselves is the most fascinating feature of the new laws. Clearly, women's prominent role in the rituals, particularly their loud laments as they passed through the streets of a town, was once accepted and is now being challenged. Why women in particular?

The explanations that were offered for the restrictive legislation before Alexiou's study ignored the issue of gender discrimination and concentrated on questions of economy and attempts to eradicate superstition.[55] Alexiou dismisses these explanations as unsatisfactory, given the fact that the money spent on funerals was not public money and that during the same period there was no attempt to curb spending on religious festivals, theatres and public works. The hypothesis that the laws were a rationalist bid to control superstition, as Alexiou points out, ignores the fact that at the same time hero worship was officially introduced.[56] She suggests that taken in the context of the reforms of the sixth century, the Athenian legislation can be seen as an attempt to contain the aristocratic clan cults.[57] The cults were based on the worship of an ancestor/founder, and ritual played an important part in such cults. The banning of *thrēnoi*, choral laments composed for wealthy patrons by poets like Simonides, seems a logical step towards reducing the attraction of the cults. Similarly, the revival of hero cults, already popular in some areas of Greece, was a means of substituting a local hero for a relative and opening membership in a cult to the public through initiation ceremonies. Solon may also have been responsible for transforming the *genesia* from an elaborate festival held on the anniversary of a man's death to a public festival for the dead, a change which, like the restrictive legislation on funerals, can be seen as part of the broad process of democratization.[58] The fact that these reforms were roughly contemporary with the introduction of hero worship and mystery cults into Athens, and with the renaming and discarding of the old clan names by Kleisthenes, is evidence to suggest at least a strong connection between the restrictive laws and the attempt to limit the powers of the clan cults.

Alexiou does not pursue the possible connections between the establishment of state-sanctioned cults and a new attitude towards the mourning of the dead, one demanded by a state that must recruit a standing army if it is to survive. The mystery cults, after all, held out to initiates the promise of eternal happiness after death, and the hero cults were both proof against defeat in war and, should they fail to keep this part of the bargain, at least they reminded worshippers of the immortal glory to be won from a fighting death. It is suggestive, to say the least, that restrictions on female mourning occur at the same time as these new cults offer promises of rewards for dying in the service of the state.

Another motive behind the restrictions, as scholars have suggested, was an attempt to consolidate private property and the right of a son to inherit.[59] The immense wealth of grave offerings found in the Mycenaean tombs had no parallels in the archaic period, indicating that the restriction of grave offerings pre-dates the legislation. Still, inheritors must have stood to lose by any valuable offerings to the dead. The old laws of inheritance during the aristocratic period protected the *genos*, a group of three or four generations who had worked the same land. As the *oikos* or family unit became more independent in the new society of the city-state, Alexiou notes that 'a struggle arose between the concentrative tendencies of the clan and the autonomous inclinations of the family.'[60] Solon's laws on property and inheritance made it possible for a testator to adopt a son to inherit and perpetuate his household, and so to dispose of his own property without reference to the *genos*. The new legislation on inheritance affected mourning, since the right to inherit was traditionally linked to the right to mourn.[61] Within the clan system, the tending of a founder's grave was the responsibility of his descendants until the fourth generation, when the great-grandsons would inherit his property. Even after the breakdown of the clan system, though, there is evidence that mourning and inheritance were linked. That being so, the restriction of mourning to immediate kin is understandable. It still does not explain the fact that women were the special targets of the legislation. Alexiou suggests two possible explanations.

As we have seen, mourning and lament at funerals had been very much under the control of women during the pre-classical period. Given the fact that mourning and the right to inherit were linked, it may be that women exercised at least a behind-the-scenes influence on decisions about property: 'If the family, based on father right, was to be established as the basic unit of society, then the power of women in religious and family affairs must be stopped and they must be made to play a more secondary role at funerals. *Restrictions on women are another sign of incipient democracy.*'[62] Alexiou also suggests that the establishment of the Thesmophoria and the Eleusinian mystery cults were a calculated compensation for women's lost authority in the rituals for the dead, one which placed their activities under state control.[63]

Another motive Alexiou sees behind the legislation is that

women's loud and demonstrative behaviour at funerals could create a danger to society by stirring up feelings of revenge. Solon's laws were passed at a time when blood feuds were still common, and Plutarch regards the legislation as being directly linked to the feud that lasted for at least thirty years following Megakles' murder of Kylon and his fellow conspirators.[64] Solon was said to have passed his restrictive laws on the advice of Epimenides of Crete, who had had similar problems at Phaistos. In both cases women were regarded as being responsible for the violent crimes of revenge.[65]

Anyone familiar with the folk laments of Mani or those of any traditional culture where vendettas are common cannot fail to see the connection between the women's laments and incitement to revenge. If the purpose was to prevent the cycle of vengeance, then Solon's legislation was well aimed. Perhaps it could be said that Solon was acting in the general interest in attempting to prevent such wasteful violence. In such a society, loyalty to a brother far outweighs loyalty to one's husband. If a husband/father no longer had to consider his next-of-kin as natural heirs, but could dispose of property as he liked, a wife/mother was already forced to fight for the rights of her children. Accustomed to gaining access to decisions about property through the old association of mourning rights and inheritance, women had an even greater incentive to play a loud, intrusive role in funerals. Only by legislation could the state hope to put a stop to their traditional authority in such matters.

To say that the state was acting in its own interest in restricting women's role at funerals is not to legitimize the laws passed by Solon, but rather to confirm that the new social order at Athens and a number of other city-states in the classical period involved, even necessitated, the careful control of women in their prominent role as mourners of the dead. It could be argued that the laws reflected a change at some deep level of the human spirit, the sort of change Ariès sees occurring in the eleventh and twelfth centuries in western Europe, when death, for the upper classes, became no longer a collective ritual but a time for anxious self-examination.[66] However, a change of legislation does not necessarily mean a change in deeply held beliefs. One could equally well argue that changes in the public character of mourning, dictated by new political or social conditions, may alter what seemed to be firmly held attitudes to death.[67]

There is evidence that the attempts to restrict mourning were ineffective,[68] but even if they were partially effective, the legislation had to be accompanied by some substitute for the laments of women if it was to gain popular support. Funerals, as we know, were not only public events of considerable importance but rituals for the dead, firmly believed to be necessary for the well-being of the community as much as for the dead. They were, as they are now in rural Greece, a unique occasion for women to raise their voices in public. Still, despite the loud voices, the extravagance of gesture, there is no indication, apart from the late classical male sources, that the women were in any way out of control. In fact, as we have seen in the Homeric poems, displays of abandoned grief were by no means the preserve of women in pre-classical Greece. On the contrary, there are indications that, as they do in many traditional societies, women took control of mourning by turning 'tears into ideas', creating powerful poetry to confront the pain and dislocation of death, inscribing the dead in the public memory. If they used their role as lamenters to stir men to violent revenge, we may be sure they did so as artists in full consciousness of their powers. And yet, during the later classical period, at least, mourning is categorized as 'unmanly', 'barbarian', un-Greek. Women lamenters are not merely devalued in the classical sources. They shift from being dangerous to being deranged to being pathetic: the Furies become the Eumenides, losing all their powers and accepting defeat with a whimper. How is such a revolution achieved? And when laments were curtailed, what did the state replace them with? How was death to be addressed? How were the dead to be remembered?

AN ATHENIAN INVENTION: THE *EPITAPHIOS LOGOS*

The answers, I believe, are to be sought in the new forms of discourse that were developed in Athens in the fifth century. Nichole Loraux has called the *Epitaphios Logos* the 'invention of Athens'.[69] Demosthenes said of the Athenians: 'They alone in the world deliver funeral orations for citizens who have died for their country.'[70] In stressing the unique character of the funeral oration, as Loraux shrewdly observes, Demosthenes echoes the formula used by the authors of the *epitaphioi*, who proclaim the Athenians to be 'unique among men'.[71] By honouring the glorious dead, just as by praising the unique character of the funeral oration, the Athenians, are, in Loraux's view, patting themselves discreetly on the back. Unique or not, there is indeed something new, if not totally original, about the genre of funeral oration of which Pericles' speech for those who died in the first years of the Peloponnesian War remains the ultimate model.

The funeral oration may have its roots in a very old tradition that tried to exorcize the dead by speaking of their glorious deeds.[72] But, as Loraux points out, there is almost no mention in the *epitaphioi* of death as a universal end to the human condition; rather, by avoiding the common verb *apothanein* (to die) and replacing it by the formula *andres agathoi genomenoi*, the speeches place the citizen soldiers that fell in combat in a realm of glory beyond the reach of death.[73] Loraux observes that 'in treating the same mythical scene, such as the aid given to Adrastus by the Athenians, the *epitaphioi* always adopt the bellicose version of the affair, while the tragedies feel free to choose between the military expedition and the peaceful solution. Nor is it mere chance that the authors of the *epitaphioi* prefer an aristocratic democracy to the democratic kings of Aeschylus and Euripides. These phenomena confirm the politico-military character of the funeral oration.'[74]

The political nature of the funeral oration is confirmed by the fact that it is delivered by a representative of the state. As Thucydides relates, 'After the remains have been laid in the earth, a man chosen by the city for his reputed wisdom and his moral standing makes an appropriate speech of praise of the dead.'[75] It is the city that occupies the centre of Pericles' oration. Its unique character is what men 'nobly fought and nobly died' for. The democratization of the army demanded a new type of loyalty to the city: the army and the city were now, in effect, one. And 'the Athenian city, which democratized military activity, opening it to every citizen, was, perhaps more than any other *polis*, a "men's club". . . . War was men's business, as were public funerals.'[76] Pericles makes plain what the state expects of women in such a society. Speaking to the widows of the war dead he offers them 'a word of advice: Your great glory is not to be inferior to what god has made you, and the greatest glory of a woman is to be least talked about by men, whether they are praising you or criticising you . . . and now, when you have mourned for your dear ones, you must depart.'[77]

It is not enough that women, who have traditionally played a prominent role in the rites for the dead, are to be removed from the centre to the periphery of the funeral. It is as if they have died themselves, and are no longer to speak but to be spoken of. Their *kleos* is both parallel and in functional opposition to their husbands' glory. In both cases, reputation in the society of the *polis* is what counts, and that is gained, in the case of the male citizens, by death and being spoken about. In the case of the widows, the most they can hope for is that, by sinking into a life so unremarkable that it is not spoken of, they will achieve the *kleos* of a death-in-life, at least in the public life of the city.

WOMEN'S MOURNING AND THE WAR DEAD

Given the extreme nature of Athens' exclusion of women, the dismissal of their role in the funeral ceremony might be viewed as simply a particular case of a general practice, but the combination of the new genre of funeral oration with the pointed rhetoric of restrictive legislation suggests that the new attitude to mourning and death demanded by the state would be at risk, were women allowed to exercise their traditional dominion over the rituals of death. In all the surviving orations, the same formula demands that the dead be not lamented but praised.[78] In all cases, it is recognized that there is a 'natural' tendency to lament. 'Nature desires us to weep over them as mortals but their valour demands that we sing them as immortal,' as Lysias contends. The funeral oration takes on a didactic function here, one that applies to both sexes, since we know that there was no shame attached to men lamenting the dead in the pre-classical period. The supposition is that men, as citizens and active participants in the new democracy, will be receptive to such exhortations and that women will not and must therefore be compelled by law to comply.

Here it might be appropriate to consider the work of Carol Gilligan, Sherry Ortner and other feminist theorists, as well as Lutz's discussion of emotion summarized in chapter 1.[79] Gilligan's distinction between the two moral perspectives of justice and care, the former more commonly associated in western society with men, the latter with women, would seem to coincide with what the early Greek state *believed* about the difference between men's and women's mourning. The justice perspective, with its emphasis on rationality, is one of measure, of controlled response, even to death. The care principle, by contrast, is based on a notion of individuality, of specificity and difference that are not amenable to abstract notions of morality but will instead insist on individual response to specific situations. It is commonly assumed that women's responses to death are less controlled than men's, but as I have attempted to demonstrate from the folk laments of Greece and other traditional cultures, there is no evidence to suggest that women's responses are uncontrolled. On the contrary, men in such societies seem less likely to take control of their grief by turning it into a formal artistic response than women. And yet the rhetoric of the funeral orations demanding control of 'natural' responses taken together with the restrictions on female mourning suggests an early formulation of Ortner's 'female is to male as nature is to culture' principle.[80]

The notion that women will not, by virtue of their nature, acquiesce with the state in its demand for men to die in its defence is one that has been the subject of much debate among feminists. As Joyce Beckman points out, women have themselves participated willingly in a number of European wars, notably the French Revolution, when a female militia, calling themselves 'The Amazons' was formed in Paris.[81] In the nineteenth century, women were active in many pacifist groups, but there was a division between feminists who supported pacifism and those who saw war as an opportunity to fight for equal status. In the period leading up to the First World War, those women who supported militarism argued that mothering required the state to be safe and strong, a philosophy that meant sons must be good soldiers and mothers pro-war.[82] Yet despite evidence for women's willing sacrifice of their children and themselves in the defence of the state, most feminists continue to argue that women are more likely to oppose wars than support them either because of an intrinsic difference in their nature or because of the type of work they do, which involves more caring for others than men's work.

Arguing that care has its own type of rationality which distinguishes it from male rationality, Sarah Ruddick claims that 'to speak of women's ways of knowing or of a rationality deriving from work that has, as a matter of history, been women's work, is tantamount to creating a "woman's reason" to rival the man's.'[83] The opposition between the 'preservative love' of mothering and the military destruction of life is not a simple opposition but in both cases the concern is with the body. In the rationality of care there is, according to Ruddick, 'a sturdy anti-militarist conception of the body. Birth is privileged over death, and with that privilege comes a commitment to protect, a respect for ambiguity and ambivalence, a prizing of physical being in its resilience and variety.'[84] Dying, Ruddick notes, whether it occurs on the battlefield or in the care of women, is also a social experience incorporating the plans and work of the living. On the military and the caretakers alike falls the task of 'remembering the history of human flesh'.[85]

REMEMBERING THE DEAD: THE FALLEN SOLDIER

To remember the dead is, then, the task of both men and women, of tenders and destroyers of the body. One of the functions of laments is to commit the dead to memory. The Athenians, unlike the Thasians, seemed to admit the 'natural' tendency of the bereaved to lament, but by granting a minimal space to ritual laments at the funerals of the war dead and substituting a civic speech, they reminded the citizens that there was another way to remember the dead. By glorifying the war dead their memory could be put to positive use. As George Mosse has demonstrated in his examination of Germany between the wars, the cult of the fallen soldier not only served the function of inspiring a new generation to fight for the fatherland (in the German case as a sort of resurrection with deliberate Christian overtones) but it could be exploited for any number of purposes.[86] It was not as individuals that they were remembered, but as a group. Even the homogeneity of their tombs in military cemeteries united the war dead in a comradeship beyond the grave, linking them to the living by making their sacrifice massively visible.[87] 'The Myth of the [First World] War Experience was,' as Mosse makes clear, 'a democratic myth centred upon the nation symbolised by all of the war dead. Only in this way could the Myth of the War Experience attempt to transcend the front-line soldiers' encounter with death, cleansing their memory of the dread of war.'[88] Similarly, in Athens, a democratic myth was constructed by the orators at the funerals of the war dead so that they could be publicly praised and remembered not as individuals but as citizens of the *polis*.

Praise was not inconsistent with lament, as the Homeric poems indicate, but the *goos* of the *Iliad* shares with the laments of tragedy and of the folk tradition a focus on the plight of the survivor and a desire to communicate with, be it to praise or to blame, the individual who has died. The *thrēnoi* or *enkōmia* of the lyric poets, combining praise for individual heroes with philosophical speculation, already show signs of diverging from laments proper. The new democracy would abandon these forms and substitute its own form of praise. The *epitaphios logos* was delivered by a male already singled out for his position in the Athenian hierarchy as one likely to combine praise of the dead with praise of the city. The *polis*'s substitution of public praise for private mourning, at least as it presents itself in the context of the funeral oration, involves a rejection of tears and laments for the dead as feminine, barbaric and trivial.[89] Like the *enkōmium* or the *elegy*, the *epitaphios* is an essentially male genre, but one that is peculiar to Athens. Usurping female mourning, the *logos* speaks for the new democracy, telling the living how to remember their dead. In contrast, the Spartans, although restraining lamentation over those who died in battle, retained the ritual lament as proper to the funerals of its kings, a fact which Herodotus notes disdainfully as reminiscent of the customs of 'Asian barbarians'.[90] Loraux suggests that in both Sparta and Athens there was a desire to preserve continuity through the process of the funeral. While the Spartans were able to ward off the disequilibrium engendered by the king's death through the suspension of political life for ten days and indulgence in loud public lamentation, in Athens

> the *logos* allowed the city to ward off mourning, even in extremis, and to leave the last word for glory. The properly civic way of the funeral oration steered a middle course between demoralizing laments and the prohibition against honoring the living; in the oration the break with the past is consummated, even if certain themes of the epitaphioi are still reminiscent of the tradition of the threnos.[91]

THE ELEGY: A MALE GENRE?

It may be that in the Athenian insistence on praise and rejection of laments as 'female' we are witnessing the beginning of a

fundamental divergence between women's and men's ways of
mourning the dead, at least in those societies like our own that
still look to democratic Athens as a model state. The division
extends from the outward show of mourning to its expression in
tears and oral and written poetry. The funeral oration is, as we
have seen, a public and political genre that displaces and rejects
traditional mourning. As such, in the predominantly male civic
society of Athens, it also effectively displaces women's role in
the funeral proceedings. It is a short-lived genre, disappearing
before the end of the fourth century, but other forms of praising
the dead are soon developed that maintain the dichotomy
between male and female responses to death.

In the literature of the western world the funeral elegy is,
according to Celeste Schenck, 'from its inception in the poetry
of Theocritus and his followers, Bion and Moschus, a resolutely
patriarchal genre' that 'women poets . . . refuse to work or
rework'.[92] Schenck sees the elegy as being 'modelled on
archaic initiation rituals of a younger man by an elder'.[93] By
singing the praises of a forebear, the young poet demonstrates
his own proficiency in the genre and announces his succession to
the master's throne. 'The writing of an elegy, even in the
absence of a corpse, is,' according to Schenck, 'a literary gesture
signifying the admittance of the male novice to the sacred
company of poets.' It is possible that the early Greek elegiac
couplets, originally accompanied by the *aulos*, the double-reed
instrument traditionally associated with mourning, suffered
from the same restrictive policies that curtailed women's
laments.[94] As a purely literary form, the elegy remains a poem
of loss and consolation, but one that differs significantly, I
would argue, from the lament. Analysing the elegy from a
Freudian perspective, Peter Sacks both confirms and refines
Schenck's observations.[95] He sees the elegy as a form that
recapitulates loss while internalizing the idealized parental
figure. As part of the 'work of mourning', the poem also acts as
a defence against death by preventing a regressive attachment to
a prior love-object.[96] Allowing that women have made use of
the elegiac form, Sacks claims that they have failed, with the
notable exception of Amy Clampitt in her poem 'A Procession
at Candlemass', to make the genre their own by 'reinstating the
female fertility goddess and her emblems'.[97] What Sacks (and
Freud, perhaps) does not allow for is the possibility that women

who mourn their dead in laments may not be so preoccupied with the transference of their affections to an idealized object as their male counterparts. Women writers, as Schenck observes, seem less willing to make a rupture with their dead, maintaining their relationship to their predecessors beyond the grave by refusing to accept the finality of death. They are also aware that the tears and cries that are their immediate response to loss go beyond the conventions of elegiac poetry but have an undeniable value. As the seventeenth-century British poet Katherine Philips wrote, in a poem on the death of her young son: 'Tears are my Muse and sorrow all my art,/ So piercing groans must be thy elegy.'[98]

We have grown so accustomed to the difference between the male and female response to death in the west that it may seem a minor, if not an inevitable, differentiation. We have also grown used to the political manipulation of our responses to mass death that Athens may have initiated. But changes in the relationship of a people to its dead are not achieved overnight, and half of the population does not relinquish its control of those responses willingly. It is left to a more subtle and brilliant Athenian invention than the funeral oration or the elegy to recognize what powerful forces can be unleashed by traditional women's grieving and to appropriate the rhetorical passion of women's laments. In the tragedies of Aeschylus, Sophocles and Euripides, we see the last vestiges of a world where women controlled the mourning of the dead.

Chapter 5

From the Erinyes to the Eumenides: tragedy and the taming of lament

THE STAGING OF REACTIONS

Tragedy makes its appearance in fifth-century BC Athens with the same apparent spontaneity as that city's other achievements. Like Aphrodite, the foam-born goddess, it seems to emerge fully grown out of the raw stuff of life. To say it is preoccupied with this or that theme seems naïve, but tragedy is, from its earliest surviving examples, selective. It is a form that deals with murder, revenge, guilt, sacrifice, retribution and lament. Aristotle will claim that through the contemplation of such themes in a form that imitates reality, men experience both fear and pity. By entering into an active relationship with the drama, they achieve a kind of purification, or catharsis of their affections.[1] Aristotle is not the first to suggest that poetry induces these emotional responses; Gorgias, in *Helen*, adds 'shuddering fear, weeping pity and sorrowful longing' to the list of more pleasant emotions induced in those who listen to 'speech with rhythm'.[2]

It is interesting that only after the institution of tragedy as a state festival do we have any articulation of the poet's magical powers extending to what might be termed 'negative' emotions. We cannot help but be reminded of Odysseus' reaction to the songs of Phemios and Demodokos, of his tears on Calypso's shore. Weeping pity, sorrowful longing – these two emotions are familiar to an audience raised on Homer. They are also thoroughly familiar in the context of the modern Greek folk lament where a special group of *moirológhia* are concerned with *xeniteiá* (absence from Greece in foreign lands which causes precisely such a sorrowful longing).[3] Fear may not be a traditional reaction to poetry. It is a natural response to lament. The singers of dirges commune with the dead. Their *mimēsis* is a terrifying foretaste of death-in-life. By the *realisation* (the sense of the word is as the French *cinéastes* use it) of fear, are the dramatists in fact assuming a powerful controlling force in society? Is it a force that subsumes traditional lament within elaborately *staged* lament, demonstrating its potential for violence and at the same time defusing it in the 'catharsis' of mass audience reaction?

It is not only the audience who must react. The staging of tragedy is largely the staging of reactions: Antigone's reaction to the ban on her brother's burial, Clytemnestra's to the impending and actual return of her husband, Oedipus' reaction to Creon's report of the oracle, and, most crucial, the chorus's reaction to the events visible and invisible around them. In the chorus we, as audience, have a curious double. They appear to react for us, and yet they almost always know more or less than we. They are more often than not female (played, of course, by males) and we, the presumed audience, are male. It is they who direct our fear and our pity. Why do we need these intermediaries? What is their function in relation to the action of the principal actors in the drama and to us?

The chorus are by no means the vanguard in the redefinition of social institutions. Old men (*Agamemnon*), quaking virgins (*Seven Against Thebes*), reluctant brides (*The Suppliants*), foreign female slaves (*The Libation Bearers*), displaced female deities (*The Eumenides*), they frequently interpret wrongly, fail to see what is obvious to us. They seem anachronistic as they are presented to the citizen audience – reminders of a world familiar but no longer viable, where women were traditionally the singers of laments, the interpreters of death and suffering. It may be that in the chorus, we see a mimesis of the audience's former selves. Perhaps it is by the double mirror effect of seeing themselves reflected in the chorus and reflecting on that image – seeing themselves being persuaded – that Aeschylus convinces his audience that traditional interpreters can no longer be relied on in the context of the city-state, that they threaten chaos and destruction. Such an explanation accords well with Vernant's view that tragedy frequently develops as a kind of dialogue between the Athenian past and the Athenian present.[4]

POLITICS AND DRAMA

As George Thomson rightly argues, it is important to keep in mind that the origin of the word for an actor in Greek, *hypokritēs*, comes not from its sense of 'an answerer' but 'an interpreter', and that the name for the leader of the dithyrambic chorus, *exarchon* , is synonymous with the *exegetēs*, the priest who interpreted what was done in the sacred ritual, the exponent of the *legomena*, or 'things said' in the Eleusinian mysteries.[5] Whether or not the immediate precursor of tragedy was the Dionysiac dithyramb or a mystery cult associated with it cannot be definitively established, but that Aeschylus and the dramatists who followed him viewed drama as both exegesis and *hypókrisis* or *erminia* (the later word for interpretation) is never in doubt. Aeschylean tragedy is both socially analytic and prescriptive. It is preoccupied with defining institutions of the new social unit: the *polis*. It is also an *agōn*, originally a word associated with assemblies of people, especially to watch games, and later extended to contests of all kinds, including lawsuits. Clifford Geertz observes, in connection with the cock fights of Bali, that all such 'deep play' is an outward display of internal truth, a way of viewing oneself in an extreme situation.[6] The relationship between the dramas played out in the theatre of Dionysos and those played out on the other side of the same hill, on the Pnyx, was an intimate one. As Josiah Ober and Barry Strauss make clear, 'political rhetoric and drama can be seen, and analysed, as closely related forms of public speech.'[7] That being so, we should not be surprised to find reflections, in the drama, of the tensions and conflicts inherent in the changing society of the *polis*, tensions the funeral legislation attempted to minimize.

In the pages that follow, I will argue that tragedy, particularly the drama of Aeschylus, does more than reflect the conflicts surrounding funerals. By appropriating the language, music and gesture of traditional women's lament and employing them in public performance, tragedy's 'deep play' involves the audience in an *agōn* that provides men with an outlet for the potential violence of grief while denying women any public role in the artistic ritual drama they customarily controlled. In the earlier dramas the curved tiers of marble seem unable to contain the fearful power of women's lament, and tragedy paradoxically threatens its own existence as a public Athenian institution. Later, during the Peloponnesian War, Helene Foley has demonstrated that plays like Euripides' *The Suppliants* seem to represent a response to lament that accords better with the spirit of the new funerary legislation and the *Epitaphios Logos*. She even suggests that these plays may be viewed as an implicit criticism of earlier tragedy for failing to distance itself from what is portrayed on stage.[8]

However momentous the historical and political events that caused the *polis* to change its attitude to women's traditional art, we see in the tragedies of Aeschylus, a profound ambivalence towards lament that suggests a lag between state prescription and public acceptance, one that continues in the remote areas of Greece to this day. It is for this reason I have concentrated on the tragedies Aeschylus at the expense of those of Sophocles and Euripides. In his plays, especially in the *Oresteia*, I believe we can still sense, behind the new masculine poetics of tragedy, a female art form, half-submerged and potentially explosive. I would also contend that these powerful echoes of traditional women's laments are what give the tragedies of Aeschylus an electrifying quality unique in western art.

THE PERSIANS: ORIENTALISM AND WOMEN'S LAMENTS

The earliest drama we have, Aeschylus' *The Persians*, is based on a play of the same name by Phrynichos. Phrynichos was the author of a lost tragedy, *The Capture of Miletus*, which so moved the Athenian audience than they 'burst into tears'.[9] Phrynichos was fined 1,000 drachma 'for reminding them of terrible things that touched them so closely' and it was forbidden for anyone to stage the play again. *The Persians* of Aeschylus may have been acceptable because it dealt with the defeat of an enemy, not of a Greek city. At first sight it seems an extraordinary act of daring to produce a play which presents the enemy defeated only eight years earlier at Salamis in an apparently sympathetic light but there is method in it. The defeated hero is a Persian, an eastern barbarian. His mourning can be staged in a way that would not be acceptable in a Greek hero. What defines classical Greek culture as it presents itself to the citizen body in the *Epitaphios Logos* or, generally speaking, in tragedy is a cluster of what we have come to think of as 'western' characteristics – rationality, a preoccupation with justice, civic thinking, mediation, masculinity. It should not surprise us to find, underlying Greek tragedy, a subtext of what has so recently been supplanted, the oriental and female. The city may find it necessary to substitute the *Epitaphios Logos* for the traditional women's lament; the theatre will appropriate its function of catharsis while stressing its essentially female, barbarian–oriental and un-Athenian nature.

The Persians opens with the chorus of elders who as yet do not lament, but speak about lament. The absence of the king and his great army has lasted too long. The lack of news is ominous. 'All Asia laments' the men who have gone to fight with Xerxes, none more than the queen, his mother, who has had a prophetic dream of her son's defeat. When the herald arrives, bringing news of the defeat, the queen does not ask directly whether her son is dead, but which of the captains are to be lamented.[10] The rest of the play is taken up with lamenting the dead and the defeat of Xerxes. Not only do women and men lament, but they use their lament to summon up the dead Darius. The play seems to be less about the Persian defeat than about lament itself and its power to affect action on stage and audience reaction. In other words, lament is not only practised in the text, it becomes thematised. In *The Persians*, as in so much of Greek tragedy, we are faced with the methodological problem of distinguishing between the explicit poetics of lament as it is discussed in the text and the implicit poetics of lament as *practised* in the text.

The *kommos* of the chorus (531) is itself a theatrical appropriation of the type of lament for dead heroes and lost cities, familiar from the *gooi* of the last book of the *Iliad*.[11] In it we hear how the women of Persia are tearing their veils, weeping and lamenting. Soon the lament becomes an imperative: 'Be mournful! Wail dismal cries to the heavens.'[12] The chorus punctuate their speech with frequent cries – *ee, oa, popoi, totoi*, presumably imitating in gesture as well as speech a frenzied lament.

There is nothing exclusively 'oriental' about the chorus's reaction, as later Greek tragedies confirm, but that Persian and oriental women have a unique reputation for extravagant lament is something that will become clear in later tragedies. The queen's reaction is to bring offerings to her husband Darius' tomb. Her propitious gifts, which Aeschylus stresses are 'unblemished', achieve what Clytemnestra's tardy, disingenuous offerings will fail to obtain in the *Choephoroi*. She is careful, moreover, to bring the chorus of lamenters – in this case male, but oriental – to help her in her task, which is none other than to summon up her dead husband from the underworld. The sounds the women are about to make, we note, are not pleasant to the ear: 'I will cry out clearly the manifold ill-sounding, dismal, barbarous chants.' Yet when the king rises from his tomb he does so because of the power of these laments: 'You stood beside my tomb and lamented, and called me piteously to rise up by your laments that lead the soul' (*psychahagogois orthiazontes gooisl oiktros kaleisthe m'* (687–8)). This is potent magic indeed. Hermes is the god associated with leading the soul (*psychē*) to and from the underworld. The word *psychē*, has both the sense of soul as living spirit, and of the dead. It is to Hermes that Electra will address her first prayer at the tomb of Agamemnon in the *Choephoroi*. The relationship between the lament and magic, *goos* and *goetia* will become clearer in the *Oresteia*, but here, in the first extant Greek tragedy, we have what seems to be a recognition of the specific magical powers ascribed to the *goos* as a musico-poetical double of Hermes. We are reminded that Hermes was credited with inventing the lyre, and passing it on to Apollo and Orpheus. Orpheus' playing is said to move the *psychē*, a power he demonstrates by literally moving a *psychē* from the underworld.

The Persians ends in an elaborate interchange of lament, with Xerxes acting as the leader and encouraging the chorus to louder, more extravagant wailing, as he reveals more and more details of the rout of his army. Is the very structure of this final section based on a funeral lament? It is an unavoidable assumption. The chorus promise to 'send an evil-omened shout for your return, an evil-practised cry, a lament with many tears, the sort lament-singers from Bithynia sing'.[13] (We must not, it seems, imagine that Greek elders would cry in this way.) Then, as woe falls on woe, the exchange contracts to that most dramatic of forms, single-line *stichomuthia*. Xerxes, now in a frenzy, tears his clothes, utters inarticulate cries and instructs the chorus to '*boa antidoupa moi*' (shout antiphonally to me). Here, if we can rely on our evidence for funerals in classical and pre-classical Greece,[14] we have a deliberate staging of what would normally be female lament: 'Lift up your voice in the lament [*goos*]. Otototoi! Dark, all merged together, oi! Groaning wounds. . . . Beat your breast and cry the Mysian [song] and I'll tear the whitened hairs of my beard' (1050–6).

How is the audience to react to this staged lament? With pity for the Persians? Fear for the power of lament to summon up the dead? A sense of superiority as Athenian males who have defeated a powerful enemy and mourn their dead in a less extravagant way? For despite the irony of depicting the Persian court as Greek-speaking and Olympian-worshipping, there is no doubt that Aeschylus is describing the Persians as 'others'. Xerxes has been made the leader of lament, his mother has dressed him in new silk robes so that he can rend them again before our eyes. The Persian elders weep and moan with him. This may be the first true literary evidence of Edward Said's '*orientalism*'[15] – the depiction of the Persians fulfilling what, to the Greeks of Aeschylus' period, was predominantly a female role. There will be no such extravagant display of male mourning in Greek tragedy. When Greek men are overwhelmed by disaster (Oedipus, Ajax, Heracles), their behaviour may be violent, they may do themselves or others violence in what may appear to a modern audience as a fit of madness. But as Foucault wisely warns us, we have little idea of what 'madness' meant to the Greeks.[16] Aristotle's view of tragedy as a catharsis of fear and pity may be some recognition of the need to channel, and in so doing contain, 'unreason'. In the elaborate sexual ambiguity of the theatre, men imitate women who imitate men (Clytemnestra, Antigone). The reverse is not true. We do not witness 'unmanly' behaviour in tragedy staged in Athens, although it abounds in comedy.[17]

SEVEN AGAINST THEBES

If Aeschylus' treatment of lament in *The Persians*, can be seen as a negative commentary on the behaviour of barbarians and their indulgence in lament, the portrayal of lament in *Seven Against Thebes*, is more ambiguous. This strangely static and ritualistic drama, first presented in 467 BC, begins with another ill-omened lament for a fallen city, this time sung by a chorus of young unmarried women. At the end of the play the same women, though unrelated to the dead Eteocles and Polynices, join Antigone and Ismene in a lament that is openly critical of both brothers and a triumphant vindication of their female skill in reading portents.

The city of Thebes is already under siege as the play begins. Eteocles seems calm and confident of his ability to steer his city safely through the battle to come. A messenger brings news of the seven bloodthirsty commanders, led by Eteocles' own brother Polynices, who are busy plotting their attack. His warning is serious but still optimistic, picking up the metaphor of the king as skilled captain of his ship. As soon as the chorus enters, the mood of masculine confidence is undermined. The young women seem helpless in their fear, without faith in their king or in any particular deity. They call, with little conviction, on all the gods and goddesses who might be sympathetic to their plight (78–180) until the king returns to upbraid them in a long tirade where he elaborates what could pass as the official Athenian line on the place of women and the threatening quality of their laments. Women are unbearable creatures who have undermined the confidence of the citizens (182–92). They should stay indoors where they belong and leave public affairs to men (200–1). Instead of clinging to the gods, they should rely on the men who rule them to defend the city, and if they insist on praying he will give them a lesson in how it is done (236–78). The king's prayer is a confident bargain, offering sacrifices and the trophies of war in return for victory. What the women must do, he insists, is to pray like him, avoiding lament and moaning. The women accede to Eteocles' demand in the form but not the content of their prayers. They continue their ill-omened lament for the fall of the city, imagining the awful fate of its women and children, but their appeals to the gods are more controlled, and there is nothing in the language of their prayers to suggest they are actually weeping or moaning.

Critics have been divided on how to interpret the violence of Eteocles' reponse to the chorus, some viewing it as an ill-founded misogynistic outburst, others as appropriate to masculine behaviour in wartime.[18] Helene Foley has suggested that the portrayal of the women's behaviour in a city under siege must have struck a familiar chord with the audience, inviting comparison with Andromache's premature lament for Hector in the sixth book of the *Iliad*.[19] The contrast is illuminating. Andromache first leads the women of Troy to pray for Athena's favour, then laments her husband before his death, alone and with her servants. It seems natural in the Homeric world that women appeal to the gods in wartime, just as Andromache's passionate grief, however ill-omened, provokes sympathy rather than anger from her husband. Eteocles' stern reaction to the behaviour of the women of Thebes in the opening scene of *Seven Against Thebes* suggests a change in attitude to women's participation in public ritual as well as towards their lament. Or does it? As the play develops, a strange reversal of roles takes place. No sooner does Eteocles discover that he will meet his brother face to face in mortal combat than the chorus become the voice for control and civic interest, warning the king against the pollution that will result from fratricide (679–737).[20] And when Thebes is victorious the women of the chorus, though not related to the dead, not only control the funeral rites but use their laments for the two brothers to voice their own political points of view.

I will reserve more detailed discussion of Aeschylus' treatment of lament for the *Oresteia*, simply suggesting that the role of lament in *Seven Against Thebes* is far from straightforward. We move from what seems an exaggerated display of male distaste for public display of emotion by women to an anachronistic display of the female control of death rituals. It is not the grieving sisters who are given the principal role in the proceedings, but the chorus, singing a song of the Furies (*hymnon Erinuos*), a lament that, as critics have remarked, takes the form but not the spirit of normal lamentation.[21] The women, who appeared so fearful and fragile at the beginning of the play, seem vindicated in their prescience and we are left wondering how the Athenian audience would have viewed their triumphant lament.

LAMENT IN THE *ORESTEIA*

If *The Persians* identifies women's lament with barbarians, and *Seven Against Thebes* seems ambiguous in its attitude to women's control of the rituals of death, the *Oresteia*, with the *Choephoroi* as its centrepiece, is Aeschylus' most complex treatment of mourning and its potential for engendering violence. Mourning, in the *Oresteia*, is always treated in a 'political' context. The *polis* and its new institutions are at some level the subject matter of all three plays. Since Aeschylus' concern seems to be to justify those institutions, particularly the Athenian law-court and a modernized, local version of the Olympian religious hierarchy, with Athena and Apollo in privileged positions and a new cult of the Eumenides, we must expect him to devalue what preceded them. The feminist critic Froma Zeitlin, examining the *Oresteia* in terms of 'the dynamics of misogyny', sees Aeschylus establishing a hierarchization of values, in which Olympian is placed over chthonic on the divine level, Greek over barbarian on the cultural level, and male over female on the social level. She concludes

> But the male-female conflict subsumes the other two, for while it maintains its own emotive function in the dramatisation of human concerns, it provides too the central metaphor which 'sexualises' the other issues and attracts them into its magnetic field.[22]

Zeitlin's reading of the trilogy is provocative, and in singling out mourning and lament as a central preoccupation of the trilogy, my reading both supports and extends some aspects of Zeitlin's feminist interpretation. It also agrees with critics who, like her, see the *Oresteia* as a fundamental examination of the institutions of the *polis*.[23] While I would not concur with any reading of the *Oresteia* that reduces the text to a political conflict, sexual or otherwise, there is, in the trilogy, an undeniably negative presentation of the potential of lament to provoke violence. Unlike the *Epitaphios Logos*, which deliberately substitutes the official praise of the dead for private, female lament, the *Oresteia* undermines lament in a more subtle way. By re-presenting traditional lament, particularly in the *Choephoroi*, the plays expose its frightening power. At the same time, the obvious failure of the final scene of the *Eumenides* to silence the ancient deities of revenge suggests we should be wary of any reading of Aeschylus that imputes to its author a view less subtle than our own.

By staging the ritual of mourning as the centrepiece of his trilogy, Aeschylus makes clear that it is an issue of immense interest in the Athens of his day. It is a theme that will be taken up again by Sophocles and Euripides, but in the *Oresteia*, we have the benefit of seeing it worked out in the full form of the trilogy. Statement is followed by counterstatement, conflict by resolution. We are left in no doubt, by the end of the *Eumenides*, that complete female control of the rituals for the dead is incompatible with the new Athenian state, but how much must be left in order not to offend? If no concessions are made, is there a price to pay? The new institutions of the state may have replaced a world Aeschylus deliberately distances from Athens in time and space, but that the aged mythical powers can be so swiftly contained and redirected for the good of the state is something Aeschylus himself seems only half ready to believe.

THE DANGERS OF EXCESSIVE MOURNING IN *AGAMEMNON*

As they watched the opening scenes of *Agamemnon*, the Athenian audience must have been immediately aware that they were being presented with the spectacle of a society out of joint. The innovation of Athens in granting a limited equality to its citizens did not extend such privileges to women. And yet the Mycenae of the play is ruled by a woman, temporarily, it is true, but a decade has gone by since Agamemnon left: enough to make Clytemnestra's rule no mere regency. Not only does she rule with political ambition (*Agamemnon*, 12–13), manœuvring the kingdom like a man, but she has betrayed her husband by taking a lover. Clytemnestra dominates *Agamemnon*, as she does her husband, her lover and the city. She is a portrait of a female who has carried mourning to a dangerous extreme. In one sense she is a mythic double of the goddess in whose name her daughter was sacrificed – Artemis the huntress, protector of the newborn, of 'the lion's tender, helpless cubs' (141). Once Calchas has interpreted the sight of the twin eagles devouring the pregnant hare as an omen requiring virgin sacrifice, Agamemnon is prepared to kill his own daughter, Iphigenia, in order to lift the curse that keeps his fleet from sailing. The chorus are quick to remind us that the war Agamemnon and his brother went to fight is one that avenged the loss of a woman (225). Helen, the 'grief that never heals', may be Clytemnestra's sister, but she is also the indirect cause of her daughter's death, turning the mother into a ravening fury, as dangerous in her anger as Artemis.

In *The Persians*, as I have suggested, extravagant mourning is permitted to Xerxes as befitting the non-Greek; in *Agamemnon*, we have a more subtle identification of the Orient with decadence, luxury and female prerogative. The play opens with the tired watchman waiting for a signal from the east, a fire to turn darkness into dawn. The queen, elaborate in her cunning, has ordered an early-warning system of beacons placed on all the high points between Troy and Argos to ensure her immediate news of a Greek victory. When the fires light up she rejoices with the innocent citizens in a speech rich in irony. Fire is on its way from east to west, a fire lit by woman's command – she is proud to call it 'unfathered (*apappon*) fire' (311). Fire is generally a male element in Greek mythology, associated with Hephaestos (so with metalworking, and specifically the anvil) and Prometheus. The unnatural quality of Clytemnestra's fire consists partly of its lack of male progenitor. In the *Eumenides*, Apollo will argue that the male is the only true progenitor, that the female is simply nurse for the male seed. Before such an argument can be advanced, though, we must be shown the dangers of female power. Darkness and light constantly succeeding one another will be associated with the female and male throughout the trilogy, but first we see the queen in her moment of triumph, as a source of unnatural light – 'torch-bearing according to my laws . . . a message passed on from Troy to me!' The 'Dawn of good news', Clytemnestra, has already informed the chorus, is 'according to the proverb, *born from the womb of the kindly time* (i.e. night)' (265). Can an audience fail to catch the allusion to the dark, female powers that have engendered this brightness? Are not the Erinyes themselves daughters of night, soon to be tamed and renamed 'the kindly ones' – the Eumenides?

The chorus, obtuse as always in this first play of the trilogy, fail to read the sign as adumbrating vengeance, and praise the queen's triumphant speech adding irony to irony: '*gunai, kat' andra sophron' euphronos legeis*' (Lady, you speak with self control, like a prudent man) (351). The sexual ambiguities are rich, as they will continue to be throughout *Agamemnon*. Male actor playing female is praised by male chorus for speaking like a man.[24] The audience knows this woman is lying, that the chorus have misread her. Her deception is as essentially female as the weapons she will use to bring down her husband: the carpet and the net.

What intricate threads are woven into that soft crimson path that leads from the outside world of men and light to the dark, inner chamber of the palace where women ply the art of weaving that belongs to them as it does to the Fates and the goddess Athena![25] Unlike the ageing chorus, Agamemnon makes no mistake in his reading of signs. This laying down of carpets associates him with what is female and foreign: 'Don't treat me delicately like a woman. And don't grovel, shrieking at me as if I were a Barbarian husband. . .'. Returning, as he is, from the east, there is a suggestion that he may be tainted by un-Greek tastes, but he quickly reassures us that he is a man, i.e. an Athenian, wanting only to be respected as a man. Besides, it would be an act of hubris inviting divine retribution. Clytemnestra's response is to compare his behaviour with the hypothetical behaviour of King Priam in similar circumstances: 'But can you imagine Priam if he were so praised?' The implication that Priam, as an eastern ruler, would revel in luxury, fearless of gods or man, places him in company with Croesus, legendary king of Lydia and renowned for his wealth, as well as with the Persians. Agamemnon's answer confirms the difference between Greeks and orientals: 'It certainly seems to me he'd be walking on the rich cloth.' Clytemnestra parries, 'And you stand in awe of public censure?'

The king may stand in awe, not the queen: Greeks, not oriental barbarians. There is no doubt where right lies, and yet a woman wins by an appeal to male pride. As she watches him take the first steps on the crimson cloth, woven by female hands, that will lead him into her dark domain the queen says: 'It is like the sea. Who will drain it dry?/ Nurturing so much porphyry, like silver/ forever oozing bloody dye' (958–9). Then, with the irony she is a master of, she continues: 'I would have sworn to tread on any number of blood-red cloths to repay the oracle, who could bring that life back' (963–5). Whose life would she bring back to the house? We know it is not her husband's. It is Iphigenia's absence that motivates her actions, her maternal grief for which she would happily have defied the gods. She makes this doubly clear by equating her husband with Zeus: 'When Zeus makes wine from the bitter unripe grape' (970). Husband, king, king of the gods, his prophet – these are the forces drawn up on one side. On the other, the 'unripe grape', the young offspring and its avenging mother, whose grief has turned to a fury unquenchable as the sea.

As the king and queen enter the palace the chorus cringe in terror, tormented by a song that will not leave them in peace. It is the lament of the Erinyes, those ancient deities who will become Clytemnestra's monstrous double. The destructive dimension of maternal grief, soon to be made manifest in Clytemnestra's violence, is given a symbolic presence in the Furies, who use lament as the main instrument of their terrifying power. In this first mention of the dirge of the Furies, the chorus describe it as a 'self-taught *thrēnos* sung without the lyre' (989–90). In other words it is the quintessential women's lament for the dead, sung at the graveside, with no instrumental accompaniment. Already it exercises a strange power over the chorus, one that robs them of hope and, as if to emphasize the comparative impotence of male song, they ask: 'Once a man has shed his dark blood on the earth by what songs (*epaeidon*) can he be brought back to life?' It may be impossible by means of normal song, but the audience remembers the Persian queen bringing her husband from the grave with her lament. It is hard to imagine more striking evidence of the force of the unaccompanied, untutored song than Darius' appearance from the grave.

Only one character on the stage understands the meaning of the terrible dirge. Cassandra chooses silence at first, and Clytemnestra makes the error of imagining she cannot speak Greek, but only in 'a barbarian voice', like a swallow. The symbolism of the swallow – the bird whose tongue was cut out – is doubly appropriate for Cassandra, who is condemned to go unheeded and to be identified with what makes one barbarian – the inability to speak Greek.[26] As she goes to her death, Cassandra will sing her own dirge (1,345). In doing so she will become a symbolic double of Iphigenia, an innocent victim going helpless to her death. Why does the queen kill her? Clytemnestra may sense in her a tongue more powerful than her own, one that will prophesy the future terror she is not ready to hear, or it may be that there is a simple exchange of victim for victim, a death that will engender more deaths. As Cassandra herself says, calling the chorus to witness, 'when woman for woman dies for me/ man falls for ill-married man'(1317–18). What we must understand, from Cassandra's words, is the repetitive nature of the blood feud, the ritual of revenge. The identification of revenge with lament is precise:

Let me speak again, a dirge –
it is my own. I pray to the sun
my last light, that those who kill my enemies
avenge my death as well.

(1,322–6)

Cassandra's dirge is her own (*emon ton autēs*) in the sense that it is for her own death, but like the song of the Furies it is also her own composition, unaccompanied by instruments. She has just proved herself a woman of magical powers, the priestess of Apollo, whose fate it is not to be listened to in life. It is through her voice that we witness the murder of Agamemnon. The chorus persist in calling her words 'Obscure, riddles' (1,113). Cassandra may speak at first in riddles because the message she has to convey, one that links past horrors to present, is impossible for the chorus to believe.[27] If they are unsure of what her words signify, they comprehend her call for vengeance and understand it is addressed to the Furies (1,119). Through Cassandra's mouth, as if from an oracle, we will witness the queen become a monster. The cow catches the bull in her cunningly woven net – a female weapon – but it is she who 'gores him with her black horn' (1,127). From this unnatural inversion of sexual roles it is an easy step to link Clytemnestra to monsters like 'Scylla', 'a sea-witch', 'a viper'. As Cassandra reveals to the audience what is happening behind the closed doors of the palace, the chorus tell her literally to 'put her mouth to sleep' (*koimēsou stōma*). Not only do they not hear, they do not wish to hear of the inevitable repetition of violence engendered by the slaughter within. In death, though, she demands and expects to be heard.

Cassandra's *thrēnos* is where the work of revenge begins. The killing of Cassandra repeats the killing of Iphigenia. By an excess of mourning, Clytemnestra has become violent. Mourning will become the means to kindle Electra's and Orestes' violence; the rituals of death, we begin to understand, beget the rituals of death.

THE *CHOEPHOROI* AND THE ORCHESTRATION OF EMOTION

In the *Choephoroi* the focus of the trilogy becomes clear. Locus and focus converge before our eyes at the tomb of Agamemnon.

Orestes, who has been in exile for some years, performs a ritual gesture of mourning at the grave by cutting off two locks of his hair. He and his companion, Pylades, hide as they notice a group of women dressed in black approaching the tomb. Orestes thinks he can distinguish his sister among them and immediately makes a vow to avenge his father with her help. In the first speech of the play we know that revenge will come and that it will take both siblings to achieve it. We know, too, that revenge involves matricide, a crime before which all of us shrink in horror. How can Orestes, and the audience, be persuaded to such an act?

Now we see the function of the female chorus of mourners. Like the players in *Hamlet*, they are about to work on the emotions not of the king, but of the lagging prince. They have no more direct involvement, as captive Trojan slaves, in avenging Agamemnon's death, than the professional actor at the Danish court has in Hamlet's predicament. What we are about to witness is, I believe, something that Aeschylus' Athenian audience were thoroughly familiar with: a lament at the grave-side led by 'professional' women mourners who 'stage' emotional response and by doing so inspire not only pity and fear but violent action. By showing us how female lament worked in Greek society and by subtly undermining it, Aeschylus affirms the function of his own art. Tragedy, like lament, is a controlled artistic response, but as part of a public festival it is a state-sanctioned outlet for violent emotions. What we see on the stage is what happens, or what Aeschylus would have the audience believe happens, without public control. It is a mimesis of the mimetic art of lament, one which has a self-conscious didactic function. We see men in the 'deep play' of theatre playing women engaged in the 'deep play' of ritual lament. But we must keep in mind that what takes place on the stage is taking place in a male space, where women have no part and must always be introduced as representations of absent others. Whatever the theatre taught the Athenians about their own society by re-enacting its elemental oppositions in symbolic form, we must remember that the ritual was a closed one, bound to reveal partial truths.

The chorus of the *Choephoroi* are both female and oriental – doubly removed from the audience, though not yet monstrous. They accompany Electra, who, at Clytemnestra's behest, brings offerings to her father's tomb. We know these gifts are too late and are inspired by fear, yet the chorus make their entry in the full frenzy of lament. They tear their cheeks with their nails making 'bloody gashes', rend their linen garments, beat their breasts and howl (23–30). Clytemnestra has had a fearful dream, interpreted, by those with knowledge of such matters, as coming from the dead beneath the earth. The offerings at the tomb are an attempt to ward off the fury of the vengeful dead but the chorus are reluctant bearers of *charin achariton* – empty gifts that will not bring favour. Any libations they may pour on the queen's behalf they know will be rejected by 'mother earth' and lie solid as the blood of the murdered victim that 'clots and will not soak through' (66–7). There is, it seems, no *akos* (remedy) for past wrong in the chorus's vocabulary. As captured women they have, themselves, been wronged. They remain slaves of masters who have destroyed their city and killed their menfolk. Behind their veils, though, they have secretly wept for Electra (82–4), nursing their fury. Now the time has come to turn their tears to some purpose. The extravagance of their gesture is no sign of lack of control; indeed it is they who orchestrate the emotions of Electra, as she comes to pour the libation, urging her to 'remember Orestes who is *thuraios*' (both 'at the door' and 'abroad') and to call for vengeance on the murderers.

Electra's call for revenge, as she pours her libation, takes the form of a prayer addressed to Hermes as an intermediary with the spirits of the dead, asking that Orestes return to avenge his father's death. As if acknowledging the inefficacy of her plea, Electra ends with these lines:

> Such are my prayers. After them I pour libations.
> It is your business to make them bloom with laments,
> Calling out your paean for the dead.

These are interesting words. Lament and praise for the dead are not in conflict here. Electra expects them to be one and the same. Later the chorus will express the hope that their *thrēnos* may turn into a paeon (343) of celebration. It would seem that the forms of lament and paeon are, for Aeschylus, not mutually exclusive, but rather distinguished by the circumstances of performance. The chorus do not immediately use the form most commonly associated with the lament in tragedy (the *kommos*) but one that is in an appropriate metre.[28] At the same time they address themselves in the imperative, a not uncommon device in lament, enjoining themselves to shed noisy tears. We have no knowledge of what their lyrics sounded like, but the Greek in which they begin the long process of working grief into action is full of musical suggestions. Repetition of sounds, particularly an assonance of o-sounds in the first section, ends in the long cry, common to laments,[29] of 'ototototototoi'. Like the *tsakísmata* or *extra metrum* exclamations that interrupt modern Greek folk-songs, such cries must have had the effect of heightening the emotional state of the singer as well as the audience. We begin to understand how 'noisy' tears can be. Immediately following this staccato exclamation comes the first explicit call for violence.[30]

Electra and Orestes are now reunited and Orestes calls on Zeus to witness their pitiable state, comparing himself and his sister with 'fledglings' and 'orphans' (250–60). The chorus's response to the self-pitying rhetoric of Orestes is to imagine a hideous death in 'bubbling pitch' for the murderers of Agamemnon.[31] In the speech that follows, Orestes tells Electra and the chorus how Apollo has urged him to revenge. It is interesting that Apollo's description of what the unavenged dead will do to the living is quite as repulsive in its detail as the Furies' will be at the end of the play. It seems madness and fear are what lie in wait for Orestes, whatever path he takes. If he fails to avenge his father's murder he will be cursed with disease, polluted. Yet his only possible revenge is a crime that will pollute him. In this cycle of endless revenge, memory lives from death to death. Lament is the vehicle for communicating with the dead. It can function as a healing mechanism, reassuring the living or calming their anger, but if the mourners take up the cause of the angry relatives and appeal to the dead for revenge, it becomes the means of perpetuating the cycle of murders.

STIRRING UP THE DEAD

As the chorus begin what Aristotle describes as the tragic form of the *thrēnos* (the *kommos*) we are at the heart of Aeschylus' trilogy. Not only does it occupy a central position in the play and the trilogy, but it is the longest, most structurally complex lyric which has survived from ancient tragedy. George Thomson has noted how far Aeschylus has progressed from the invocation to Darius in *The Persians*, which effects the appearance of the

dead king, to this long lyrical exchange that 'effects a revolution
in our attitude of mind'.[32] What no critic has paid sufficient
attention to is the fact that the women mourners are in charge
of this 'revolution'. They are performing a role which is
certainly familiar to the audience, and the reason their power is
so singularly displayed may itself be an attempt at revolution –
the undermining of women's traditional role as mourners.

There are suggestions that the *kommos* had Asiatic
connections.[33] Although Aristotle confines its use to tragedy, it
almost certainly pre-dates it. Alexiou suggests it may have
evolved 'as a dramatic form of the ritual antiphonal lament
between the professional and predominantly choral mourners
on the one hand, and the mainly solo and narrative improvisations of the kinswomen on the other'.[34] In this case the
chorus begin with an invocation to the Fates. In doing so they
may also be repeating a formula which is derived from funeral
practice.[35] The modern Greek word for a lament, *moirolói*, does
not appear in the language until Pseudo-Callisthenes' *Life of
Alexander* (c.300 BC – the versions we have of it all date from
300 AD or later), but in that context, as in many of the
modern folk laments, *emoiróloghisa emautón*, the concept of
prophesying one's own fate, is remarkably similar to Cassandra's 'lament for myself'.

The connection of fate with death, of *moira* as the inescapable
Fate of us all, sometimes personified as a single goddess, sometimes as the Three Moires, has a long history in the learned and
popular tradition.[36] The association of the Moires with the
Erinyes is not uncommon. Apollo has warned Orestes of how he
can expect to suffer at the hands of the Erinyes if he does not
avenge his father. The chorus's appeal to the Fates seems to make
them synonymous. Similarly Zeus and Dikē (the personification
of justice, whom the chorus of the *Choephoroi* immediately link
to the Fates) are frequently paired.[37] The concept of justice, at
least here, is a fierce one. She cries out for retribution:

For hostile words, let hostile words
be paid, Justice cries aloud,
demanding retribution –
Let blow be struck for murderous blow
By acting we suffer
Three generations the saying goes.

The equation of justice with fate is powerfully reinforced by the language in which the chorus presents it. The series of reciprocal phrases reinforcing one another creates a perfect union of form and meaning. The killings in the house of Atreus balance one another in an endless cycle.

In a speech full of interest for its explicit recognition of the power of the lament to communicate with the dead, Orestes responds:

> Oh father, wretched father
> what can I possibly say or do
> to speed you back from where
> you lie at anchor so far away?
> The realms of darkness and light
> are opposed. And yet men say
> the lament that brings glory is welcome
> before the house of Atreus.[38]

Orestes is stating what seems to be a commonly held belief that the bridge between the upper world of light and the darkness of the underworld is not to be found in words or deeds but in the singular power of the sung lament accompanied, as it always is, by ritual beatings of the breast, tears and other outward displays of grief. It is an idea common to the folk tradition, and one that Aeschylus has already adumbrated in *Seven Against Thebes* (854 ff.), where the chorus lament the sons of Oedipus:

> But, my friends, down the wind of groans
> with hands that beat the head
> ply the speeding stroke
> which sends through Death's waters
> the dark-sailed ship of mission
> to the shore, untrodden by Apollo, and sunless,
> the shore unseen, that welcomes all at last.[39]

The two passages are strikingly similar. The world of life is one of light, separated by a great body of water from the dark underworld. *Goos* is the magic incantation that can traverse the shadowy realm between. In this sense its magic is linked to that of Orpheus, charming his way by means of music to the underworld. *Goos, goeteia, thelgein* – lament, charm, to charm – words that seem distant in mood begin to converge.[40] Nor is this something peculiar to Greece. In Egypt, where 'lamentations' were a major feature of religious ceremony, music was thought to have an influence on people through a power called *heka'* or *hike* which was similar to a spell.[41] Similarly the Latin *cantus* and *carmen* are, of course, related to 'enchanting' and 'charm'. The word 'tragedy' itself – *traghodia* – is a compound which includes the word 'song', and has become the general term for song in modern Greek.

The reply of the chorus carries the association of *goos* and magical power forwards:

> Child, the ruthless jaws of fire
> can never conquer the spirit of the dead
> He shows his anger later
> the dead man is lamented
> revealed as an avenger
> the just lament of fathers and sons
> will hunt out the guilty,
> stirring and embracing all.
>
> (324–31)

As in the first choral lyric, a cluster of 'o' sounds surrounds the verb *ototuzetai*, reminding us that the words of a lament are cries in themselves, pure expressions of feelings that defy articulation in the language of everyday speech or of literature. These cries will raise not the body of Agamemnon, as Darius was raised in *The Persians*, but his disembodied *psychē*. The power of the *goos* is extended by the chorus to one of active participation in the process of revenge. *Goos* is semi-personified, again following a precedent in *Seven Against Thebes*, where a lament escorts the dead brothers from their house, becoming a *psychopompos* (915 ff.), and with *The Persians* (697) where the phrase *psychagogois goois* appears. Now we have a *goos* not only performing a bridging function between two worlds, but actively involved in the process of revenge. The word *tarachthēs*, from *tarasso*, to stir-up, perhaps best defines the active principle of lament. The *goos* stirs up, or troubles, the emotions of the living and the dead, drawing them out of their inertia.

The chorus, confident in their powers, realize the *thrēnos* can be turned into a paeon (342). Both Electra and Orestes do not immediately advance the mood of revenge. Instead, as in many of the traditional folk laments, where wishes rapidly turn to curses, they wish Agamemnon's fate had been different.[42] The

chorus, beginning the central, anapaestic section of the *kommos*
remind Electra and Orestes that these irrational wishes will not
advance their cause; it is the 'sound of the double lash' that can
be heard below (375).[43] In other words the lament is not a song
to dream with, but a powerful weapon that will raise the dead
to revenge. Orestes is immediately inspired, saying: 'That
pierced the ear like an arrow', but he calls on Zeus for revenge,
rather than contemplating action. This is the turning-point in
the *kommos*. The chorus anticipates its own cry of triumph for
the moment when 'the man is struck, the woman killed'. The cry
is no longer the *otototoi* of despair but the *ololugmon*, a cry
specifically associated with female victory, with sacrifice and
violence.[44] The same cry is heard a number of times in the
trilogy, memorably in Cassandra's account of the murder of
Agamemnon, and it will be heard again at the end of *The
Eumenides*. The word which accompanies it here, *peukaent'*,
may be connected with musical pitch.[45] Its root is from the
word for a pine, and it seems to indicate a shrill, sharp
vocalization. *Ololugmos* is certainly a plausible transliteration
of a female cry that often accompanies laments in the Middle
East and north Africa involving a free vibration of the uvula. In
any case the cry is part of a physical expression, an exterior-
ization of what has long been repressed. 'Why hide what keeps
whirling in my mind and shaking it?/ The fierce head wind of
my anger/ blows before my heart's prow/ malignant hatred.'

It is Electra who responds immediately to the change in
rhetoric. She calls on Zeus to 'crush the skulls' of the murderers
and cries, like the chorus, *pheu pheu*. The chorus remind Electra
that bloodshed demands bloodshed in return: 'For murder
calls to the Erinyes, who, from those long dead, bring ruin on
ruin' (400–4). Orestes is still full of despair, but Electra,
lamenting as a woman among female mourners, has become
strong and fierce. Of her mother, she says:

> She may fawn, but she can never charm those who suffer
> The wolf is savage, not to be tamed –
> my anger comes from my mother.
>
> (419–21)

The analogy is multiply effective. Electra, her new-found
strength acquired by howling, has taken on her mother's
monstrous anger, becoming a she-wolf now immune to her

mother's fawning. The dog image is one Aeschylus commonly links to deceit[46] and has used before in connection with Clytemnestra (194). The monstrous imagery associated with Clytemnestra in *Agamemnon* has passed down the female line, through the medium of lament. The purity of Electra's motivation in avenging her father's murder is suddenly in doubt. Are we to understand she is tainted, being her mother's daughter, or that her mother's monstrous behaviour has forced her, against her nature, into violence? It is certainly a question that Sophocles will follow up in his version of the story (*Electra*, 616 ff.), but whether or not Electra's inheritance plays a role does not affect our perception of the power of lament in awakening her anger. Once aroused, Electra becomes the equal in fury to and ally of the chorus in urging Orestes to action.

EASTERN STRAINS AND THE MAKING OF MONSTERS

The second principal section of the *kommos* begins with a re-enactment, for Orestes' benefit, of the lament and burial of Agamemnon. As they did in the *parodos*, the chorus describe their own lament, with its traditional self-flagellation and they spell out the connection between such extravagant behaviour and the Orient, specifically Persia. This is the most detailed description of the lament in tragedy, a peculiarly self-referential text in which the women, undoubtedly singing in lament form and actually beating their breasts, both re-enact their former grief and describe how they do it:

I struck myself in Arian fashion
in the mode of a Kissian wailing-woman.
(423–4)

There is no doubt that this was familiar terminology for Aeschylus' audience. What does it mean? *Arioi* was, according to Herodotus, an old name for the Medes.[47] Kissia, another Persian name, was in the direction of Susa.[48] The chorus are Trojans, already 'oriental', but they look to Persia as a more legitimate source for the extravagant gestures of lament. Aeschylus was not alone in thinking that such laments were 'oriental' in nature.[49] Was the connection made between the mystery cults, recently introduced into Athens, in which women played a prominent part, and another sort of rite that was traditionally controlled by women? Were Persian women more extravagant in their laments than Greek women? Or was the association of lament with Persian 'orientalism' an attempt to discredit both women and their performance of funeral rites? It is a difficult question, but one to which musical practice may offer some clue.

I have deliberately translated the word *nomos* as mode, because it suggests both a manner of performance and a musical term denoting a certain tonality and even mood. Later in the play (822) the term is used again in what seems to be another musical context, although the Greek is not altogether clear. It is an important passage because it deals with the power of lament, this time at the moment of vengeance:

> And then, at once, we shall let out
> the famous song for the deliverance of the house.
> Laments (*goeton*)[50] in female, high-pitched mode
> bringing fair winds – so it is well for the city[51]
> mine, mine will be the greater gain
> and ruin stays far from those I love.

As in most monophonic traditions, including the bulk of modern and presumably ancient Greek music, there is an elaborate system of modes which are not only equivalent to certain tone rows but are characterized by patterns of melodic ornamentation and particular emotive qualities. The word *nomos*, as Aeschylus uses it, seems to indicate such a musical mode. Laments in the classical period were sung, according to Plato, in a certain mode or cluster of modes.[52] The word Plato uses is *harmonia*, which probably meant a melodic type and a certain type of tuning, rather than simply a tone-row. He says the Mixolydian and High Lydian 'and suchlike' were favoured. These *harmoniae* were, in the ideal state, to be banned as 'unprofitable for women who are respectable, let alone for men'. It is interesting that in present-day Greece, and in a wide area of the Balkans, many of the modes used by folk musicians are derived from the East, some from Arabic and Persian prototypes. It is hard to date the beginnings of such a tradition, but it is probable that certain musical modes, particularly those with oriental place-names, came to Greece from the East, and that certain of them were associated with lament. The two neighbours of ancient Lydia, Caria and Mysia, are both linked to female lament in classical times. It would seem that the whole area of the eastern Aegean coast had a reputation for exporting laments to the Greek mainland. The dirge, if it is to be suppressed, must be identified with what is unworthy in the 'men's club' that classical Athens has become.[53] To insist that it is eastern, as well as female, makes it doubly unwelcome.

The chorus in the *Choephoroi*, having succeeded in rousing Electra's fury, join with her in describing to Orestes the disgrace of his father's burial. Not only did he go without the proper mourning rites, but his body was mutilated, a traditional practice apparently followed by Clytemnestra to prevent him returning as a revenant and taking vengeance (439–40). It is this obscene reversal of proper burial and mourning practice that provokes Orestes to fury. Brother and sister address their father as they pour libations together and plan the murder of their mother. Before they act, the chorus sings a long ode in which they make use of mythical material to develop the theme that female passion is the most terrible thing in nature. Men, they contend, are capable of high feats of daring, but women's passion goes beyond all bounds. What drives them is sexual passion, an unnatural excess of love that both overpowers and empowers.

To illustrate this perversion, the chorus first use the case of Althaea, daughter of Thestius, king of the Curetes, wife of Oeneus, king of Calydon, and the mother of Meleager. When Meleager was a week old, the Fates appeared and said that he would die when a brand, flaming in the hearth, had burned away. Althaea hid the brand in a chest, but when Meleager killed his mother's brothers in a quarrel, she threw the brand into the fire and caused her son's death. The second example that the chorus introduces is Scylla, not the Homeric monster, but the daughter of Nisus, king of Megara, who had a magical lock of hair on which his life depended. Bribed with a golden necklace by the forces of King Minos, who was besieging Megara, she cut off the lock of hair and so ensured her father's death.

Next follows the story of the women of Lemnos, who killed their husbands and all their menfolk because they had taken Thracian concubines.[54] Aeschylus expects his audience to be familiar with the story and merely alludes to it, but as Zeitlin has pointed out, the story of the Lemnian women, coming as a climax in a series, 'completes the misogynistic progression by moving from one to all'.[55] Woman's fury can perhaps be matched only by the female Fury. The chorus, after mentioning Zeus, Justice and Fate, end their ode with Fury: *kluta busso-phrun Erinyes* – renowned, deep-thinking Furies – and we understand from these three words, echoing her very name, that Clytemnestra is Fury personified.[56] Orestes may be the agent of her destruction, but it is only the dread female powers, aroused by the magical lament of the chorus, who can match her ferocity. This is, as Zeitlin sees correctly, a progression in a terrifying portrayal of women that leads us to consider Clytemnestra as a monster, but we understand, too, that the Furies, who are responsible for stirring Orestes to action, are no less culpable in the perpetual cycle of violence.

FROM MONSTERS TO MADNESS

When the murder is planned, the chorus sing another ode, this time appealing to the Olympian powers to help bring justice and freedom to the house. It is here that they utter their triumphant *ololugmos* and urge Orestes to be like Perseus killing the Gorgon. Again, the choral ode ends with the association of Clytemnestra and a monster surrounded by snakes. The snake-mother sees her son in a dream as a viper biting her breast, and after he has killed her, Orestes, like Perseus, will be pursued by the Gorgon-like, nightmarish figures of the Erinyes.

In the climactic scene of the play, the confrontation between mother and son, we are in no doubt that Orestes will kill his mother, and only curious to see what the arch-strategist can pull from her store of cunning. What she does is, as usual, both masterly and feminine: she bares her breast, and calls on her son's pity. Since Orestes' nurse has appeared and informed us she was the one who suckled the baby and cleaned his clothes when he wet them, we are somewhat sceptical of her claim to have nursed him for hours at her breast. Clytemnestra may be expected to use some gesture to remind her son of their undisputed relationship, but given the fact that Orestes has matured in exile, the exposure of her breast (in contrast to Hecuba's similar gesture in *Iliad* XXII) can be construed as more than maternal. There is at least a hint of sexual appeal in this scene, of the threatening power of a woman's weapon.[57] Its effect is to cause Orestes to hesitate and turn to Pylades, who reminds him of Apollo's curse. The horror of matricide seems to pale beside the wrath of the god.

In the ode that follows the violent climax, the chorus sing a song of liberation for the house of Atreus. Apollo, the god of light, has triumphed over darkness and the power of the Furies. Orestes displays the bodies of his mother and her lover, reminding us how they killed his father. Comparing the queen to an eel and a viper, he displays the net in which she trapped Agamemnon, and says he would rather die childless than have such a wife. Now Orestes is free to mourn his father, and he clutches the fateful robe to him, but as he does so he is aware that the doing of the deed involves an endless pain, one that affects the whole of his clan. The bloodstained garment is both victory and curse. He sees himself as a charioteer, whose bolting horses (his own wits) pull him off course. Fear sings near his heart, accompanied, as in a dance, by anger (1,024–5).

The musical imagery is complex, and we are reminded of *Agamemnon* (990) where the chorus's song of fear becomes the dirge of the Furies as Clytemnestra enters the palace to commit murder. Knowing, as we do now, that the lament is a song with magical powers, as capable of arousing anger as sadness, we see that again there is a failure to mourn correctly. Perhaps Orestes can now mourn his father, but he cannot mourn his mother and so the song which puts one death to rest stirs vengeance for the next. There is no solution to Orestes' dilemma, and it has literally driven him out of his wits. As he leaves for Delphi, to escape the blood of Argos, he sees 'women like Gorgons, dressed in black and wreathed in serpents' (1,048). The chorus appear not to see the terrible vision that pursues Orestes and prepare the audience for the next play of the trilogy. Their last words reiterate the curse of the house. 'Where will it end?' they ask, 'Where will this furious ruin end?'

THE *EUMENIDES*: WITCHES EXPOSED TO THE LIGHT

What do the terrible female monsters of Orestes' vision represent? If Clytemnestra was the Gorgon, or serpentine monster, as the chorus has reminded us more than once, then what could be more natural than that he should be hunted by the spirits who are her counterparts in the world of the dead. The last play of the trilogy extends the identification of female power with monstrosity to its dreadful limit, then attempts to contain the horror it has unleashed by turning the witches into good fairies, the Erinyes into the Eumenides. The didactic structure of the trilogy becomes clear only with its final play. The first play was set in a mythical kingdom whose bloody history was known to the audience, a prelude to the unthinkable murder of the king. In it the queen was seen to have over-mourned her daughter, under-valued her husband through adultery and her son by sending him into ignominious exile, and finally to have carried out her long-planned murder. The second play is set at the tomb of the dead king, where foreign women, known to be good at laments, rouse the son and daughter of Agamemnon to revenge by the use of magical song. The murder of Clytemnestra and her lover seems as if it will end the cycle of violence until, at the very end of the play, the Furies appear and strike terror into Orestes. Something must now be resolved, and that means leaving the old world of darkness and magic. The palace of Mycenae, whose dark interior reeks with blood, is succeeded by Delphi, sanctuary of the god of light. Delphi will be succeeded by Athens, a new source of enlightenment.

The movement from darkness to light, so fundamental to this, perhaps to all tragedy, is graphically represented by a scene shift. In the clear morning light of Delphi, the Erinyes' dark magic is at a disadvantage. Phoebus Apollo, whose very name, we are reminded in the opening chorus, derives from light, transforms Orestes' nightmarish vision of the Furies into a huddle of obscene old maids lit by the glare of his bright shrine.

The Erinyes, or Eumenides, are perhaps the nearest the Greeks came to representing madness. Foucault maintained that there was no contrary to the Greek *logos*[58] but *logos* itself, as de Romilly argues,[59] is a form of magic that can induce a temporary loss of reason. Antithesis is a favourite device of classical rhetoric and of magic spells. Turning things upside-down, disguise and *apatē*, are the deceits which are the very essence of the theatre.[60] The Erinyes, or Furies will become the Eumenides, the kindly ones. The reversal of their name would not have been enough to allay the fears of an Athenian audience of the fifth century any more than it would in contemporary Greece, where it is still customary to give what is most feared a 'good' name. The old hags are immediately recognizable as witches, and correspond to what seems an almost universal stereotype.

It is only in *The Eumenides* that we fully understand Clytemnestra and the wailing women of the *Choephoroi*.[61] As Zeitlin says: 'In the primitive portrayal of the Furies there is a regression to the deepest fantasies of masculine terror.'[62] Aged children who produce no children, virgin daughters of night, living under the earth, their disgusting physical appearance is elaborated in irresistible detail: their eyes ooze, their breaths rasp, they are like wingless gorgons. In *The Fate of Schechem*, Julian Pitt-Rivers describes a witch as 'a woman who has become a man thanks to her occult powers and . . . inverts the basic premise of society, which is the moral division of labour.'[63] The broomstick symbolizes her inverted role, the domestic tool protruding from her loins. The prevalence of widows among witches condemned in the seventeenth century, and the common association in the Mediterranean of widows with predatory sexuality, can be explained, Pitt-Rivers believes, in terms of the fact that they are seen as women who have 'escaped from proper male authority'.[64]

At the beginning of the trilogy, Clytemnestra is a wife who already behaves like a widow. In her strategies, her control of the court, her choice of an unmanly lover, she has usurped her husband's role, and she flaunts her sexuality at her own son in an attempt to save her life. By murdering the King she becomes a monster and a witch. The chorus of the *Choephoroi* are her enemies but also her counterparts. They, too, are widows – oriental widows, whose magic song of mourning puts them in direct contact with the powers of the underworld. Like the Eumenides, they are dressed in black, they howl, tear their hair and scratch their cheeks till the blood runs, they sing magic songs. Other excrescences, different garments, songs, but how alike the elements! Black clothing, night, the underworld, female songs, excess – we begin to see Aristotle's 'universal mythopoiesis' converging in this last play of the trilogy. Clytemnestra, the lamenting chorus, Electra, the Eumenides are all part of the same monstrous vision, and we understand that the trial which will take place on the Areopagus is an attempt to contain the terrible nightmare of uncontrolled woman.

In a curious reversal of the *Choephoroi*, it is the ghost of Clytemnestra that rouses the chorus of the Eumenides to sing their dirge. They moan in their sleep until the 'she-dragon' wakes them but their opening chorus is not a song of fury;

rather it is a lament for their own pain, and as de Romilly notes in their famous 'binding' song (330), the very rhetorical structure is a form of magic.[65] Words are repeated, or nearly repeated, like incantations – in three lines we have *epathomen*, *pathousa*, *epathomen*, *pathos*, together with the exclamations *popax* and *popoi* – the muttered spells of witches, but also the *goeteia* of the *goos*. It is a lament for lost power, female power that Apollo and the 'younger gods' have usurped. There is, as many critics have observed, a clear suggestion here of a mythical matriarchy preceding historical patriarchy, combined with elements of an initiation ritual, with Orestes as the ephebic initiate.[66]

Apollo tells the Furies to leave his shrine and go to where heads are cut off, eyes gouged out, men castrated, justice and slaughter one, bodies stuck on spikes. Where can this be? Surely we are expected to equate this with a barbarism that is un-Greek, despite the mutilation of Agamemnon's body. Again, there is an unmistakable connection of female with barbarian, with woman as an enigma who attracts and repels like the foreigner himself.

THE SONG THAT BINDS

The debate between the Furies and Apollo as to Orestes' guilt turns on the question of the relative guilt of Clytemnestra and Orestes. It is properly to be argued in Athens since it is as much an apology for the city and its new institutions as it is a clash between male and female power. Hounded by the Furies (they compare themselves with dogs thirsting for blood (246)), Orestes clasps the knees of Athena, asking for sanctuary. The shrine of Apollo has not been enough to protect him, but Athena is a more formidable threat to female power, a virgin goddess herself, yet known to support men in battle – embattled men. What do the Furies do to claim their victim? They do what one expects of witches, crones, professional singers of dirges: they sing a magic 'binding song' while dancing in a ring. Again, it is as 'magic' in its rhetoric as it must have been in its music – clusters of trisyllabic words accented on the same syllable produce a thick texture and hypnotic rhythm impossible to reproduce in translation. If fear and pity were emotions fundamental to tragedy and regarded as being induced by poetry itself,[67] imagine the effect of this macabre song and dance on an audience sitting only a stone's throw from where the Furies formed their terrible ring around Orestes. This is *goeteia* produced not by a *goos*, but by a chorus who are both the very powers appealed to by the oriental dirge singers, the chorus of the *Choephoroi*, and who call on similarly ancient female powers to help them: on their mother, Night, and on the Fates. It is a *moirolói*, a song of fate, one that belongs to the female world and should not be witnessed by men. Tragedy, itself perhaps derived from ritual song, is staging a ritual song, mimicking the forbidden. Does this make it in some sense a form of initiation, or is this rather voyeurism? Should we, witnessing it, suffer the fate of Pentheus? There is a sense in which the form of tragedy can no longer hold its material, as if it is, after all, female. It is females who have traditionally, by the authority of the Fates, controlled the great mysteries of birth and death. Their control over death has been exercised through poetry and song, by a magic rhetoric that induces terror and pity. Tragedy is usurping a female art form. To do so it must make it its own. In this last wild dance of the Furies, we see tragedy both unleash and contain the dark witchy power of women. In the last tragedy that has come down to us from the classical age, *The Bacchae*, by Euripides, the dance will be repeated, and the Athenian audience, the symbolic doubles of Pentheus, will realize the terror of bearing witness to mysteries not meant for male eyes.

NEW BONDS: JUSTICE ON TRIAL

How does Aeschylus set about containing what will, as the Furies remind us, remain till the end of time (383, 393)? On one level the shift is a rhetorical one. The magic song and dance end. Enter Athena, fresh from tidying up her business at Troy. Unlike Orestes or Apollo, she shows no sign of fear or disgust at the sight of the Furies, a fact she underlines herself (407). Instead she cross-questions them like a good lawyer and respectfully suggests a trial. Already, she has cut the ground from under their feet by failing to be afraid of the Furies' physical appearance. Now, the brisk *stichomuthia* of the goddess with the chorus leader interrupts the frenzied rhythm of the dance, and establishes her authority. Rhetoric undercuts magic just as Athena's response has broken the binding spell. The trial is set, and we know that Orestes must be absolved so that the endless repetition of slaughter can end. Before the trial begins, though, the Furies sing a last song, a dirge for their own inevitable loss of power in the contest to come and a warning of what the consequences of that loss will be.

The opening words of their song break the circle of their dance – their *hymnon desmion*, or 'binding song', is being destroyed by *neon thesmion* – the verbal echo of their magic song is impossible to ignore. A shift has taken place from what binds by custom and what binds by law.[68] The magic rhetorical devices of the *stasimon*, are, by comparison with the binding-song, few. Instead there is uncertainty, suffering. The metaphor of the Fates as *brotoskopon*, watchers of mortals, is echoed at 517 by *to deinon . . . episkopon*, terror as watchman to the heart. Without this guard, parents will be forced to lament, not with a *goos*, but *oikton oiktisai*, wailing a piteous cry. (Is there a suggestion here that there will be no mourners to sing the customary dirge, since the old law of revenge induced by lament will be overturned?) Already the Furies seem tamed as they anticipate defeat, their 'female' qualities seem less marked. They advance their own view of *dikē* in words that contrast with their former excess; they plead for balance, the middle ground. It becomes clear in the subtle shifts of meaning of the word *dikē* that they are no longer advocating simply the principle of death for death, but rather a sense of appropriate punishment for the sinner who should suffer a shipwreck, crying in vain in the storm, while demons laugh at him, and worst of all, should die unwept, unseen – *olet' aklaustos, astos*.

In the trial that follows, justice itself, or rather *dikē* with all its shifting meanings, will be judged. Once Orestes has pleaded guilty to killing his mother, the case, as far as the Erinyes are concerned, can be only about appropriate punishment. When Orestes asks why they did not harry his mother for killing her husband, they reply that Clytemnestra and Agamemnon were not *omaimos*, not of the same blood. To them, the question is one of blood relationships.[69] Orestes then asks the strange question, 'Am I of my mother's blood?' The Furies answer in scorn, wondering how his mother could have borne such a murderer, yet affirming that a mother's blood is nearest in kin (*philtaton*). For Apollo, acting as Orestes' legal representative, the task will be to defend his client by demonstrating a hierarchy of murder in which the killing of husband or father outweighs the killing of mother. This he will do by denying the importance of women's control over birth as well as death. He must do away with the bloody female business of birth (there is a consistent association of the fluid and the female in the trilogy – even the aged virgins drip fluids, perverse tears, from their eyes) and to establish man as the true progenitor. *Tiktei d' o thrōskōn*, he says – a phrase so concise, so rich in imagery that it defies translation. *Tiktein*, to beget, has strong agricultural associations, and is used of bearing fruit. It reinforces the image preceding it of woman as nurse to male seed, an argument more fully developed by Aristotle.[70] *Thrōskōn* literally he who mounts, is a military term for an attack or assault.[71] Thus the most basic of male activities, agriculture and war, are present in the phrase which establishes man as true progenitor. And standing right beside him, Apollo has living proof of the redundance of woman in the birth process: Athena, not 'bred in the darkness of the womb' but born of her father, Zeus, 'like a shoot' and fully armed. The double imagery of agriculture and war is reinforced by this ideal birth, which does away with woman entirely and effects, as Zeitlin notes, 'a total reversal from female as begetter of male to male as begetter of female'.[72]

Instead of summing up the evidence, Athena offers the jury her own myth of the foundation of the areopagus, reminding them it was named for the god of war by the Amazons, female warriors like herself, but uncontrolled by males until Theseus defeated them. As she casts her vote[73] for Orestes, she upholds male superiority. As a virgin with no mother she rejects marriage, otherwise she praises the male (*to arsēn*) in all things. As a female who is both idealized and unnatural, she is probably the only credible mediator of the male/female opposition that has played such an important part in the trilogy and crystalized in the trial. As Orestes looks towards the sun god and wonders if he will survive to 'see light', the Erinyes call on 'Night, dark mother', for protection. Appropriately, what follows is a lament, the magical song of the Furies bewailing their loss and turning swiftly to revenge. Instead of personal vendetta, though, the exchange of a death for death, the circle has been widened. Now, just as they have moved from the old world of mythical kingdoms to be judged in a modern city, their revenge will extend to mass destruction. They will poison the land, make it and its inhabitants barren. And this poison will be *antipenthi* (792) – in revenge for grief. How precise and economical is the conjunction of grieving and revenge in this single word! Singing a dirge that is a spell in itself, the Furies threaten to 'enchant' (a precise translation) the land. Athena's task is to persuade (with veiled threats of her father's own potential for violence) the Furies to give up their powers over death. The spell of the Furies' words must be broken by a new spell. Athena invokes Persuasion, a goddess suited to the lawcourt, adopting her voice as *meiligma* and *thelktirion* (a soothing song, a charm) (886).

A NEW SONG FOR AN OLD

The spell seems to work (*thelxein m'eoikas*), especially as the Erinyes are bribed by Athena with a new power, the respect and friendship of the citizens. But they still have their old ways and ask what song they must sing to their new land to bind it to them. The word they use, *ephymnesei* is one used commonly of dirges. Athena advises them to sing a song of peace and prosperity. The Furies now have a new leader. They sing her song, a thoroughly civic song praising the virtues of the well-kept city, the fertile countryside, reversing their threat to make it barren. Athena allows the Furies, or rather a single personi-fication of fate, the clear apportioning of punishment 'in the end', of 'songs to some, a dimmed life of tears to others'. Here, the control of death is still recognized as belonging in some sense to the old powers. One's *moira* is, in the end (in death?) in their hands. The songs and tears are contrasted, but their conjunction in mourning and death mutes their opposition. The Furies now extend their traditional control from death to marriage, calling on the Fates to grant their prayer.

Athena thanks the goddess Persuasion for helping her to achieve her goal through her own 'tongue and mouth', delighting in the spell that has reversed the magic of the Furies, turning them into beneficent deities. Honoured with tokens of respect, with torches lit, escorted by a procession of women, the Furies are farewelled and return to darkness and night. As they go, the escorts demand of them that they *ololyxate nun epi molpais* – sing out now to the gods and dance. We remember the *ololugmos* of the *Choephoroi* – the songs and cries of women that echo through the trilogy. 'All-seeing Zeus and Fate come down together,' the play ends, 'sing out now to the gods and dance.' Placated, the Furies are of value to the city. The opposition of old power (Fate/Fury) and new (Zeus), of Female and Male, is resolved by androgynous Athena, but not without threats of her father's thunderbolts and the use of magic spells. What is most feared must be propitiated. Magic chants that began at the tomb of Agamemnon are still powerful weapons. To keep them in control, the city must have its own enchanting songs.

WOMEN'S LAMENTS IN LATER TRAGEDY

In examining how laments are treated in Attic tragedy, I have focused on Aeschylus because he is the first to raise the issue of the threat of female mourning to the state and to male authority. He is also the dramatist who most effectively turns women's laments against themselves and, by appropriation of a female form, allows us to see that tragedy is itself an ambiguous art, attacking its own roots as it supplants old ritual with new. Sophocles and Euripides both explore the theme of female mourning, but they use less traditional means to do so, creating female heroines that are singular individuals rather than stereotypes of the female principle. What we have learned of traditional laments and attitudes to death, of women and mourning, is still able to offer us valuable insights into the plays of later tragedy, but it must be used with caution.

ANTIGONE

George Steiner noted that:

> No literature knows of more audacious or compassionate insights into the condition of womanhood. . . . It may well have been that those elemental rights of femininity, even of female primacy in certain capabilities and situations, which were denied to women in everyday life, in law, in Platonic politics and the Aristotelian classification of organic beings were one of the impulses behind, and extra-territorial licences of, Greek tragic drama.[74]

Steiner is thinking, in particular, of *Antigone*, and it is certainly in Sophocles' drama that the issue of female authority over the rituals of death receives its most sympathetic treatment. But can we go so far as to see a defence of female rights and an expression of female primacy in certain realms of activity in the play?

Despite her preoccupation with death, Antigone does not appear before the audience lamenting in a conventional manner for her brother. We are informed by the guard that she let out 'the shrill, sharp cry of a bird', at the sight of Polynices' body and 'cried with long groanings, crying a great curse on the people who had done the deed' (471–5). Sophocles seems careful to dissociate Antigone's mourning from any taint of oriental dirge and irrational possession. But the absence of an antiphonal chorus of lament, except at the end of the play when Antigone laments for herself, is only one of the signs of her singularity. She is one who cannot be a model for the citizens of a state, since she laments alone, pours her libations alone, and confesses her guilt in terms that reiterate her *auto*-motivation: 'I say I did it and I don't deny it'; 'I knew I must die; how could I not?' Antigone's way is never traditional; it has the stamp of the extraordinary. She pursues her own doom with the same stubborn self-will of her father. Her antagonist is similarly self-motivated, but not larger than life.

In her great *agōn* with Creon, the cards are unfairly stacked in Antigone's favour. Creon's victory can only be Antigone's *kleos*, her glory, since she desires death and already claims familiarity with the dead (515, 519). He is doubly humiliated because she is both a woman and one who has dared 'to think alone'(510). When she claims: 'I cannot share in hatred but in love,' Creon's response is not so much to call her bluff as to accede to what he comprehends as her own blind desire: 'Then go down there,' he tells her, 'if you must, and love the dead.' Even in her determination to die, Antigone remains fiercely individual, refusing to share her martyrdom with her sister. It is as if she belongs only to her dead: 'Death and the dead, they know whose act it was/ . . . don't die along with me nor make your own that which you did not do. My death's enough'(452, 545).

Antigone's burial lament is introduced by a hymn to Eros. The paradoxical relationship between wedding songs and laments for the dead and the association of Eros and Thanatos have already been noted in connection with Greek folk laments (chapter 2).[75] The lament shares other features with the modern tradition. Like the village women whose names have become legendary, Antigone has dared to defy authority in the name of a superior claim. Brother may have been killed by brother, but to forbid burial is to dishonour her male relative and she is bound by laws much older than Creon's to perform the essential rites for the dead. Funeral and wedding song are combined, again with the authority of tradition but, unlike her village counterpart, Antigone does not have the full support of the community. There is an antagonism between her and the chorus that is never resolved. The Theban elders deny her the glory she seeks in death, merely granting her respect for doing her sisterly duty (872–5):

You showed respect for the dead. So we for you
But power is not to be thwarted so
Your self-sufficiency has brought you down.

Even in her own death Antigone is self-reliant, self-mourning; despite the fact that her sister and her betrothed will mourn her, she insists there is 'No-one to weep for me/ no tears for my destiny.' There has been considerable speculation about possible interpolations in the speech (853–90) in which Antigone advances the superior claim of brother/sister love over love of husband or child. In a recent article, Matt Neuburg convincingly argues that not only is it unlikely the text was amended, but that the argument is essential to our reading of the play as a whole.[76] As Neuburg points out, Antigone's lament for herself draws attention to the very real conflict between blood ties and marriage ties. Marriage may have lain at the centre of a woman's life, as contemporary epitaphs stress, but when it conflicted with the duties of a daughter to her parents and siblings, particularly the most sacred duty of burial, the ties of blood proved stronger. To anyone familiar with the revenge laments of Mani, there is no surprise in the superior claims of sibling love. In fact, reading this as a lament of revenge makes clear the direction of the rhetoric. There is no need for Antigone to justify herself to the chorus – she has, after all, sought death from the beginning, and clearly feels no sympathy towards the living. But if she is to avenge her brother's dishonour she must not only bury him but bring about the downfall of Creon. Her remarks are calculated not to save her life but to destroy his. For that she needs to use her artful lament to persuade the chorus of his culpability, her own rightness. Foley notes Antigone's use of the rare word *koiranidai* in her address to the chorus, as if she is investing them with special status as witnesses.[77]

> Look leaders of Thebes, I am the last of your royal line
> Look what I suffer, at whose command
> Because I respected what was right before the gods.
>
> (490 ff.)

By appeal to authority, by the assertion of her own royal heritage (and by implication Creon's suspect authority) and by the certainty of her own ethical position, Antigone attempts to win the support of the chorus and set revenge in motion.

The measure of her success is apparent in the choral ode that follows. Antigone joins the ranks of legendary martyrs. There is a strange juxtaposition of characters here. Antigone is first likened to Danae, an apt enough comparison perhaps, since both were imprisoned by angry kings, but the next character seems to have more to do with Creon than Antigone. Lycurgus, like Pentheus, tried to suppress the worship of Dionysos, pursuing his women worshippers and mocking the god. In a fit of madness inflicted on him as punishment, he killed his own son because: 'Fool, he has tried to stop the dancing women/ possessed of god/ the fire of Dionysos, the cries and flutes' (1,060–5). Here we have more than a hint of what Euripides will make explicit in *The Bacchae*. Creon's refusal to provide a proper burial for Polynices and his persecution of the sister who has performed a burial and mourning are dangerous, the chorus seem to be saying, because they interfere with the traditional rituals of women. Mourning and possession by the gods are linked. Any interference in such matters is bound to lead to violence, perhaps the very 'moral chaos' the city of Athens had hoped to avoid by its restrictive legislation.

The message of the chorus is reinforced by Tiresias, who reminds Creon that 'Furies sent by Hades will get even with you and your victims' (1,075). The chorus offer a last address to Dionysos as healer and patron deity of the city, asking him to be manifest with his maenads. But his healing, if healing it is, comes in the form of terrible revenge. The link between that revenge is made through female mourning and its potential for violence. That mourning, like the god, has its healing and destructive sides is made clear in a brief exchange between the chorus and the messenger after Eurydice learns of her son's death:

Ch.   What do you make of this? The queen has gone
       in silence. We know nothing of her mind.

Me.   I wonder at her too. But we can hope
       that she has gone to mourn her son within
       with her own women, not before the town.
       She knows discretion. She will do no wrong.

Ch.   I'm not so sure. This muteness may portend
       as great a disaster as a loud lament.

Me: I will go in and see if some deep plan
       hides in her heart's wild pain. You may be right.
       There can be grave danger in mute grief.
                                        (1,179–91)

Mourning among women, in the private domain of the house,
offers no threat. But failure to lament at all, like loud lament, is
also threatening. The chorus may acquiesce with Antigone's
desire to perform the traditional rites for the dead, but they also
understand that lament opens a channel of communication with
the dead and with the ancient powers of the underworld – the
Furies, the Fates, Thanatos, Hades. Dionysos, reigning with
Demeter over the Eleusinian mysteries, is himself linked to the
underworld and to women's ritual behaviour. The 'leader of the
dance' whose maenads' cry is 'but your name' is a god who
shares with the heroines of tragedy, a capacity for excess.

What, then, are we witnessing in the theatre of Dionysos? A
self-referential representation within the context of a Dionysian
festival in which the ritual text warns of the consequences of
interfering with the god's ritual? A defence of the traditional
control of death by the aristocratic clans? A heroine who, in her
excessive loyalty to family death rites, is ultimately irrational?
A king who, in his apparent devotion to the good of the state, is
ultimately irreverent? It is important to relate this great act of
representation to its setting, its players and its audience.
Antigone's lament for herself is displayed before an audience
whose response to laments must always have been induced by
an art of poetry and song. We must presume that they are
familiar with Antigone's terms, as well as her means of expression through funerals of their own dead. The originality of this
self-conscious representation of the traditionally female authority over death is precisely the context of the display. The

audience may be predominantly composed of male Athenian citizens, likely to respond favourably to Creon's defence of earthly authority, but the god who is honoured by this display is both healer and frenzied destroyer. Women, in their role as traditional mourners of the dead and devotees of the god, share his potential for violence and, more important, the laments they sing have both therapeutic and destructive potential. At some level, the portrayal of Antigone's defence of traditional piety and Creon's arrogant secularism may be motivated by a desire to keep the benign face of Dionysos turned towards the city.

LAMENT AS THERAPY IN THE *MEDEA*

The power of the *goos* that Aeschylus had attempted to placate and control in the service of the *polis*, may have been recognized by Sophocles and Euripides as both a source and a counterpoint of their own art, a form of representation that ultimately derives from the confrontation of women, rather than men, with death. Only such a theory can account for the centrality of female mourning in tragedy. There is much that could be said about lament in the plays of Euripides, but I will confine myself to a few brief remarks about *Medea* and *The Suppliants*.

The nurse who elicits our pity for her mistress in the opening speech of *Medea* is conscious of satisfying her desire for lament and so gaining relief.[78] The nurse suggests that Medea's grief has no such outlet, and theorizes about the ability of poetry and song to heal grief. The usual type of songs, she contends, are powerless to heal the griefs that destroy families, yet 'it is a gain that men heal these by means of song' (191–203). As Pietro Pucci points out, the terminology used (*kerdos akeisthai*) is modern and medical. This, according to Pucci, has the effect of overturning the usual Greek assumptions about poetry as an inspired unveiling of the truth and so a cognitive discourse. Instead of deriving from a divine source and operating as a revelation, the Euripidean notion of poetry, in this passage, is as a sort of narcotic which blunts rather than sharpens rational enquiry.[79] As Pucci elaborates, the idea of gain (*kerdos*) through lament is found in a number of Euripides' plays, including *The Suppliant Women*, *Hecuba* and *The Trojan Women*. Taking the passages together he concludes that 'Euripides presents tragedy as a song aiming at the paradoxical *kerdos* (gain) of tears as medicine for grief.'[80]

One might conclude that Euripidean tragedy has, according to its own claims, usurped the position of woman's lament and appropriated its forms and functional aesthetics for its own ends. But although Euripides may be writing a 'therapeutic discourse', as Pucci contends, the plays themselves remain ambiguous sources of antidotes to the pain of loss. Grief, as we have seen from our survey of traditional laments, is not necessarily placated or dulled by tears. The final horrors of *Medea* and *The Bacchae* suggest that Euripides is fully aware of the frailty of his own discourse about the therapeutic possibilities of his art.

CIVIC VIRTUE IN *THE SUPPLIANTS*

In *The Suppliants*, written at the height of the Peloponnesian War, we have perhaps the most explicit thematization of a changed Athenian attitude to lament in tragedy. The mothers of the seven champions who were killed at Thebes present themselves to Theseus, asking him to help them bury their sons, a request Thebes has denied. Aethra, the mother of Theseus, is moved by their plight and intercedes with her son on their behalf. As a mother she understands them, and as a mother she uses her feminine tears to awaken her son's pity (286–90), but she is cautious in her plea, appealing to him to act for the good of the city by obeying Panhellenic custom. Faced with the intransigence of the Thebans, Theseus is forced to go to war to recover the bodies of the dead champions. In victory, he is temperate, halting his attack at the walls when he has achieved what he came for: the recovery of the bodies in order to give them a proper burial (723–5).

Rituals for the war dead have become, in the play as in the contemporary *polis*, an affair of state. Even so, as critics have pointed out, the degree of control exercised by Theseus in carrying out the funerary procedures himself, and thereby excluding the female relatives of the seven from their traditional roles, exceeds even the most stringent proscriptions of the new regulations.[81] When Adrastus, the Argive leader, is about to lead the mothers in their laments, Theseus intervenes. Such laments, he contends, will be 'useless' and make the women weep (770). Adrastus agrees, admitting he was taught to lament by women, but no sooner do the bodies appear on stage than he begins a lament focused, as so often noted in folk tradition, on the plight of the survivors (799–836). Again Theseus intervenes, this time deliberately drawing Adrastus away from the feminine, private world of the grieving mothers into the masculine, public world of the city, where the young men must be set a good example. Praise, not lament, is what the young must hear if they are to emulate the champions in glory. 'Manliness can be taught', Adrastus insists (912) and since Theseus has reprimanded him for the arts he learned from women, we presume this martial virtue can be taught only by men.

One last intervention makes clear how little the mothers now have to do with the burial rites for their sons. After he has concluded his oration, Adrastus asks the women to draw near their children. Theseus interjects: 'Adrastus! That was not well said.' 'Why?' Adrastus asks in surprise. 'Must parents not touch their children?' Theseus replies that it would cause them pain. Adrastus agrees that wounded bodies and blood are a bitter sight. 'Why then,' says Theseus, 'would one increase the women's sorrow?' Again Adrastus' scruples are swiftly overcome. '*Nikas*' (you win!), he concedes and tells the women to be brave and stay away. They obey, swayed, we can only conclude, by the force of this new rhetoric which has deprived them of the right to tend the dead bodies of their sons. At the conclusion of the play the grandsons of the dead refuse the mothers permission even to touch the funerary urns (1,160, 1,165–7, 1,855–8). In both cases the strictures against the women's physical contact with the dead go well beyond Athenian custom.[82]

Despite Adrastus' speech, the mothers continue to lament and in a dramatic gesture of rebellion against the injunctions to moderation, Capaneus' wife Evadne commits suicide by leaping onto her husband's funeral pyre. The sons of the dead men then return with the ashes of their fathers and, in what has been noted as an odd reversal of the tragic norm, argue for revenge.[83] The paradoxes of the final scene remind us that from its opening scene, where the women interrupt Demeter's festival with their loud cries, *The Suppliants* seems to present an ambiguous view of women's lament. Foley, in her detailed study of the question, has concluded that some aspects of the play may be explained by the fact that it was probably produced after the battle of Delium in 424 BC when the Boeotians refused to allow the Athenians to recover and bury their dead.[84] She also cites evidence from later plays to suggest that Theseus' response to female lamentation finds a parallel in contemporary practice and attitudes. Such laments for the dead as the mothers sing in *The Suppliants*, Foley maintains, not only fail to give proper praise to the dead, but undermine the role of women in the classical state by doubting the value of producing children at all.[85] Theseus seems to be a mouthpiece for the establishment of wartime Athens in condemning such negative rhetoric. On the other hand, the play ends with the young men urging revenge and the women restraint.

CONCLUSION: LAMENT AS A DRUG

Whatever Euripides intended his audience to think about Theseus' restriction of women's control of the rites of death, we have moved into an entirely different world from that of the *Oresteia*. Even an ironic reading of Adrastus' funeral oration reduces women's role to a private counterbalancing of official oratory by private grief. Lament, in Euripides, poses a danger because of what it says or fails to say, and because of its associations with Dionysiac possession.[86] It is an unreliable device, as we have noted in *Medea*; a drug that may cure or harm. It is no longer possible, in Euripides, to think of lament as a powerful dialogue with the dead, as the fundamental impulse behind art itself. Even in the terrible finale of *The Bacchae*, the temporary madness of the women possessed by Dionysos is a nightmare from which they wake in horror. They are no longer in control of death itself, the creators of an art that shakes fear and pity into all who hear it. Tragedy, the invention of Athens that is so preoccupied with the lament and appears to subsume its ritual function, ends by reducing the magical power of women's voices to a civic danger with at best private therapeutic value.

It may be that in the course of the development of classical tragedy we are witnessing the transformation of Greek, perhaps of western art in general, from an art where women's voices are heard in all the remembered force of their pain and anger as they addressed the community over the bodies of the dead, to one where their rhetoric is only a memory of dubious significance. In cultures like that of modern Greece, where the art of lament is still alive in the countryside, one can see something of the same appropriation and simultaneous diminishing of the art of lament. It is a process that even women writers seem unable to reverse. From an awesome ritual, essential to the community's well-being, women's lament has become a private, shameful therapy, a drug of dubious value that the state must prescribe and, when necessary, proscribe.

Chapter 6

Epitaphs and photographs: laments in modern Greek literature

In Christian Greece it has been the Orthodox Church, rather than the state, which has attempted to control lament, but there are parallels to the classical suppression of women's mourning in the rhetoric of condemnation as well as in the appropriation of the forms of lament by another literary tradition. Women mourners were hired by the church in the early Christian period, but their professional practice of tearing their hair and clothes and dancing in the funeral procession was seen as a pagan, specifically Bacchic, impiety.[1] John Chrysostom, for example, called the lament 'self-centred and self-indulgent' and referred to hired mourners as 'this disease of females'.[2] As Alexiou rightly comments, 'the frequency and vehemence of these condemnations in the Byzantine period are proof of the persistence of ritual lamentation.'[3]

The church soon developed its own expression of ritual mourning to substitute for the Bacchanalian lament. The psalms and hymns, an important part of early Christian worship, were sung by choirs of men and often by women who had taken holy orders. At funerals, choirs sang official laments which competed with the popular tradition. They were followed by the Christian version of the *Epitaphios Logos*, a speech that was concerned with praise, not pity, for the dead. The term *Epitaphios Thrēnos* was used of another funeral, one that lay at the heart of the new religion: the funeral of Christ. Part of the litany of the service consists of the lament of the Virgin over her dead son. She is portrayed, according to this tradition, as weeping *dakrious thrēnous* (tearful laments) for the dead Christ.

Romanos the melodist, greatest of the Byzantine hymnographers, was one of the many liturgical composers who saw the dramatic potential of the laments for the Virgin. In his sixth-century hymn he portrays Mary weeping and wailing before the crucifixion until her son interrupts her saying: 'Put aside your grief, mother, put it aside; *ou gar prepei sou threnein* (mourning does not become you).'[4] Mary argues with her son, begging him not to embrace death. It is only when he promises to reveal himself to her after death that she consents to wipe her tears.

The *Epitaphios Thrēnos* which is now sung in the Orthodox services on Easter Friday and Saturday has been in existence at least since the fourteenth century, although its origins may be older.[5] In its use of imagery, particularly of the contrast of light and darkness and the participation of nature in the grieving of the Virgin, it is sufficiently close to the folk laments to indicate some popular influence.[6] Perhaps by transforming the folk laments into an integral part of the Christian ritual, the church thought to appropriate for itself the role of official mourner. It also condemned excessive mourning as inappropriate to a religion based on the promise of resurrection and the rewards of an afterlife. But whatever the official attitude of the church, the folk laments continued to flourish in Greece, creating a double, often incompatible structure of mourning at funerals. Both traditions are reflected in the literature of modern Greece.

LAMENTS IN MODERN GREEK LITERATURE

Laments make their appearance in the works of a number of modern Greek writers, both male and female. The complex interrelation between the ritual lament of the Virgin in the *Epitaphios* service of the Orthodox Church and the folk *moiróghia*, is nowhere more apparent than in the writings of these nineteenth- and twentieth-century authors. In a village context, where the two traditions have existed side by side for centuries, the parallels and contradictions between the Christian and folk laments may have periodically bothered the church, but they have not been perceived as incompatible. Rather, the existence of a folk tradition of ballads based on the Virgin's lament, and the evidence for popular elements in the Orthodox hymn itself both point to a long tradition of interdependence.[7]

The dramatic possibilities of the parallel between the two lament traditions are consciously exploited by a number of Greek writers including Palamas, Varnalis, Ritsos and Kazantzakis. In a different and more complex form, women poets like Katerina Anghelaki-Rooke and Kiki Dimoula draw on the Christian and folk laments to compose their own. What is so striking about the use of laments by modern Greek writers is the difference between the male writers' conscious adaptation of a traditional female form, and the female writers' sense of formlessness, of their inability to fall back on the formulas of lament to express their grief. And yet in their very doubts and ambivalence, their sense of a pain that is incurable, their focus on themselves as survivors rather than on the dead, the women writers may be closer, in sentiment, to the *moirologhístres* of Inner Mani or northern Epirus than their male counterparts. It is their sense of nostalgia for a lost tradition combined with an awareness of having consciously broken with whatever was traditional in their upbringing that causes a sort of paralysis when the women poets lament their dead. Unlike the male poets, it seems, they cannot rework the forms of their grand-mothers and yet they have a similar functional aesthetic: the desire to communicate with the dead, and to preserve their memory in poetry. As they address their dead, re-creating a new language of mourning, the women writers cannot prevent the echoes of traditional lament from intruding, but this only emphasizes the differences between their own groping un-certainty and an earlier generation's resources for ritual expres-sion and communal catharsis.

PALAMAS' 'DEATH OF A BRAVE LAD'

The *Epitaphios* ceremony, where women play such a prominent role, the wailing of women at the cemeteries, the promise of resurrection, the grim vision of Charos and the underworld – these are the unavoidable inheritance of modern Greeks and it would be strange if such echoes should not be detectable even in the least traditional of writers when they deal with the subject of death. In the work of a conscious traditionalist like Kostis Palamas laments are used not only as a source of form and inspiration for his own poetry. In the short story '*Thánatos Pallikarioú*' ('Death of a Brave Lad') Palamas has given us the most detailed description of the lament and its relationship to the *Epitaphios* ceremony in modern Greek literature. In it we are left in no doubt that the lament is a female song of ritual magic, a form of possession. The fact that it is an unnatural lament, demanded by a dying son of his mother, only heightens the parallels to the Virgin's lament.

The story opens on the evening of the *Epitaphios*. The hero of the story, a young fisherman called Mitros, is drinking with his friends in a wine shop when they remember they have forgotten the fireworks for the *Epitaphios*. Mitros runs to fetch them and falls, breaking his leg. The local doctor tells him to rest for three months, but the leg does not improve and a series of quack doctors and healers are called in. The young man's widowed mother, Kyria Dimaina, believes herself to be god-fearing but '. . . να πούμε την αλήθεια, περισσότερο έτρεμε τα μάγια και τα ξωτικά, χωρίς κι αυτή καλά να το καταλαβαίνει.' (To tell the truth she was more afraid of magic and hobgoblins, without really being aware of it.)[8] When the wound becomes gangrenous and she is told she must take her son to Athens, Kyria Dimaina instead believes her son is under the influence of a magic spell cast by the mother of a local girl who has fallen hopelessly in love with the handsome Mitros. She decides to consult a series of witches and wizards, all of whom attempt to exorcize her son. When Good Friday comes round again, Mitros realizes he is about to die. Remembering his old pride in his appearance, he dresses himself with care, combs his long curly hair, twists the end of his moustache and asks his mother to sing his lament:

> Now, poor Mother, I've been brave for so long, saying I wouldn't die. . . . I've one favour to ask you. Cry for me, so that I can listen to you.[9]

The mother at first refuses to comply to this unnatural request, but her son insists, prompting her with a traditional lament formula:

> Youth turns into earth
> And youthful joys to grass
> The body, strong as a hawk
> Becomes ground where people walk.

Not wishing to die alone, the young man throws open the window, and the villagers, emerging from the Easter service, hear:

'a slow, pitiful sound, so pitiful it made your hair stand on end and tore you apart, a sound that seemed to come from an animal or from a person; a sound that rose and fell, and was drowned and flowed and lashed; a sound that was both speech and howl, lament and complaint, cry and laugh, curse and song, the song of a terrified, crazed, hopeless soul. And the passers-by heard it, stood still, shuddered, listened hard, felt, shook their heads, and said to each other: 'Moirolói! Who can have died?'

The terrible sound is immediately recognizable to the villagers. They presume that Mitros has died and head towards his mother's house, the women still carrying flowers from the *Epitaphios*, to be greeted by the extraordinary spectacle of a mother lamenting her son while he is still alive. Extraordinary, but not unprecedented. The same women who view the spectacle have spent the previous night singing the Virgin's lament for her son. In the version sung in the Orthodox Church the Virgin at the cross addresses her already dead son, but there are both literary and popular sources familiar to most Greeks for a lamenting Virgin entering into a dialogue with her dying son, both before his crucifixion and while he is on the cross.[10] Moreover the parallels between the physical beauty of the young man in Palamas' story and the dead Christ of the *Epitaphios* make such associations inevitable. In case we miss the point, Palamas, whose virtues do not include subtlety, reminds us:

You would say that the passion of Christ had taken place inside the house and another *Epitaphios* had been staged. And a lot of people were still holding flowers in their hands, flowers from the *Epitaphios* ceremony, and you'd say they were going to strew them on the dead man's bed, to make his last sleep fragrant, to sanctify the dead.

Kyria Dimaina, who has summoned the villagers to the bedside by means of her unearthly song, is now visible. Her son may be glorified in death. She, on the other hand, is entirely negated as woman and becomes 'the remains of a body, without a soul, without tears. All her life had become a voice, but not the voice of a woman, the very voice of despair, and she sang a tune of her own that had never been heard before':

Ομορφονιός ψυχομαχάει, ομορφονιός πεθαίνει,
ανάψτε πράσινα κεριά και κίτρινες λαμπάδες,
να φέξουνε τ'ομορφονιού να κατεβή στον άδη.
Σκαλή, σκαλή κατέβαινε, σκαλή, σκαλή ανεβαίνει.

A fair young man fights death, a fair young man lies dying,
light green candles for him, and yellow funeral tapers
to light the fair young man, as he descends to Hades.
He went down stair by stair; stair by stair he rises.

Here we have an imitation of folk lament, with its antithetical
structure, its contrast of light and darkness, its journey to the
underworld and the (rarer) promise of resurrection. The only
unusual feature of this lament is that it is orchestrated by the
dying man, who prompts his married cousin to join his mother
by giving the first antiphonal response:

Κ' ηύρεν τον ένας σκώλικας, μα και τον ερωτάει:
Που πας, ασήμι, να χαθής, μάλαμα να θολέψης;
Που πας, αργυροκούδουνο, να χάσης τη λαλιά σου;

And a worm came and found him there, but stopped to ask
    him this:

Where go you, silver, to be lost, gold to turn all dull?
Where go you, little silver bell, to lose your pretty toll?

And from the mother's lips:

το μοιρολόγι ξεφύτρωσε στα χείλη των γυναικών των άλλων,
καθώς τα δάκρυα φέρνουν δάκρυα και τα γέλια, γέλια,
καθώς το κερί ανάφτει από άλλο κερί. . . .

the lament sprang to the lips of the other women, just as tears
bring tears and laughs, laughter; just as one candle is lit from
another.

The description of the *moirolói* seems to have come to an end,
but at the young man's death, there is yet another detail that
makes the picture of the lamenting mother complete. Silently,
'like a snake', the spurned girl slips into the room and stands for
a moment at the foot of the bed, seeming to smile at the dead
Mitros. Catching sight of her, the mother leaps up to attack her,
but the girl disappears as she has come. The mother's final
words are a curse on the girl:

Αχ! μωρή στρίγγλα! Ως κ'εδώ βγήκες, μπόισσα! Μου τον
έφαγες! αχ! αν είχα κουμπούρι σ'εσκότωνα! Ας είναι! δεν
τον πήρες μια φορά, κι ας τον πήρε ο Χάρος.

Ach, you crazy witch! Even here, you've turned up, hoyden!
You've destroyed him for me! Ach, if I had a knife I'd kill
you! So be it! You didn't catch him the first time, let Charos
take him!

The mother, whose belief in God – Palamas has already
informed us – is secondary to her faith in magic, has been at
least partly responsible for her son's death. Her lament, too, is
a magical song, the song of a witch that moves the villagers to
fear as much as pity. Now we have the missing element, the call
for revenge so familiar from the folk laments of Mani. The
contrast between the Virgin's lament and the village woman's
lament must be underlined so that this parallel *Epitaphios* be
understood for what it is: a ritual controlled by ignorance and
primitive belief, one transformed for a passing moment by the
beauty of its victim, by the ability of the mother to express her
grief in song. In the end, though, we are left in the realm of
sorcery and spells, of the *stríngla* whose greatest insult is to call
another woman *stríngla*.

THE TOMB

Only a few years after 'The Death of a Brave Lad', Palamas was
to write his own *moirológhia* for the death of his younger son.
Describing his inspiration for the cycle of twenty-four poems
entitled *The Tomb*, Palamas confesses that in the struggle
between the pain of his loss and the value of such an experience
for his development as a poet, it is the latter that dominates:

Η στοργή του πατέρα; Η προσήλωση του ποιητή; Νομίζω
και τα δύο. . . . Ομως – πρέπει να την ομολογήσω την
αλήθεια – ο ποιητής κυριαρχεί.[11]

The love of the father? The engrossment of the poet? I think
both. . . . But – I must confess the truth – the poet dominates.

Palamas goes on to describe his collection of poems as:

a cry, call it an improvised *moirolói* of the house hit by death
and at the same time and above all a technically careful

construction using styles that frequently appear and charac-
terise my intellectual work.[12]

When he enumerates the sources of his inspiration they are as
unlikely a combination as this marriage of art and improvization:

Demotic tradition, religious belief, rational thought, the
Olympus of Art, the Blessed Isle of Love, Love of the Fatherland, the Forefather, both subservient to the paradigm and
disobedient, towards broader horizons, unteachable and the
terrestrial house; all in a paradisical dematerialisation.[13]

Perhaps it is the grandiose ambition betrayed in this eclectic list
of sources that is responsible for the failure of the poems of *The
Tomb* either to cohere as an artistic whole or to convey any of
the stark intensity of the folk laments. The inspiration of folk
models is obvious in a number of poems. Besides using demotic
verse forms, the traditional imagery of the underworld songs is
invoked in several of the poems: the mother of Charos sends her
son to fetch the children she eats for her supper (13); the child is
warned not to eat and drink on his journey to the underworld
with the hope that he can cheat Charos and return to the living
(8); the natural world joins in the lament for the dead (14); Eros
and Charos, in a variation of the folk tradition, fight on a
marble threshing floor; and the focus of the poems, as in
traditional laments, is on the pain of those left behind. In this
case the poet has turned the pain of his dying child into a
religion:

μ'ανυψώνει ο πόνος σου
και μούγινε θρησκεία. (21)

your pain elevates me
and has become a religion.

There are parallels, here, with the bereaved mother in a
lament collected by Petropoulos[14] who, in order to carry her
pain with her forever, decides to take it to the goldsmith's and
have it gold-plated:

να φτιάσω 'να χρυσό σταυρό κι εν' ασημένιο γόλφι,
να προσκυνάγω το σταυρό και να φιλώ το γόλφι.

to make a gold cross and a silver amulet
so I can worship the cross and kiss the amulet.

But what the mother of the folk lament makes concrete, the poet dematerializes. The imagery of the bereaved mother is taken from everyday experience. It is Palamas' 'paradisical dematerialisation' which removes his poems of death from the realm of women's funeral laments. Unlike the voice of Kyria Dimaina in 'Death of a Brave Lad', we have no sensation, in these poems, of listening to a medium addressing another world. It is rather the poet, conscious of his art, making use of the traditional material he is familiar with to transform the experience of his child's death into a memorial. Despite the inspiration Palamas claims to have derived from his grief, it is not the romantic poet's self-styled *moirolói* that leaves a lasting impression, but his prose description full of dread, ambivalence and awe, of a village woman's lament.

RITSOS' *EPITAPHIOS*

A generation after Palamas published his 'Death of a Brave Lad' and the cycle of poems that comprise *The Tomb*, a young Greek poet was to publish perhaps the most influential work of his life, a cycle of poems inspired by the death of a young man killed by police during a strike of tobacco factory workers in Salonika. On 10 May 1936, a picture was published in the Communist newspaper *Rizospástis* of a mother bending over the body of her son as he lay on his back, arms outstretched, in the street. For the young Marxist poet who had grown up in a small provincial town and watched his own mother die of tuberculosis when he was 12 years old, the image was charged with personal as well as cultural associations. In Monemvasia, Ritsos had absorbed the roots of his poetics from the litany of the Orthodox Church as well as from the folk songs of the region. Like a number of his contemporaries in Greece – Varnalis, Sikelianos, Kazantzakis – and several of the writers he admired in Russia and France, Ritsos remained fascinated all his life by the figure of Christ. (Alexander Bloch's 'The Twelve' had been translated into Greek in 1929 and Ritsos would translate it himself nearly thirty years later.) The newspaper photograph of the mother lamenting her dead son was an irresistible subject – a proletarian *pietà* to which Ritsos responded immediately, publishing three song-like sections under the title 'Moirolói in *Rizospástis* on 12 May.

Dedicating his poem 'To the heroic workers of Salonika', Ritsos added a small prose introduction emphasizing the mother's central position in the tableau: 'Salonika. May 1936. In the middle of the road a mother sings a lament (*moirologái*) over her dead son. Around her and over her, waves of demonstrators – the striking tobacco workers – roar and break. She continues her lament.' Ritsos felt he had only to listen to the voices of his youth, voices he had heard in the Orthodox services as well as in the local laments, to find a suitable form for his lament: 'my feelings, my acoustic foundations came from the people. . . . They came from inside me; I sang them, I'd listened to them since I was a child.'[15] The fifteen-syllable rhymed couplets of Ritsos' verse as well as its imagery of traditional lament are all familiar enough. The young man is likened to a bird who has flown away, the mother is left thirsty, like a withered tree, etc., but Ritsos handles the form with consummate skill. The first poem opens with a couplet that defies translation:

Γιέ μου σπλάχνο των σπλάχνων μου, καρδούλα της καρδιάς μου
πουλάκι της φτωχειάς αυλής, ανθέ της ερημιάς μου.

My son, core of my being, heart of my heart
bird of the poor courtyard, flower of my desert.

The use of the word *spláchnon* (literally guts but the word has come to have a broader meaning) occurs in the Virgin's lament from the *Epitaphios* service. It is as if the lament is being torn from the mother's entrails before being softened as the four metonymies diminish in size and power. The four uses of the possessive pronoun that accompany them leave us in no doubt as to whose business it is to mourn him. The mother's anger at the terrible silence of her son is also a familiar motif. She lets down her white hair in the middle of the street and when he still refuses to speak to her she says:

Δε μου μιλείς κ'η δόλια εγώ το κόρφο, δες, ανοίγω
και στα βυζιά που βύζαξες τα νύχια μπήγω.

You don't speak to me and I, poor wretch, look! I open my dress
and into the breasts that suckled you, my son, I plunge my nails.

It is a shocking image, especially in the context of Greek society. Just as the woman in the photograph has been driven by her son's unnatural death to expose her grief to the camera, so the language of the poem forces the reader to bear witness to the violence of a mother's lament, something that normally belongs to the exclusive world of female ritual.

When Ritsos published his poem in book form later the same year he changed the title to *Epitaphios* and added eleven new sections. The change of name as well as the size of the new work are indications of a more ambitious and somewhat different approach to the subject. The title suggests the ancient model of an encomium for the dead hero composed and delivered by a male figure of authority, but in the modern Greek context the more immediate associations are with the Good Friday service of the Orthodox Church. The physical beauty of the dead Christ, dwelt on so lovingly in the Orthodox hymn and linking it, perhaps through a long tradition, to the laments for the dead Adonis or Osiris, is echoed in a series of sensuous epithets the mother applies to her son. He is 'bull and nightingale', his mouth is 'sweet-smelling', his strong thighs are like partridges. In her disbelief and anguish over her son's death, the Virgin asks 'How is it that you, Life, are dead in the tomb?' The doubt and feeling of abandonment are reiterated by Ritsos' lamenting mother who asks 'Where has my boy flown? Where is he leaving me?' She vacillates between enumerating his charms as if playing with a string of worry beads and stringing them into a dirge:

Πότε τις χάρες σου, μιά-μιά, τις παίζω κομπολόι
πότε ξανά, λυγμό-λυγμό, τις δένω μοιρολόι.

(VIII)

Sometimes I play with your charms, one by one, like a *komboloí*
sometimes I thread them, sob by sob, into a *moiroloí*.

The mother has lost her joy and faith in God (IX) and wonders where to turn for help. In the sections Ritsos added to the poem in 1956 (X–IV) the mother seems helpless without her son who taught her everything she knows and made her life meaningful. Like the widows and bereaved mothers of the folk laments, her social worth depends on her son, and with a touch of anger she asks him to look at 'this wretched old beggar-woman/ who neither man nor God gives a damn for' (XII). All she has left is a disembodied voice she can hardly recognize but which is her only pleasure:

Και χαίρομαι ναν τη γροικώ, για να ανεβαίνει νάμα
πιό δυνατό απ'τη ρίζα μου και πιό στριγγό το κλάμα.

(XII)

And I delight to hear it, rising like a spring
stronger than its source in me, a shriller cry.

It is this voice that reminds us of Palamas' lamenting mother. For the most part Ritsos's mother is gentle, homely, humble. She has lived life through her son, and with his death she becomes less than nothing, but as she sings, her voice takes on a power of its own and it is not long before she cries for vengeance:

Ω, γιέ μου, αυτοί που σ'έσφαξαν σφαγμένα να τα βρούνε
τα τέχνα τους και τους γονιούς και στο αίμα να πνιγούνε.

Και στο αίμα τους η φούστα μου κόκκινη να την βάψω,
και να χορέψω. Αχ, γιόκα μου, δεν πάει μου να σε κλάψω.

Oh, my son, may those who slaughtered you find
their children and parents slain and drown in their blood.

And in their blood I'll dye my skirt bright red
and dance, ah, son, it's not for me to weep.

The sudden transformation of grief into anger is familiar from the lament, but the mother's call for revenge becomes generalized as part of the proletarian struggle. Seeing her son's likeness in the thousands of other young men who throng the streets, she wishes he could see the 'forests of fists, oceans of cries, mountains of hearts and breasts'. The khaki shirt of the young soldier mingles with that of the workers and the mother, fired by the strength of her dead son, lifts his body and raises her fist. Instead of tearing her breasts with her nails, she marches with the crowd, carrying her son's rifle.

Reading the poem today, it is hard not to find the concluding sections of Ritsos' poem pathetic. In a Greece which had recently seen village women shoulder rifles and take to the mountains to fight in the resistance and the Civil War, it becomes at least understandable. One cannot help but wonder if Ritsos' decision to extend the poem and turn it into a revolutionary call to arms might not have been dictated by a negative reaction, among his left-wing readers, to the mother's initial *moirolói*, a desire to appropriate the strength of her disembodied voice as a weapon for an essentially male political struggle.

Revolutionary as the last sections of Ritsos' *Epitaphios* may be, it was not, I suggest, for these final songs that the poem was publicly burned by the Metaxas regime, banned for another twenty years, then, after being set to music by Theodorakis, banned for another seven years. It was the mother's *moirolói* for her dead son that caught the imagination of the Greek public, and it was the Theodorakis' settings of the more poignant sections of the poem that were to transform the Greek popular music of the 1950s into the dynamic protest music of the 1960s. When they were recorded by the bouzouki singer Grigoris Bithikotsis in 1959, the songs caused an immediate sensation.[16] It is difficult, in retrospect, to sort out the various threads that caused the *Epitaphios* furore, but listening to the songs today, one cannot help but be aware of the curious anomalies of this modern lament.

In a mixture that is rich and strange, we hear a setting of a section of a poem by a Marxist inspired by the death of a striking worker. The poet deliberately uses the form and motifs of traditional village laments together with elements from the Virgin's lament for the dead Christ. The verses are set to music by a composer who until this point has thought of himself as a classical musician. Sharing the poet's Marxist beliefs, he sees the possibilities for the poem becoming popular music, and having discovered, while interned in various prison camps, the beauty of the mostly male music of the *rembétika* songs, he decides to use the rhythms and instrumentation of that music to reach his audience. Like Ritsos, he has been raised in the Orthodox Church and has sung as a cantor in the choir. He immediately responds to the echoes of the *Epitaphios* hymn and bases his melodies on the material of 'Life in the Tomb' and other hymns. He sets eleven of the songs in neo-*rembétika* style and has the outrageous idea of using classical musicians in combination with a bouzouki.[17] Then he decides to employ a male night-club singer to perform the songs. The orchestra refuse to play with such riff-raff so he is forced to use a smaller group of popular musicians. Theodorakis' fellow composer Hadzidakis thinks he has taken leave of his senses and suggests a more refined version of *Epitaphios*, using a piano and female singer. Theodorakis agrees to a second version being made, but the two records emerge simultaneously and it is the Bithikotsis version that wins with the Greek public despite the fact that this is a mother's lament and what we hear is a rough male voice from Piraeus.

The reasons for the immense popular success of *Epitaphios* probably have as much to do with the politics of the period when it was written and with the popular taste for the *rembétika* as they do with Theodorakis' and Ritsos's individual genius, but somewhere, under the layers of transformation and appropriation, lies a powerful female voice, one with which the Greek audience who listened to *Epitaphios* were familiar. The echoes of the *moirolói* were at least an important factor in the emotional capacity of these songs to move Greek audiences to respond so strongly that the authorities felt compelled to ban them.

WOMEN POETS AND LAMENT

If the male poets and prose writers of Greece have sensed the awesome quality of women's laments and used them as inspiration for their own expression of grief or anger, what of the women writers? One would imagine that lament, as an essentially female form, would be still more freely adopted and adapted by them, but instead it seems as if the women writers, at least the writers of the post-war generation, have rejected the use of traditional forms to confront their dead. At some level, though, it may be their very consciousness of not being able to sing a traditional lament that links them with *moirologhístres* of Mani or Epirus. Just as the women who sing laments express their sense of abandonment, anger and frustration, often addressing the dead directly:

Ε, Μιχαλάκη, δε μιλάς
πως γίνεις ακατάδεχτος

Eh, Michalaki, you don't speak
why have you turned so scornful. . .
(Petrounias, 1934, no. 66)

so Katerina Anghelaki-Rooke angrily confronts her mother in the poem 'My Mother and Satan' (1971):

ΜΕ ΒΑΣΑΝΙΖΕΙ
Τι έκανα λάθος
ποιό λάθος;

SHE TORMENTS ME
What did I do wrong?
what mistake?

and Kiki Dimoula, in the poem 'No Star Cognac' (1988), is frustrated by a sense of the futility of attempting to express her grief:

Χαμένα πάνε εντελώς τα λόγια των δακρύων
οταν μιλάει η αταξία η τάξη να σωπαίνει
– έχει μεγάλη πείρα ο χαμός.

Τώρα πρέπει να σταθούμε στο πλευρό
του ανώφελου.
Σιγά-σιγά να ξαναβρεί το λέγειν της η μνήμη.

The words of tears are completely wasted
when disorder speaks, order should hold its tongue
– death has a lot of experience.

Now we must stand on the side
of futility.
So that memory can slowly find its way of saying something.

It is in the work of these modern women poets that we realize most fully the changes that have separated them from their mothers and grandmothers. Unlike Ritsos, who adopted a lamenting voice from the remembered traditions of his youth, women writers have rejected such solutions as inappropriate to their modern urban world. At the same time, like the women who have composed laments for centuries, they struggle to find some functional aesthetic of their own to inscribe memory, assuage guilt, and exorcize their pain and loss. It is the sense of their inner struggle that links these women's poems to traditional songs of mourning. In the folk laments the focus is not on the dead so much as on the person of the lamenter who examines her own response to death, sometimes admitting her inadequacies, but wholly absorbed in the effort to record her pain.

ANGHELAKI-ROOKE: THE INVERSION OF TRADITION

In 'My Mother and Satan' (1971), Anghelaki-Rooke struggles to find the inner core of her mother and in doing so she offers a penetrating insight into the limits of all such attempts to revive the dead:

Μάνα μου, κηδεία πολυπρόσωπη
καπέλα και συναστροφές
οι ιστορίες δεν σε σκάβουν
μόνο σε ονοματίζουν
σε τοποθετούν, σε αναφέρουν
όμως εγώ θέλω το μέσα, μέσα, μέσα
το εισωτερικό από το δέρμα σου
το μηχανάκι της αναπνοής σου
και εκείνο το άλλο
το καλικαντζαρένιο
της σκέψης σου.
Πόσο είχες απ᾿αγιοσύνη
πόσο από σκουριά
πόσο είχες την ειρήνη
την εκ γενετής.

Mother
funeral with many faces
hats and social rounds
stories don't dig down into you
they just name you
place you, refer to you
but I want the in, in, in
the inside of your skin
the mechanism of your breathing
and that other one –
the hobgoblin workings
of your thoughts.
How much holiness was in you
how much rust
how much of the peace
one is born with?

It is in her recognition of what 'stories' do and don't do that Anghelaki-Rooke indicates the inadequacy of traditional laments to fulfil her needs. One of the salient features of laments wherever they occur is that they are full of proper names, particularly place-names. The Maniot narrative laments tell the story of a death, fixing it in some inner map of memory by relating it to a precise landscape. Beyond its mnemonic value, the naming process seems to fulfil some emotional need, perhaps providing a sense of order amidst the chaos created by death. For Anghelaki-Rooke, though, it is not enough to hear stories about her mother that name or place her. She wants to penetrate her mother's skin and understand in her death what she failed to understand in her mother's life. Above all, like most rebellious, sensitive spirits, she wants to be judged, to have her sense of sin restored and to 'revive the conflict/ mother–desire/ mother–passion'.

Memory, though, has its own hobgoblin mechanisms, and it is not by conscious attempts at psychological penetration, but by the precise enumeration of details, even by naming, that Anghelaki-Rooke succeeds in restoring her mother with her 'fourth finger, fat-tipped like my own'. . . 'spreading the evening Nivea on her face'. . . 'Eleni, Eleni'. And it is from these details that the poet shrinks: 'φρίκη οι ακριβείς αναμνήσεις/ όστρακα/ με το θαλάσσιο τέρας φευγάτο' (how horrible precise memories are!/ shells/ abandoned by sea-monsters). We realize that what the poet wants is not to resurrect her mother in memory but to recreate a mother, reading her in the grounds of an upturned coffee cup: 'μαντεύω εγώ/ μαντεύεις εσύ/ μαζί εφευρίσκομαι τη μάνα μου' (I make a guess/ you make a guess/ together we invent my mother). Invention by inversion: turn mother into a secret sinner, and find redemption for one's own desires, take the traditional Easter symbols and up-end them so that the doubts of the Virgin's lament can be appropriated by the sinning child in the 'miserable Easter of memory' where 'life hangs again from the wood' and 'I lament/ voluptuously/ in the mystery rite of time'.

It is only from within the confines of tradition that tradition can be inverted. By situating her provocative confrontation with her mother's memory in the context of the Orthodox Church, Anghelaki-Rooke has broken the most sacred of Greek taboos. The virginal mother-as-icon tradition of the Orthodox tradition has been shattered, and the woman who scatters its shards has won an ambivalent victory. 'I've come out/ I risk it', she says, but by obeying her own needs she has lost her inheritance, the 'things' which are the heirs of a traditional mother: 'my snout is rubbed on things/ like a cat that dirtied the living-room'. Her revolt ends in a nightmarish vision: a gaping hole surrounded by beetles from which the consecration of her mother's memory is the only means of rescue:

Μάνα κινδυνεύω
αιώνια σου η μνήμη.
Κινδυνεύω πολύ
αιώνια σου η μνήμη.

Mother, I'm in danger
eternal be your memory
I'm in great danger
eternal be your memory.

This extraordinary poem that began on Good Friday, with the Virgin as the 'personage of the day', ends with a combination of traditional επίκληση – the direct appeal to the dead found in most folk laments, and an Orthodox prayer for the dead. It is surprising to discover in Anghelaki-Rooke, one of Greece's most sophisticated and daring modern poets, a *moirologhístra* with dishevelled hair, but her presence is unmistakable. 'ηδον-ικά/ θρηνώ/ στη μυσταγωγία του χρόνου' (sensuously/ I lament/ in the mystery-rite of time), she tells us, and like her village counterpart who prefers to lament than eat or drink, she takes indulgent pleasure in her artful confrontation with death. However she may have defied the traditional relationship role of a Greek daughter in life, her mother's death provides the poet with an opportunity she cannot resist. She knows she has the ability to inscribe her mother's memory and only the magic incantation of lament can exorcize her spell.

In the poem 'Notes for Father's Book', written as her father is slowly dying, Anghelaki-Rooke is able to compose a less ambivalent lament but she does not let us forget her song is magical 'τούκανα μάγια του πατέρα πούφευγε/ ξόρκια της αγάπης' (I cast a spell on my departing father/ magic spells of love). The spell of love in this case is memory, the poet's need to inscribe, to name her father. At first she cannot bring herself to name him; in the vagueness of his senility, the contradictions of his personality, he seems nameless: 'He has grass, ants/ but no name.' But names are the magical signifiers of memory, and so she must call her father: 'Yianno/ with a heavy emphasis, a heavy accent/ with something of the Bosphorus/ of Greek mythology/ of the Hellespont.' Anghelaki-Rooke is aware that her father is not the usual stuff of poetry: 'Poetically he doesn't exist,' she tells us. 'Nothing of his was ever transubstantiated/ nothing was ever transformed/ into things beyond the physical.'

But, like all laments, this poem is not so much for her father as for herself. The exercise of writing it, like the singing of a lament, is a way of coping with her loss and making her memories concrete:

Περιμένω να μεγαλώση το φεγγάρι,
για να μαλακώσουν όλα μέσα μου
να θυμηθώ
να θυμηθώ όλα τα θάυματα

I wait for the moon to grow big
for everything to soften in me
to remember
to remember all the miracles
                    ('Unexpected Things')

However untraditional her means, Katerina Anghelaki-Rooke's poems for her dead contain many of the essential elements of folk laments. The direct appeals to the dead, the inscription of memory by the concrete amassing of detail, the focus on the person of the lamenter and her pain are all familiar. So is the poet's evident confidence in her ability to 'cast spells'. Like her village counterpart, the *moirologhístra*, she knows that she has a talent for expressing her own pain, and that the act of expressing pain has its own inexpressible pleasures.

KNIVES, FORKS AND PHOTOGRAPHS: KIKI DIMOULA AND LAMENT'S LAST REMAINS.

In her collection of poems *Never Farewell*, another of Greece's contemporary women poets, Kiki Dimoula, expresses her sense of loss for her dead in ways that are as unconventional as Anghelaki-Rooke's and yet still subtly linked to the female tradition of mourning. For her, photographs become the unsatisfactory substitutes for memory in her struggle to recreate the dead:

Νέα σου δεν έχω.
Η φωτογραφία σου στάσιμη
Κοιτάζειφ σαν ερχόμενος
χαμογελάς σαν όχι.
Ανθη αποξηραμένα στο πλάι
σου επαναλαμβάνουν ασταμάτητα
το άκρατο ονομά τους *semprevives*

semprevives – αιώνιες, αιώνιες
μην τύχει και ξεχάσεις τι δεν είσαι
Οπως βρέχει χωρίς να βρέχει.

Νέα σου δεν έχω
Η φώτογραφία σου στάσιμη
Οπως σκιά μου επιστρέφει σώμα
Κι'όπως θα συναντιθούμε μια μέρα
εκεί πάνο.

I have no news of you.
Your photograph fixed.
You look as if you're coming
you smile as if not.
Dried flowers beside
you keep repeating ceaselessly
their unadulterated name *semprevives*
semprevives – everlasting, everlasting
in case you forget what you are not.

I have no news of you
Your photograph fixed
Like it's raining without really raining.

It returns the body to me like a shadow.
And like we'll meet one day
Up there.

The ethereal meeting will be, in Dimoula's imagination, as
unsatisfactory as the photograph. It will lack the soul of the
party: the flesh. Like the lamenter who complains of being
abandoned, Dimoula cries out to the ash, to the death of her
dream, 'the dream of the youngest child', her 'most painful
dream: not to grow old alone'. And yet dreams are all she has to
confront her loss with. She gives her dead no name and her
photograph only gives back an empty smile. There is an irony
and detachment in the tone of Dimoula's poems as she imagines
the dullness of any reunion 'up there' but there is also a
helplessness in the face of loss that causes her to abandon her
rational irony and accept her need for comfort: 'Love me for as
long as you don't live/ Yes, yes, the impossible will do for me.'
    In another poem of the series, 'Sole Heir of Porcelain', an
orchestra of miniature china figures takes the place of the

photograph as a static image to both summon and thwart
memory, covering with its silent music the 'melancholy noise' of
'our empty sorrows that follow sorrow':

Ιδιοκτησία πορσελάνης αυτή
η χρυσή στασημότητα.
Πρόσεξε θα το σπάσεις, μου φώναζε
η μάνα μου
τότε που ακόμα διηύθυνα εγώ
την ηλικία της ορχήστρας.

Αυτή την ορχήστρα καλώ τα μεσημέρια.
Την βάζω να μου παίξει τη μάνα μου.

Δυνατά, πιό δυνατά παρακαλώ

The ownership of this porcelain
is golden immobility.
Be careful, you'll break it,
my mother used to shout at me
when I was still directing
the age of the orchestra.

I summon this orchestra at noontime.
I make them play me my mother.

Loud, louder please.

Most of the poems in Dimoula's collection are concerned with
remembering her dead. Like Anghelaki-Rooke her sense of loss
is complicated by guilt, but she has none of Anghelaki-Rooke's
confidence in the art of her lament. Photographs become the
recurrent reminders of the impossibility of a satisfactory dialogue with the dead:

Μου φαίνονται πιό γκρίζα τα μαλλιά σου
μπερδεμένη καθώς τα χτενίζω με σκέψεις.

Τι έπαθες. Σε γέρασε η πολύ φωτογραφία
η μη σου είπε τίποτε εναντίον μου
η φαρμακόγλωσσα ενοχή μου.

Your hair seems greyer to me tonight
as I comb it, confused, with thoughts.

What's the matter? Has all that photographing aged you
or did my poison-tongued guilt tell you
something against me?

('Hostile Reconciliation')

Dimoula uses the metaphors of medicine and alchemy to explore the mystery of survival. Obeying the dark speech of a 'magician alchemist', she makes poultices mixing 'the roots of life with the roots of the unbearable', but although the medicine bottles write directions for preserving their contents:

Δεν είναι καρτερία. Είναι μία συμφιλίωση
εχθρική ανάμεσα ζωής και αβίωτου.

It is not preservation. It is a hostile
reconciliation between life and the unbearable.

In this process, the poet becomes the 'blind helper of the magician word'. He, it is, who 'hypnotizes insupportable pain into peripatetic pain'. The functional aesthetics of lament as healing could not be more clearly spelled out, but it is not possible for the poet removed from a traditional village environment to take comfort from her affinity with tradition. 'What more do you want, what more do you want?' she asks. It is this word-magician who:

persuades
those all-black mothers to live
to live to live on their children's tomb
into the depths of old age.

Dimoula understands the language of the lamenting women. She has been hypnotized too, the first night she felt 'your pillow empty' and slept with the magician. But she is not seduced for long. The images in the photographs continue to elude her, taking on a life of their own. In *Passe Partout* the speaker 'opens the windows of the photograph to air because they had remained closed for a long time like a lot of old country houses'. The subject of the photograph remains unnamed. We know its gender only from the masculine endings of an occasional adjective. The speaker herself, who was once in the photograph, now seems to be a recent addition, already wearing her 'black look'. 'How did the photograph find out?' she asks: 'How did true time turn into paper time?'

Unlike Katerina Anghelaki-Rooke, who inverts the tradition of lament from within but clings to a number of its essential elements, still sensing her power to summon or exorcize her dead through her poetic art, Dimoula's fascination with the deceptive photographic images of the dead signals a more drastic rupture with tradition. The entire collection of *Never Farewell* is a thoroughly modern attempt to express the pain of loss. As an attempt to communicate with the dead or to inscribe them on memory, her poems are as unsuccessful as photographs. But in their refusal of the comforts of religion, their unflinching acceptance of the pain of surviving, we recognize the same determination to preserve *ponos* that plays such an important part in the folk laments. The psalms' promise of a hereafter where ουκ έστι πόνοφ is as unimaginable as a reunion of souls without flesh:

Ώστε μας αποχωρίζεται η λύπη, παει
βουβαίνεται αυτός ο εθνικός
ύμνος της ύπαρξής μας;

So sadness is segregated from us, goes away
shuts up, this national
anthem of our existence.

If sadness and sorrow are lost, 'with what knives and forks, what taste, will we gobble up these marvellous circumstances?' Pain is, Dimoula seems to say, our identity, perhaps as Greeks, as women, as human creatures and life is unimaginable without it.

What Dimoula, like a number of other Greek women writers who write laments for their dead, lacks is a sense of belief in her own powers. The *moirologhístra* in the village is rightly regarded by the male writers with a certain fear. She has an authority that is recognized by all around her to communicate with the dead. She is both poet and priestess, spellbinder and exorcizer of spells. When we hear her song our hair stands on end. Male poets and prose writers have understood the force of this female art of lament and made use of its forms to communicate with a broad audience. Women poets in Greece have been less willing to draw on their own traditions. Theirs is, we feel, a private dialogue with the dead in which they sense the inadequacy of their own attempts at communication. The result is a diminishing of the living. As another modern Greek woman poet, Maria Laina, says in 'At Night I Disinter You': 'At night I dig into time/ I open roads, brush aside the spiders/ and carefully raise you from the dead. . ./ But, each time, I hold something less in my hands.' And Kiki Dimoula's final poem of *Never Farewell* begins with the words: 'I am moving towards less.'

There is a courage in the rational recognition of these women writers' inability to communicate with their dead, but there may also be a new kind of conformity involved in their acceptance of the restrained male aesthetics of irony and detachment towards death. In their lonely exercise of a poet's art they have renounced the traditional community of women who supported and wept with each other in the village cemeteries, in the prisons of the Civil War period, and have lost the *hēdonē* of *ponos*. Instead of the art of lament that has served women in cultures all over the world as the means of dealing with death, these modern Greek women poets have accepted a prevailing modern aesthetic that has left them diminished, surrounded by the cheating photographs, the collections of porcelain figurines, the knives and forks of their dead.

Perhaps there is no return to tradition; once it goes, it disappears, like a species of extinct animal. Perhaps the Greek women writers are the clear-eyed ones, who see the futility of a return to the community of women who sang laments in their grandmothers' villages. When women's voices were heard only in the high-pitched wails of laments, perhaps they had no other language to express their pain and anger. Now that Greek women poets, singers and prose writers are free to express themselves more broadly in public, they may begin to invent new genres, a new language to address the dead and commit them to memory. Without such new means they will be tied to the universal aesthetics of the modern or post-modern western world where we live with the photographs of our dead, lamenting our failure to lament.

Notes

INTRODUCTION: DANGEROUS VOICES: WOMEN'S LAMENTS AND GREEK LITERATURE

1 This occurs not only in specific historical situations such as military conquest (cf. Deuteronomy 21: 10.4) where one would expect the abducted bride to mourn, but also in traditional societies where marriages are arranged.

2 Schieffelin (1976: 172–96) describes the *Gisaro* ceremony of the Kululi people of Papua New Guinea, in which men moved to weeping by the performance of the dancers retaliate by jabbing the burning ends of torches into the dancers' shoulders. According to Schieffelin the wounding of the dancers is a reaction of anger for having been publicly provoked to tears.

3 There are numerous examples from Greece where wives express anger at their husbands for abandoning them to economic and social hardship. See chapter 1.

4 For a full documentation and discussion of the legislation, see Alexiou 1974: 3–23.

5 Hegel, *Lectures on the Philosophy of Religion* (II: 3a).

6 See Alexiou, 1974: 23 & ch. 3.

7 Kassis 1979: vol. 1, 74.

8 Despite the familiar biblical examples (e.g. David and Jacob), the comparative anthropological evidence suggests women are more often the lamenters of the dead.

9 Levi 1984: 18.

10 Ariès 1974.

11 Martins 1983: v–xxii.

12 Ibid., xiii.

13 Ibid., xiv.

14 Alexiou, 1974: xi.

15 1984: 250.

16 In Moffat 1982: 272–3.

17 In a review of a biography of Maria Callas (*Elle*, February 1990), Andrew Harvey says: 'I know one survivor of a concentration camp

and one young man dying of AIDS who both say hers [Callas's] is the only voice they can bear to listen to for long because it does not lie and makes, from unshrinking unconsoled confrontation with the facts of abandonment and despair, a final beauty.' Perhaps it is some echo of the voices she heard lamenting in her childhood that gives Callas's singing such a quality.

1 DEATH, TEARS AND IDEAS: LAMENT IN CROSS-CULTURAL PERSPECTIVE

1 Ariès 1974
2 Vovelle 1983.
3 Ariès (1974) saw five 'death systems' as having been evident in Europe from the Middle Ages on. These systems reflected variations in four underlying attitudes in the society that he characterized as awareness of the individual, the defence of society against nature, belief in an afterlife and belief in the existence of evil.
4 Hertz 1907: 48–137.
5 Carmichael 1976
6 Ibid.
7 Danforth 1982: 80–1. For other examples, see Politis 1978.
8 *Encyclopedia Judaica*, vol. 8, 1,461.
9 Unpublished lecture given at Cornell and informal discussions with Feld 1990.
10 Feld 1990: 88.
11 Ibid., 92.
12 Ibid. One is reminded of Valery's definition of poetry as 'an attempt to represent or to restore by articulate language that thing which tears, cries, caresses, kisses, sighs, etc., try obscurely to express'.
13 Ibid., 92.
14 Schieffelin 1976: 190.
15 Geertz 1973.
16 Ibid., 450.
17 Ibid.
18 Hélène Monsacré (1984) has explored the difference between men's and women's crying in the Homeric poems, pointing out the active, energetic force of male outbursts of grief compared with female. The depiction of tears and lament in Homer are discussed in chapter 4.
19 Schieffelin 1976: 78.
20 Abu-Lughod 1986: 197–204.
21 Ibid., 198.
22 Ibid. An equivalent distinction is made in parts of Greece between singing and 'crying' laments.
23 Ibid., 198–9.
24 Canetti 1973: 168–81.
25 Nenola-Kallio, 1982.
26 Caraveli-Chaves 1980; Seremetakis 1990, 1991.
27 Caraveli-Chaves 1980: 157.

28 Nenola-Kallio 1982: 111
29 Bachoven 1967.
30 Foucault 1965
31 Ibid., ch. 1.
32 For an interesting discussion of witches and widows in Andalusia, see Pitt-Rivers, 1977.
33 In these barefoot women who go 'over the mountains' and drink blood, there is an unmistakable echo of classical maenads. We are also reminded of Jephta's daughter taking to the hills with virgin friends to lament her own fate. For a discussion of this see Alexiou and Dronke 1971.
34 Partridge 1979: 25–37.
35 O'Riain 1972.
36 Death is not unique in granting temporary licence to women to behave in ways that would otherwise appear socially unacceptable, even outrageous. For the duration of certain festivals they controlled, women in ancient Athens were loud, raucous and sexually provocative. During the festivals devoted to Demeter and Adonis (the *Stenia*, *Thesmophoria*, *Haloa* and *Adonia*), as Winkler points out (1990: 188–209) normal taboos on female behaviour were lifted. During these festivals, according to a number of sources, the women seem to have enjoyed a sexual liberation denied them at normal times. Winkler quotes a scholium to Lucian describing the *Haloa*, where 'the priestesses covertly sidle up to the women and whisper into their ear – as if it were secret – recommendations for adultery. All the women utter shameful and irreverent things to each other. They carry indecent images of male and female genitals. . . ' (195). For further discussion of women's behaviour during the *Adonia*, see chapter 4. As Winkler is careful to emphasize, the women's temporary bawdiness, like their return to acceptable seemliness, should not be seen as indicative of their own acceptance of a male-dominated norm of female behaviour. Being aware of what the males in one's society expect of you is entirely different from concurring with their vision. 'Behind the facade of public docilty women had lives of their own and, arguably, a more comprehensive understanding of men than men had of women' (209). Judging by my own observations of modern Greek society, I would say that very little has changed. Discussions of men's behaviour, especially of their sexuality, are more common and frank among Greek village women than most I have heard among 'liberated' western women.
37 Danforth, 1982: 73.
38 Ibid.
39 Vouras. Photographs from Olynthos, Karpathos, 1968.
40 Lutz 1988: 53–80.
41 Dodds (1951) remains the best introduction to the question of how rational the Greeks were. Even in the classical period, as he points out, there is ample evidence to suggest that rationality was not so highly valued as later commentaries have led us to believe. On the

other hand, it is fair to say that the Greeks were preoccupied with the dichotomy between rational and irrational motivation for human behaviour, assigning both negative and positive values to 'divine madness' or the promptings of one's *thumos* (cf. chs 3,6).
42 Lutz 1988: 62.
43 See, for example, Keller 1985; Harding 1986.
44 See Ruddick 1990; Gilligan 1982.
45 Lévi-Strauss, 1963: 71.
46 There is a broad literature on this subject summarized by Lutz 1988: 72–5.
47 Ibid., 79.
48 Chatwin (1987). Chatwin whose mind had its own fertile map of cross-referenced memories, relates the Australian songlines to similar phenomena in a number of other cultures, pointing out that they seem to be a universal means of marking out territory and organizing the social life of a tribe. cf. pp 281–3.
49 Kassis 1981: vol. 3, 84.
50 Kassis 1979: vol. 1, 179.
51 Feld 1982: 108–29.
52 Nadia Seremetakis comes to a somewhat different conclusion about the use of landscape imagery in Maniot laments (1990: 481–511, 1991.). In contrast to the imagery of 'shared substance (food, clothing, shelter, and labour)', Seremetakis sees the metaphors of roads, travel, journeys, storms, etc. as representative of an outward movement, an exposure of the kin and household to the outside world. The wake, in her structuralist analysis, becomes a mediating space between the 'opposing topographies' of social orders and death' (1990: 488). Seremetakis' otherwise thought-provoking analysis of laments ignores the non-metaphorical references to landscape, where the movement is distinctly an inward one. The concrete details of the physical world inhabited by the dead person become internalized triggers of memory allowing the bereaved to re-create the dead by re-reading the landscape. The process can be seen more clearly in chapter 3, where I analyse specific Maniot laments.
53 Ibid., 129.
54 Susan Auerbach (1987) deals with some musical aspects of lament, but not with the relationship of these musical qualities to emotional expression. Nadia Seremetakis makes a useful contribution to the field by an analysis of the importance of acoustic (sobbing) and corporeal (breathing, breathlessness) to an understanding of how non-verbal elements function, although I cannot agree with her claim that the stylized sobbing that accompanies the sung text functions as 'a signifying system *autonomous and independent* of any specific verbal content' (1990: 499–501, author's emphasis).

2 THE PAINFUL ART: WOMEN'S LAMENTS FOR THE DEAD IN RURAL GREECE

1 Alexiou 1974: 110.
2 Ibid.
3 The connection between weaving and writing becomes explicit in the tradition of the three *Moirai* in the Greco–Roman period, as Alexiou notes (ibid., 116), but it is hinted at in tragedy (see chapter 5 in this volume).
4 Herzfeld, 1981: 44–57.
5 Ibid., 47.
6 There is a whole class of laments for ξενητειά (the word means foreign lands, but has a negative connotation of being in forced exile from Greece). In the funeral laments, the metaphors of marriage and exile are frequently used for death and the underworld. Formulas common to both wedding and funeral laments are σκοτείνιασε τό σπίτι σου (your house has darkened) and Χορτάριας' η αυλή σου (your courtyard is overgrown with weeds) (Alexiou, unpublished ms., 181). In an article about Chinese marriage laments (1979 'The Feelings of Chinese Daughters towards their Mothers as Revealed in Marriage Laments', *Folklore*, 90:1) Fred Blake analyses how Chinese brides lament their fate for two or three days before their marriage. The texts of these songs, usually addressed to the bride's mother, frequently express a combination of grief at leaving home and bitterness at having been given or sold in marriage against one's will.
7 Herzfeld 1981: 50.
8 Kassis 1979: vol. 1 248. Kassis' view is in sharp contrast to Seremetakis (1990:482) who maintains that the taxonomy is strictly observed by the Maniots. I find Kassis' evidence more persuasive, especially since he is descended from a long and distinguished line of lament singers.
9 Both Chianis and Alexiou have recorded examples of the same songs sung as laments and played as instrumental pieces in the very different context of a πανηγύρι. Alexiou recorded a woman singing the Epirot lament Σήκω Μαριώ in a high-pitched voice as a dirge and later heard a gypsy violinist and clarinetist perform the same piece at a festival (personal correspondence with sources).
10 Kassis's collection is both more extensive and less edited than the standard anthologies by Pasayianis, Petrounias and Politis (see Bibliography).
11 The best-known source in English on this subject and on the culture of Mani in general is still Patrick Leigh-Fermor's *Mani: Travels in the Southern Peloponnese*, first published in 1958.
12 Kassis 1979: vol. 1, 24.
13 Seremetakis 1990: 482. See also Seremetakis 1991.
14 Caraveli-Chaves 1980: 129–57, 1986: 170–94.
15 1980: 130.
16 Ibid.

17 Ibid., 144.
18 Ibid., 146.
19 Ibid.
20 Taken from the personal archives of Professor Chianis at the State University of New York, Binghamton.
21 Quoted in Nenola-Kallio 1982: 101. The gloom of these Ingrian laments exceeds anything I have found in the Greek repertoire and invites comparison with the lament of Job for his children. There are not only funeral and wedding laments by women expressing a wish for death rather than the miserable life of a woman, but laments that express a wish for the death of girl children.
22 Danforth 1982: 137. There have been a number of anthropological studies of the position of women in rural Greece. See Campbell 1964: 31–5, 263–301; Friedl (1967); du Boulay (1974: 100–41).
23 Kassis, 1979; vol. 1, 287. The strange paradox of the 'satirical' lament is not unique to Mani. Yiannis Tsouderos's anthology of Cretan *moirológhia* (1976) contains a group of 'satirical laments', 'and the writer Vizyenos, in his essay 'Aνά τον Eλικώνα' (March 1893) cites some examples of satirical songs or *balismata* from his native Thrace where women used to go on dancing while their husbands were dying (I am grateful to M. Alexiou for this reference to a little-known essay). In her collection of gypsy folktales, Diane Tong (1989) points out that Greek gypsies tell wondertales during the all-night vigil of the wake, when laments are forbidden. The paradoxical juxtaposition of the satiric and absurd with the tragic, so common in Greek folklore, reminds one that bawdy, comical satyr plays followed perfomances of the three tragedies in antiquity.
24 Kassis 1981: vol. 3, 33.
25 For some more recent and revised approaches to the question of women's spheres of authority in rural Greece, see Hirschon 1978: 72–88; Dubisch 1986.
26 For the most thorough discussion of the common formulas of laments in the Greek traditon, see Alexiou 1974, chs 7, 8 and 9.
27 Taken from the personal archives of Professor Chianis at the State University of New York, Binghamton.
28 For examples of this and the following common elements, see Alexiou 1974
29 Ibid. Alexiou quotes examples from antiquity and from the modern folk tradition (pp. 189–93). In a number of examples where a grown son or husband is the subject of the lament, the dead man is himself compared to a ship or a helmsman, and his departure leaves the family 'without a helmsman'. In other laments, the two metaphors of death as a voyage with Charos as helmsman, and a journey by road are interwoven.
30 See Kassis 1979: vol. 1, 247. I have no idea why speaking of oneself in the third person should be known as speaking 'in Indian fashion'. I reproduce here the second of the five versions published

by Kassis. The first version he publishes is a compilation and
exceedingly long. This version is by a relative of Liakakos.
31 Kassis 1979: vol. 1, 187–8. I reproduce Kassis's transliteration of
Maniot dialect, with some minor alterations in punctuation.
32 García Lorca 1960: 133.
33 Petropoulos 1959.
34 Kassis 1979, vol. 1, 24.
35 Kassis 1979: vol. 1, 248.
36 See, for example, Herzfeld: 1985.
37 Kassis 1979: vol. 1, 248.
38 This version is from Theros 1952: 205.
39 Kassis, 1980: vol. 2, 232.
40 This version of the song was recorded by Kassis from Lias
Kaloyeroyannis. He cites a number of other versions, including one
recorded in 1977 by a 93-year-old man which begins with the
address to the crow and then reverts to the couple's hopes for their
son.
41 See, for example, Beaton 1980.
42 From the lament 'Tou Vaghaki', from Theros 1952.
43 Seremetakis (1990, 1991) links the 'screaming' of the dead to the
condition of *anastatosi* or topsy-turvy induced by death. She sees
the wild cries as being linked to the burning, melting metaphors as
indicative of bodily disintegration (501–2). My interpretation
suggests there is more of conscious dramatic art in these cries than
is immediately apparent to the observer.
44 Seremetakis argues that 'the technical dynamics of breathing in
moirolói communicate with the moral connotations of breathing. . . . The passage of the lamenter's discourse in a teleological
movement toward the sob is a simulation of death, an expression of
the mourner's *social death* as a response to the personal loss she has
sustained' (500, author's italics). I find the argument somewhat
strained, especially considering the universality of sobs and sighs in
response to pain.
45 Alexiou (1974) conjectures that Echembrotos, the Peloponnesian
poet famous for mournful elegies, may have been one of a school of
elegists. His music to the *aulos* for the Delphic festival in 578 BC
was disqualified because of its mournful character (104). For a
Freudian interpretation of the connection between wind instruments, mourning and male sexuality see also Sacks 1985: 2–18.
46 Kassis recorded this from its author, Vassiliki Petrongona, shortly
before she died in 1980. She was 85 years of age when she recorded
it. See Kassis 1981: vol. 3, 41.
47 Alexiou (1974: 110–18) deals briefly with the connections between
writing and weaving. They continue to be linked in modern Greek
poetry (cf. 'Penelope Says' by Katerina Anghelaki-Rooke (1984).

3 THE POLITICS OF REVENGE IN THE LAMENTS OF INNER MANI: DUTY, HONOUR AND POISONED EGGS

1 Kassis 1979: vol. 1, 266.
2 Kassis 1981: vol. 3, 80.
3 Petrounias 1934: 61.
4 This version was recorded for Kassis by Petros Alevromayèri-Laou. He cites a number of other versions, including one where it is confused with the lament for Vetoulas. According to Kassis' many informants, the version published by Politis is incorrect, suggesting, as it does, that the father-in-law was innocent and approved the revenge. Kassis 1979: vol. 1, 274–8.
5 Failed baking is a bad omen in many cultures, including the American South. See Gloria Naylor's *Mama Day* (1988: 169) where Miranda's day begins with a series of bad omens including the failure of her cakes to rise: 'Them cakes took one look at her evil face and refused to rise.'
6 Stilpon Kyriakidis published a version of the lament in his Αι Γυναίκες εις την Λαογραφείον, where Fotos Politis discovered it and compared it, amongst other literary works, with the *Oresteia* and the revenge of Electra.
7 See Kassis 1979: vol. 1, 273–4. This has not apparently been published elsewhere, and it is not known who composed the lament. Paraski died defending the tower but the lament is composed in the first person as if she had sung it for herself.
8 The relationship of *koumbáros* and *koumbára* is not a blood relationship but a tie involving considerable obligations. It is sometimes established at weddings, sometimes at baptismal ceremonies. It includes the notion of sponsor, best man or woman and, in the case of family feuds, of protector.
9 Kassis 1979: vol. 1, 267–70. Kassis found the best source of information for this lament, which he dates as being from the middle of the last century, was an 86-year-old woman, Vassiliki Petrongona.
10 See Kassis 1979: vol. 1, 154. The lament is discussed by Fotos Politis in his collected works (1969: vol. B, 117) and also apppears in the collections of Pasayianis and Fteris. Kassis quotes a verse by Nifakis(?) referring to a leader in the Greek War of Independence of that name who fought with the well-known leaders Kolokotronis and Venetsanakis and was killed shortly after them.
11 Kassis 1979: vol. 1, 378–85. Kassis gives a number of versions of this lament followed by a second lament said to have been composed by Yiorgatza himself, in which he eventually exacts revenge and wins back the respect, if not of his wife, at least of his mother.
12 See Campbell 1964; du Boulay 1974; Auerbach 1987; Danforth 1982.
13 These laments conflict with the observations of Herzfeld in a Cretan village, where he relates an incident when a mother came to

the defence of her son in a dispute with the proprietor of a cafe. According to Herzfeld, the mother was ironically referred to as an *athilikarsernikia'* (a female-male woman). While Herzfeld admits that women sometimes get the better of men in singing bouts, he concludes that 'the married woman who takes on a male role not only dishonours herself but also brings ridicule to her husband's agnates' (1985: 71). The circumstances described in the laments are extreme, but they corroborate accounts of women fighters in the resistance or during the Turkish occupation who were admired for taking on male roles. Certainly there is ambivalence, on the part of Greek men, towards women who act like men, but it is interesting that such women are often admired, and that the ideal of female beauty in Greece often verges on the androgynous.

14 Kassis 1979: vol. 1, 272.
15 Kassis 1979: vol. 1, 304.
16 Kassis 1981: vol. 3, 189–90.
17 Ibid., 190–4.
18 Kassis 1980: vol. 2, 278–83. The version of Panagou Frangakou's lament that Kassis gives here is, according to his own information (281), confused with other laments of the period. This would suggest that it is not unique in its sentiments.
19 Kassis 1981: vol. 3, 218–21.
20 Ibid., 221–7. According to Kassis, 'ταν 'πιτάν' is a corruption of the ancient Spartan 'ταν η επί ταν'.
21 Ibid., 314–15.

4 MOURNING IN A MAN'S WORLD: THE *EPITAPHIOS LOGOS* AND THE BANNING OF LAMENTS IN FIFTH-CENTURY ATHENS

1 Plutarch, *Solon*, 21.
2 Ibid.
3 The association seems disparate to modern sensibilities, but there is evidence to suggest it is not exclusive to Greek culture. Jewish law curtailed women's wailing on festival days: 'On Purim, women sing dirges for the dead but do not wail' (Mishnah Moed Qatan, 3.9). Similarly Nehemiah (Nehemiah 8: 9) suggests the incompatibility of religious festivals and mourning as if there were a need to separate the two (cf. Ta'an 2: 8, 10).
4 Alexiou 1974: 55–7; Detienne 1977; Winkler 1990: 188–209.
5 Winkler 1990: 200.
6 Detienne 1977; Winkler 1990: 204.
7 Winkler 1990: 205.
8 Ibid.
9 Winkler, whose bibliography gives evidence of wide reading in modern Greek anthropology, ends his chapter on the *Adonia* with an account of a study of women weavers in the north African town of Azrou (Messick 1987). The rituals women perform in connection

with the *aztta*, or loom, parallel those of birth, child rearing and death. Women straddle the prepared loom as if giving birth, beat the stretched warps as they do their male children to give the loom 'fear', and mimic Muslim death rites by daubing water across the warps while uttering a testimony of faith before cutting off the finished cloth. Such a conscious structuring of what Messick calls a 'world-frame constituted by women' within an ostensibly male-dominated society offers a suggestive parallel for how ancient Greek women may have viewed their own position in society.

10 Winkler 1990: 208.

11 See Tong 1989: 35. It is customary all over Greece to break off lamenting at sunset.

12 Again, Alexiou has examined the relevant sources and my conclusions, in this section, depend on her and Vermeule's (1979) careful attention to the details of representations on vases as well as literary sources.

13 Ariès 1974.

14 Vernant 1980: 19–25, 45–70.

15 Ibid., 50

16 Women's strong participation in mystery cults, according to Vernant (1980: 108) may have been a reaction to their lack of integration into the public life of the city.

17 Alexiou 1974: ch.1; Vermeule 1979: 15–16, Garland 1985: 29–31.

18 Odyssey XI, 72–3. See Alexiou 1974; Vermeule 1979; Garland 1985.

19 The ψυχορραγείν, or struggle of the soul to break loose, as Alexiou points out, was thought to be hampered if such obligations as proper burial and lament were unfulfilled. Plato considered it to be the sinful soul which was reluctant to depart. In modern Greece, the ψυχομάχημα is a struggle with death or Charos, but the notion of the sinful soul having a more difficult death-struggle is also common. In both cases this is a period of danger during which the family and other observers carefully observe the dying person's last agony.

20 Alexiou 1974: 6.

21 Ibid.

22 Ibid., 7.

23 Ibid., 9. Garland distinguishes between offerings of food, which he concludes were a means of giving sensuous pleasure to the ghosts of the dead, and wine offerings, which seemed an effective means of summoning the ghost to attend the rite (110–15).

24 Ariès 1974: 142.

25 Ibid.

26 Ibid.

27 Ibid., 143. Despite the fact that his warrior companion dies of an illness rather than on the battlefield, Gilgamesh's lament for Enkidu is similarly extravagant (1960: 93–6). He himself remarks that he weeps 'like a mother mourning' and that 'the young men your brothers/ as though they were women/ go long-haired in mourning'

(95). When he realizes Enkidu is finally dead Gilgamesh lays a veil 'as one veils the bride' on his friend, then begins tearing off his clothes and pulling out tufts of hair.

28 *Iliad* XVIII, 22–7.
29 Ariès 1974: 143.
30 *The Epic of Gilgamesh*, Penguin edition, p.95.
31 *Iliad* XXIV, 513–24.
32 Achilles accuses Patrocles of weeping 'like a young girl, who runs after her mother's skirts, begging to be picked up', when he comes to report the heavy losses of the Argives, but suggests there would be good reason for his tears if the Myrmidons were dying (*Iliad* XVI 2–4).
33 Monsacré 1984.
34 Ibid., 181. Monsacré allows that the phrase *krueros goos*, which I have translated as 'cold laments' may have a double meaning, suggesting the trembling of the weeper and the chilling effect produced by the sound on the listener. My own interpretation (see above) does not negate the usual connotations of *krueros* but adds the dimension of time.
35 Ibid., 199.
36 Ibid., 201.
37 It is just as likely that the folk tradition borrowed such imagery from the Homeric poems as the other way round.
38 Nancy Sultan has explored the opposition of *kleos* and *goos* in a recent paper (1991).
39 Alexiou 1974: 11–13, 132–4.
40 Alexiou 1974: 12. Alexiou underlines that Solon's legislation is aimed at the professional singers of 'set dirges' (*threnein pepoiemena*) and his limiting of the right to mourn to kinswomen is further evidence that the legislation was, at least initially, not directed at all women mourners. There is no way to know the sex of the professional mourners at Hector's funeral, but the biblical parallels may be instructive. Jeremiah speaks of a professional class of women who composed and chanted lamentations (*mekonenot, mequonenot*, Jeremiah 9: 16). Their art was regarded as a branch of wisdom and so they are called 'skilled' (*hakhamot*) (*Encyclopedia Judaica*: vol. 12, 485 ff.)
41 Alexiou 1974: 13.
42 Ibid., 133.
43 Segal 1971: 33–57.
44 According to Ariès, the 'tame' death, one which is accepted as inevitable, belongs to a tradition as old as Homer. Changes in this view of death are apparent from the late Middle Ages onwards in western Europe, but only among the middle classes, at least until the nineteenth century. Without discussing Ariès' argument at length it is possible to see, in the Homeric poems, an illustration of the 'tame' death. As Ariès says: 'The ancient attitude in which death is close and familiar and yet desensitized is too different from our own view, in which it is so terrifying that we dare not say its name' (1974: 28).

45 Ariès, 1974: 6.
46 Ibid., 158–9.
47 Ibid.
48 Again there are biblical parallels. Comforting the mourner by offering him bread and wine was customary (II Samuel, 3: 35; Jeremiah, 16: 7). The bread was called 'the bread of agony' (*lehem onashim*) (Ezekiel, 24: 17), and the wine 'the cup of consolation' (Jeremiah, 16:7). cf. *Encyclopedia Judaica*, vol. 12, 485 ff.
49 Alexiou 1974: 14.
50 Vermeule 1979: 12.
51 Both Alexiou (1974: 14–23) and Humphreys (1983) examine the legislation in some detail. See also Garland 1989: 21–2 and 1989: 1–15.
52 Plutarch, *Moralia*, 608a ff., Lysias i, 8.
53 *Leges Graecorum Sacrae* (eds H. von Prott and L. Ziehen), 1896, 1906. Similar restrictions were passed by the Romans. David Daube (1969) suggests that in the Roman case, the purpose of legislation ostensibly aimed at curbing extravagance was what he terms 'the protection of the non-tipper' (117–28). According to Roman tradition, extravagance at burials had been legislated against by King Numa. It was also curtailed in the XII Tables, and may have been inspired by religious belief (Daube, op. cit.). By 200 BC, however, Daube suggests that restrictions on conspicuous extravagance, either at funerals or in other areas of Roman life, were inspired by parsimonious members of the tight club of upper-class society.
54 Alexiou (1974); Garland (1989); Humphreys (1983).
55 Dareste, B., M. Hassoullier and T. Reinach, *Recueil des inscriptions juridiques*, Paris, 1891–5, 1898–1904; F. B. Jevons 1895, 'Greek Burial Laws', *Classical Review* 9: 247–50.
56 Alexiou 1974: 18.
57 Ibid. Alexiou notes that Aristotle saw as a democratic trend the reduction of the number of such cults and the opening of them to the public.
58 Alexiou 1974: 19.
59 See Humphreys 1983: 83–8; Alexiou 1974: 19–20.
60 Alexiou 1974: 20.
61 Humphreys 1983; Alexiou 1974.
62 Alexiou 1974: 21 (my emphasis).
63 Ibid.
64 Plutarch, *Solon*, 12B.
65 Alexiou 1974: 14–15, 21–2.
66 Ariès 1974: 95–293.
67 As Humphreys notes (1983: 86): 'Convention required that men should maintain self-control in mourning, whereas women were encouraged to display wild grief: therefore to restrict female participation in *prothesis* and funeral processions (*ekfora*) to kin and women over sixty markedly reduced both the oral and the visual impact of the procession.' But since the Homeric literature

suggests a very different convention, some explanation of the change must be sought in the social conditions of the new state.
68 Ibid., 22.
69 Loraux 1986. As Humphreys points out (1983: 88–9) evidence for 'public' funerals goes back as far as the history of the *pólis*, and presumably military commanders had made speeches honouring the dead in battle before burying them on the field. What is new is the institution of the funeral speech as a civic discourse.
70 Demosthenes, *Against Leptines*, 141.
71 Loraux 1986: 1. Loraux regards the *epitaphios logos* as self-referential, and notes that 'an Athenian finds it difficult to evoke the *epitaphios logos*, even in the context of a political speech, without borrowing from its language' (ibid).
72 Ibid., 2.
73 Ibid., 9. Loraux examines the case of Plato's *Menexenius* where the *epitaphios* is attributed to a foreign woman, Aspasia, and to Socrates. She suggests that by doing so, Plato wanted to 'dissipate the mirage of the funeral oration by turning the speech against itself'.
74 Ibid., 11.
75 Thucydides, *Histories*, II, 34, 1–8.
76 Loraux 1986: 24.
77 Thucydides, *Histories*, II, 46.
78 Thucydides, II, 44; Lysias, 77, 80; Menexenius, 248, c7; Hyperides, 42.
79 See Gilligan 1982; Ortner 1974; Keller 1985; Lutz 1988.
80 Ortner 1974.
81 Beckman 1990.
82 Ibid., 151.
83 Ruddick 1990, 236.
84 Ibid., 248.
85 Ibid.
86 Mosse 1990: 70–106.
87 Mosse's analysis of the symbolism of war cemeteries in Germany, England and France between the wars is a fascinating one, showing how similar the cult of the fallen was, both in iconography and sentiment during the period.
88 Mosse 1990: 99.
89 See Pollux, 6,202: 'To gynekeion genos esti threnoies kai philothrenon', Plutarch, op. cit.
90 Herodotus, *Histories* VI, 58.
91 Loraux 1986: 47.
92 Schenck 1986.
93 Ibid.
94 Alexiou speculates that Echembrotos, the Peloponnesian musican whose music to the *aulos* was disqualified from the Delphic festival of 578 BC on the grounds that it was too mournful, was one of a school of Dorian elegists who used the form for a kind of lament.

The fact that the genre survived only as a literary form suggests that perhaps it suffered from the religious reforms of the sixth century that curtailed funeral laments (104).
95 Sacks 1985. Sacks' analysis is concerned with the English elegy, but his account of the origins of the genre is centred on Ovid's *Metamorphoses*. He sees the elegy as an exercise in what Freud calls 'the work of mourning' – i.e. the successful transference of attachment from the dead to a new object of affection. I would argue that while he may be right about the elegy, the traditional lament is not concerned with transference of affection but its opposite, i.e. the continuation of attachment to the dead through memory.
96 Sacks quotes, as an example, the following lines from Emily Brontë's 'Remembrance':

Then did I check the tears of useless passion
Weaned my young soul from yearning after thine;
Sternly denied its burning wish to hasten
Down to that tomb already more than mine.'(15)

97 Sacks 1985: 13.
98 Quoted in Schenck 1986: 14.

5 FROM THE ERINYES TO THE EUMENIDES:
TRAGEDY AND THE TAMING OF LAMENT

1 Aristotle, *Poetics*, 20, 6.
2 Gorgias, *Helen*, 9. See also de Romilly 1975: 3.
3 Similarly, in the Hebraic tradition, exile and mourning are linked from the Book of Lamentations to late nineteenth-century Zionist poetry. The Biblical Lamentations are centred on the personification of Zion as a bereaved mother mourning her lost (exiled) children. Elsewhere, in a reversal of the same metaphor, it is the exiles who mourn their lost Zion. Exile and the emotions aroused by it are inevitably expressed on the model of mourning and lament.
4 Vernant 1988: 29–48.
5 Thomson 1941: 181–3.
6 Geertz 1973: 432.
7 Ober and Strauss 1989: 237. Using the combined methodology of political sociology and cultural anthropology, Ober and Strauss examine the relationship between the rhetoric of politics and drama in an illuminating study that shows how cross-referential and interdependent the two genres were. The elaborate code of symbols and paradigms enscribed in the 'deep play' of theatre were as much a part of the orator's stock-in-trade as the rhetoric of public speaking resonating through the speeches of Sophocles and Aeschylus. The authors argue that the two sets of texts, political and dramatic, were not only 'informed by political culture, but were

also primarily responsible for generating the new signs through which it evolved' (270).

8 Foley (forthcoming) 29–30.

9 Herodotus, *Histories*, VI, 21,2.

10 Aeschylus, *The Persians*, 296.

11 *Iliad* XXIV, 239, 523, 524, 722–3, 740–1, 746–7, 759–61. Folk examples of the genre are also abundant. See Alexiou 1974: chs. 4, 5.

12 *Iliad* XXIV, 570–80.

13 We must presume that these inhabitants of Bithynia were known, like the Carians, for their laments, and perhaps acted as professional lamenters outside their own territory.

14 See Alexiou 1974: ch. 1.

15 Said asserts (1978: 56) that the demarcation between orient and west is already 'bold by the time of the *Iliad*', but he does not elaborate and I find it hard to see any profound differences between the treatment of a Hector and an Achilles, except to the latter's disadvantage. Certainly Priam's grief for his son is intense, but he is an old man, and even the Greeks cannot help but respect his prostration. By Aeschylus' day, the orient may have come to represent a sort of decadence associated with female qualities, but Said's discussion of 'orientalism' in antiquity should be treated with some care. The Greeks looked down on all foreigners as 'barbarians' for not speaking Greek, and to project later notions of race onto the Greeks may be an easy trap to fall into. Likewise, Kenneth Dover's (1984) description of a scene on a vase published by Schauenburg in 1975 betrays what may be his own unconscious 'orientalism': 'This expresses the exultation of the "manly" Athenians at their victory over the "womanish" Persians at the River Eurymedon in the early 460s; it proclaims: "we've buggered the Persians." ' (1984: 105).

16 Foucault 1965: xi. Perhaps we have very little idea of what madness means to any age, except as a sort of antithesis to reason. To quote Foucault again: 'the Reason–Madness nexus constitutes, for Western culture, one of the dimensions of its originality.'(ibid.).

17 Heracles' veiling at the end of the *Trachiniae* and Ajax's suicide are arguably exceptions. Euripides' *The Bacchae* was not staged in Athens. Its portrayal of the victory of the 'oriental' god Dionysos and his female followers over the scornful Pentheus, who must play a woman in order to observe a secret female ritual, would have been an exception. If tragedy is in part an appropriation of a female ritual – lamenting the dead – then this play is a fearful warning of its possible consequences.

18 For a discussion of the literature on this point see Foley, op. cit., 48n.

19 Foley (forthcoming) 24. Foley's discussion of the play is detailed and insightful; her discussion of tragic lament in its historical context makes an important contribution to the subject.

20 Ibid. Here I find Foley's argument for an abrupt role reversal at this point convincing. The article contains a summary of contrary

points of view. She also points out that the women's control of the funeral laments is in marked contrast to Euripides' *The Suppliants*.

21 Foley (forthcoming) 27.
22 Zeitlin 1978.
23 See, in particular, Thomson 1946.
24 The Shakespearean comedies are also full of such ambiguities. Think of Rosalind's epilogue in *As You Like It*, where she (through the mouth of a boy actor) says: 'It is not the fashion to see the lady in the epilogue. . . . If I were a woman I would kiss as many of you as had beards that please me. . .'. Here, it is deliberately written to amuse, whereas it is hard to say what effect such lines must have had on the Athenian audience. In any case, the audience must have been aware of such ambiguities and to ignore them is to lose an important element of their irony.
25 For a fascinating discussion of weaving as a woman's art and its relation to writing and music see Ahl 1985: 224–8. See also Alexiou 1974: 115–16.
26 The complex bird symbolism of this passage and its relation to the *Agamemnon* is discussed in Ahl 1985: 223–4.
27 Ibid., 230–4.
28 Garvie 1986: 82.
29 Ibid., 84.
30 The passage is a difficult one (see Garvie, p. 84) but there is no doubt about the reference to close combat, weaponry and Ares.
31 See Garvie, p. 111, where he points out that it is not clear whether they refer to death on the funeral pyre or in a coat of molten pitch but, given the context, the latter seems a more convincing interpretation.
32 Thomson 1946: 68.
33 See Alexiou 1974: 123, where she says that 'the examples collected by Diehl suggest that it was accompanied by wild gestures and associated with Asiatic ecstasy, like the *ialemos*'.
34 Ibid., 103.
35 Schadewalt 1932: 312–54; Thomson 1946: 268 ff.
36 For a full discussion of this question see Alexiou 1974: 110 ff.
37 Homer *Iliad*, XIX, 87. Also see Dodds 1951: 8.
38 My translation of this and other passages is based on Garvie's commentary.
39 Here I have used David Greene's translation (*Aeschylus II, Complete Greek Tragedies*, 1956).
40 The *Suda* refers to a connection between *goeteia* and *goos*. (goeteia ff.).
41 Farmer 1969.
42 See Alexiou 1974: 178.
43 In the modern Greek novel, *Achilles' Fiancée* by Alki Zei (1987: 129–30), there is a curiously precise parallel to this passage. Eleni, the heroine of the novel, is watching the French actor Gerard Philippe in a performance of *The Prince of Hamburg*. His voice comes to her: 'Warm, clear, melodic, but like the crack of a whip

and it disturbs (the verb is *taràzo*) me.' In this case it is a certain voice quality that causes the stirring of Eleni's memory; no doubt Aeschylus has in mind vocal qualities, musical tonalities, in addition to the words of the *goos*, as producing this effect.

44 For a discussion of *ololugmos* and its associations, see Garvie 1986: 146. It is used on a number of occasions in the trilogy, and has been associated with Agamemnon's murder (*Agamemnon* 1, 118).

45 See Garvie p. 146.

46 cf. *The Persians*, 97, *Agamemnon*, 798.

47 Herodotus, *Histories*, VII, 62.

48 Herodotus, *Histories*, V, 49, 7; Strabo 15, 3, 2. Kissian women may have been especially known for their laments – we have no evidence except Aeschylus' *The Persians*, 120 ff.

49 See Euripides, *Orestes*, 1395 ff. *The Suppliants*, 179 ff., *The Phoenician Women*, 1304ff.

50 Here I cannot agree with the insertion of *boëton* for *goeton* because it 'does not fit the context of rejoicing' (Garvie, 1986: 69). The *goos*, as we have seen above, is precisely the instrument of such magical change and in this case it is the lament which has roused the children to avenge the death of Agamemnon.

51 Or, perhaps, 'so it sails', continuing the metaphor. See Garvie, p. 269.

52 *Republic*, 398d–9a.

53 See chapter 1.

54 The single exception was Hypsipyle, who spared her father. The other story of the Lemnians concerns the Pelasgian inhabitants of Lemnos, who carried off Athenian women from Brauron and had children by them. When their mothers brought them up in the Athenian way, the fathers became afraid and killed both the children and their mothers. Because of both these deeds, the word 'Lemnion' was associated with anything bad (see Herodotus, *Histories*, VI, 6, 138).

55 Zeitlin 1978: 155.

56 See Garvie, 1986: 222–3.

57 For an interesting discussion of this scene see Murnaghan 1987: 33. Murnaghan sees the threat not so much in sexual terms but still menacing in that it reminds Orestes of his own vulnerability and the vengeance that must ensue if he destroys the body so intimately bound to his own.

58 Foucault 1965: xi. He poses hubris as the nearest to an opposition and says that the *sophrosune* of the Socratic reasoners owes something to the threat of hubris. I suspect that a much greater threat, as de Romilly suggests, was *goeteia*, and other forms of magical enchantment produced by song, poetry and words themselves. Magic and poetry were not, as de Romilly demonstrates, far apart, and the state induced by them is not incompatible with descriptions of madness or dementia in later ages.

59 de Romilly (1975) gives ample illustration from Gorgias, Plato, Aristotle and other philosophers to support the view that the *logos*

was thought to have magical properties associated with witchcraft.

60 See de Romilly 1975: ch. 2.

61 As Chioles says (1988): 'Klytemnestra as character acquires monumental significance as the Mother with a community of Kindly Ones turned Furies in the deepest recesses of her private history' (p. 59).

62 Zeitlin 1978: 159.

63 Pitt-Rivers 1977: 82–3.

64 Ibid.

65 de Romilly 1975: 17.

66 Zeitlin points to Bamberger's comparison of the Myth of the Rule of Women and puberty rights which 'aim at detaching the boy from his natal household and his maternal associations and retraining him for his social and political roles' (1978: 60). In this case, Apollo can be seen as an initiating priest. George Thomson, in his *Aeschylus and Athens* also uses anthropological evidence to establish a parallel between initiation rites and Aeschylean tragedy.

67 Before tragedy, as de Romilly points out, poets claimed to produce only pleasant emotions, but Gorgios added 'shuddering fright and weeping pity' to the list. Aristotle singled out these two emotions as being both the purpose and result of tragedy (see de Romilly 1975: 5).

68 Goldhill discusses the critical literature on the ambiguity of the genitive *neōn thesmiōn'* in some detail (1984: 240), but does not mention the aural echo. His view is that the ambiguity may in itself be important, marking 'the interplay between the chorus's acceptance of the process of law, their submission to the trial, and their refusal to accept the decision of the court (unless they win!). This seems not implausible.

69 Such a view seems to be based exclusively on an exogamic social organization, but, as Pitt-Rivers points out (1977: 120 ff.), patrilinear endogamy was not uncommon in Greece, at least as early as Homer.

70 This is interesting if we remember the nurse in the Choephoroi. By suckling Orestes, and performing the task of *trophos*, she may have been more 'mother' in Apollo's terms than Clytemnestra. The argument of the male as true progenitor of the child, giving it form, whereas woman supplies only matter, is taken up in detail by Aristotle (*De generatione et corruptione*, 1. 20, 729a, 738b).

71 In the *Iliad*, the verb *thrōsko* is used for the attack on Troy and for the flight of arrows.

72 Zeitlin 1978: 169. It is interesting that Dionysos, a god associated with women's rituals and with the orient, should also have had an unnatural birth with Zeus's intervention.

73 Whether or not she physically casts a vote is the subject of much debate (see Goldhill 1984: 257–9 for a discussion of the literature).

74 Steiner 1984: 237

75 Seaford (1987: 106–30) suggests that tragedy seems particularly interested in the disruption of normal wedding preparations and

their transformation into a wedding-in-death. Besides Antigone, he cites the example of Iphigenia in *Iphigenia in Aulis* and the Danaids in *The Suppliants*. He believes that Antigone was probably dressed in bridal attire as she went to her tomb (113).

76 Neuberg 1990: 54–76. His argument is complex, and I have only given the barest outline of his reasoning.

77 Foley (forthcoming) 8. Again we are reminded of the folk tradition, where the lead lament singer will call on the women around her to 'witness' (the verb used is *martyríso*, which has the double association of bearing witness and suffering for) her lament. In Sophocles' *Electra* the heroine will also use her lament to political purpose (379–82), causing Aigisthus to consider shutting her away.

78 Pucci (1980) points out the innovative qualities of this first speech, eliciting, through the nurse's lament, our pity for Medea.

79 Ibid. (I am using Pucci's translation here).

80 Ibid., 28.

81 See Foley (forthcoming) 14–20. Foley's discussion of the play focuses on its relation to contemporary events, especially to the new legislation. See too Loraux 1986: 48 ff. who calls the drama 'a dramatised reflection on the funeral oration'.

82 See Foley (forthcoming) 16–18. She maintains that despite the reduced role played by women in the public funerals of the war dead, women relatives of the dead still played a prominent role in the lamentation and burial of the remains.

83 Ibid. and Loraux 1990: 67.

84 Foley (forthcoming) 20.

85 Foley (forthcoming) 21.

86 In support of this, Foley notes the use of Ionic rhythms in the *parados* of *The Suppliants* and the comparison of Evadne to a Bacchant of Hades, as well as passages from *Hecuba* and *The Phoenician Women* (forthcoming: 44).

6 EPITAPHS AND PHOTOGRAPHS: LAMENTS IN MODERN GREEK LITERATURE

1 Alexiou 1974: 28.

2 Ibid.

3 Ibid.

4 An English translation of Romanos's *kontakion* 'Mary at the Cross' appears in Trypanos 1971: 404–14.

5 Alexiou 1974: 65.

6 Ibid.

7 For a discussion of the vernacular elements in the Virgin's lament, see Alexiou 1974: 62–82.

8 Palamas 1960: vol. 4, 14.

9 Ibid., 47.

10 Romanos' *kontakion* 'Mary at the Cross' is the earliest example that can be dated (sixth century AD). In it there is a dramatic

dialogue between the Virgin and Christ. Once the fifteen syllable line had been established as the standard meter for folk poetry in the Greek-speaking world, examples begin to appear in the vernacular. (cf. Alexiou 1974: 62–78). In the ballads that are still part of the popular tradition in Greece, the Virgin pleads with her son not to die, even threatening suicide.

11 Palamas's introduction to iambs and anapaests was prepared for a new edition that did not appear. The introduction was first published in two issues of *The Journal of Free Speech* (6 & 21 April 1925). The poet's son included them in the second volume of his father's collected papers published in 1940. Cf. Palamas 1960: 376–7.

12 Ibid.

13 Ibid, 380.

14 Petropoulos 1959: 235.

15 Prevelakis 1978: 71 The poet is quoted from an interview in 1978.

16 For an account of the controversy occasioned by the Theodorakis settings of *Epitaphios* and the reasons behind it see Holst 1980: 57–70.

17 See Holst 1975 for an introduction to the *rembétika* and why they were looked down on by the upper classes of Greek society.

Bibliography

Abu-Lughod, Lila. 1986. *Veiled Sentiments*. Berkeley: University of California Press.

Ahl, Frederick. 1984. 'The Art of Safe Criticism in Greece and Rome.' *AJP*, 105.

——. 1985. *Metaformations*. Ithaca: Cornell University Press.

Alexiou, Margaret. 1974. *The Ritual Lament in Greek Tradition*. Cambridge: Cambridge University Press.

Alexiou, Margaret and Dronke P. 1971. 'The Lament of Jephta's Daughter: Themes, Traditions, Originality.' *Studi Medievali*, 12.2, 819–63.

Anagnostopoulos, Ioannos. 1984. Ο Θάνατος και ο Κάτο Κόσμος στη Δημοτική Ποίηση: *Εσχατολογία της Δημοτικής Ποίησης*. Athens: Ποτομήτης.

Anghelaki-Rooke, Katerina. 1971. *Ποιήματα '63–'69*. Athens: Ερμής.

——. 1974. *Μαγδαληνή το Μεγάλο Θηλαστικό*. Athens: Ερμής.

——. 1984. *Οι Μνηστήρες*. Athens: Κέδρος.

Ariès, Philippe. 1974. *Western Attitudes to Death from the Middle Ages to the Present*. Baltimore: Johns Hopkins University Press.

——. 1980. *At the Hour of Death*. New York: Knopf. Trans. of *L'Homme devant la Mort*. Paris: Editions du Seuil, 1977.

Auerbach, Susan. 1987. 'From Singing to Lamenting: Women's Musical Role in a Greek Village', in *Women and Music in Cross-Cultural Perspective* (ed. Koskoff). New York: Greenwood Press.

Beaton, Roderick. 1980. *Folk Poetry of Modern Greece*. Cambridge: Cambridge University Press.

Beckman, Joyce. 1990. 'Feminism, War and Peace Politics', in *Women, Militarism and War* (eds J. B. Elshtein and S. Tobias) Maryland: Rowman & Littlefield.

Bernal, Martin. 1987. *Black Athena: The Afroasiatic Roots of Classical Civilization. Vol 1: The Fabrication of Ancient Greece 1785–1985*. London: Free Association Books.

——. 1991. *Black Athena. Vol. 2: The Archaeological and Documentary Evidence*. New Brunswick.

Blake, C. Fred. 1979. 'The Feelings of Chinese Daughters Towards

Their Mothers as Revealed in Marriage Laments.' *Folklore*, 90.1.

Campbell, John K. 1964. *Honour, Family and Patronage*. Oxford: Clarendon Press.

Canetti, Elias. 1973. *Crowds and Power*. Harmondsworth: Penguin Books.

Caraveli-Chaves, Anna. 1980. 'Bridge between Worlds: The Greek Women's Lament as Communicative Event.' *Journal of American Folklore*, 93: 129–57.

——. 1986. 'The Bitter Wounding: The Lament as Social Protest in Rural Greece', in *Gender and Power in Rural Greece* (ed. J. Dubisch). Princeton, New Jersey: Princeton University Press.

Carmichael, Calum. 1976. 'On Separating Life and Death: An Explanation of Some Biblical Laws.' *Harvard Theological Review*, 69.1–2.

Chatwin, Bruce. 1987. *The Songlines*. New York: Viking Penguin.

Chioles, John. 1988. 'Aeschylus and O'Neill: A Phenomenological View,' in *Critical Approaches to O'Neill* (ed. John Stroupe). New York AMS Press.

Coleman, Steve. 1989. 'Poetry and the Constitution of the Self and Emotions in Irish Tradition.' Draft for Submission to CAE Symposium, University of Chicago.

Danforth, Loring. 1982. *The Death Rituals of Greece*. Princeton: Princeton University Press.

Dareste, R., Hassoulier, B. and Reinach, T. 1891–5, 1898–1904. *Recueil des inscriptions juridiques*. Paris.

Daube, David. 1969. *Roman Law: Linguistic, Social and Philosophical Aspects*. Edinburgh: Edinburgh University Press.

——. 1972. *Civil Disobedience in Antiquity*. Edinburgh: Edinburgh University Press.

de Ghelderode, Michel. 1960. 'Mlle. Jaire', in *Seven Plays*. Trans. G. Hanger. New York: Hill and Wang.

de Romilly, Jacqueline. 1975. *Magic and Rhetoric in Ancient Greece*. Cambridge: Harvard University Press.

Detienne, Marcel. 1977. *The Gardens of Adonis: Spices in Greek Mythology*. Trans. Janet Lloyd. New Jersey: Humanities Press.

Dimitrakos-Messiklis, D. B. 1949. *Οι Νυκλιάνοι*. Athens.

Dimoula, Kiki. 1988. *Χαίρε Ποτέ*. Athens: Στιγμή.

Dodds, E. R. 1951. *The Greeks and the Irrational*. Berkeley: University of California Press.

Dover, Kenneth. 1984. 'For the Heroes Are at Hand.' *Journal of Hellenic Studies*, 104.

Dubisch, Jill. 1986. *Gender and Power in Rural Greece*. Princeton: Princeton University Press.

du Boulay, Juliet. 1974. *Portrait of a Greek Mountain Village*. Oxford: Clarendon Press.

Durkheim, Emile. 1965. *The Rules of Sociological Method*. Trans. S. Solovay and J. Mueller. New York: Free Press.

Encyclopedia Judaica. 1971. (ed. Cecil Roth). Athens: Keter Publishing House.

Evlamvios, G. 1973. *Ο Αμάραντος: Ρόδα της Αννναγεννήθεισης*

Ελλάδας. Trans. of Russian prologue and notes by P. Koundhouros and A. Politis. Athens: Καραβία.

Farmer, Henry G. 1969. 'The Music of Ancient Egypt', in *The New Oxford History of Music*. Vol. 1. London: Oxford University Press.

Feijo, Rui, Martins, Herminio and de Piña-Cabral, João. 1983. *Death in Portugal: Studies in Portuguese Anthropology and Modern History*. Oxford: JASO Occasional Papers no. 2.

Feld, Steven. 1982. *Sound and Sentiment: Birds, Weeping, Poetics and Song in Kululi Expression*. Philadelphia: University of Pennsylvania Press.

———. 1990. Unpublished lecture given at Cornell and informal discussions.

Foley, Helene. P. (forthcoming) 'The Politics of Tragic Lamentation', in *Proceedings of Conference on Tragedy, Comedy and the Polis* (eds A. Summerstein *et al*).

Foucault, Michel. 1965. *Madness and Civilization: A History of Insanity in the Age of Reason*. New York: Pantheon.

Frazer, James G. 1890. *The Golden Bough*. New York: Macmillan (1963 edn).

Friedl, Ernestine. 1962. *Vasilika: A Village in Modern Greece*. New York: Holt, Rinehart & Winston.

———. 1967. 'The Position of Women: Appearance and Reality.' *Anthropological Quarterly*.

Fteris, G. 'Ο Φώτος Πολίτις και η Μάνη' Ταΰγετος και Μανιάτες.

Garciá Lorca, Federico. 1960. 'Theory and Function of the Duende', in *Lorca*. Trans. J. L. Gili. London: Penguin Books.

Garland, Robert. 1985. *The Greek Way of Death*. Ithaca: Cornell University Press.

———. 1989. 'The Well-ordered Corpse: An Investigation into the Motives Behind Greek Funerary Legislation.' *BICS*, 36: 1–15.

Garvie, A. F. 1986. *Choephoroi/Aeschylus*, with introduction and commentary by A. F. Garvie. Oxford: Clarendon Press.

Geertz, Clifford. 1960. *The Religion of Java*. New York: Free Press.

———. 1973. *The Interpretation of Cultures*. New York: Basic Books.

Gehr, Richard. 1989. 'Mourning in America: Diamanda Galas.' *Artforum*. New York.

Gilligan, Carol. 1982. *In a Different Voice: Psychological Theory and Women's Development*. Cambridge: Harvard University Press.

Goldhill, Simon. 1984. *Language, Sexuality, Narrative: The Oresteia*. New York: Cambridge University Press.

Greene, David. (trans.). 1956. 'Seven Against Thebes' in *Aeschylus II*. Chicago: Chicago University Press, 2956.

Harding, Sandra. 1986. *The Science Question in Feminism*. Ithaca: Cornell University Press.

Hegel, Georg W. F. 1895. *Lectures on the Philosophy of Religion*. London: K. Paul.

Hertz, R. 1907. 'Contribution à une étude sur la réprésentation collective de la mort.' *Année Sociologique*, 10: 48–137.

———. 1960. *Death and the Right Hand*. Glencoe, Illinois: Free Press.

Herzfeld, Michael. 1981. 'Performative Categories and Symbols of Passage in Rural Greece.' *Journal of American Folklore*, 94: 44–57.
——. 1982. *Ours Once More: Folkore, Ideology and the Making of Modern Greece*. Austin: University of Texas Press.
——. 1985. *The Poetics of Manhood: Contest and Identity in a Cretan Mountain Village*. Princeton: Princeton University Press.
Hirschon, Renée. 1978. 'Open Body/Closed Space: The Transformation of Female Sexuality', in *Defining Females* (ed. S. Ardener). New York: John Wiley.
Holst, Gail. 1975. *Road to Rembetika*. Athens: Denise Harvey.
——. 1980. *Theodorakis: Myth and Politics in Modern Greek Music*. Amsterdam: Hakkert.
Humphreys, Sally. 1983. *The Family, Women and Death*. London: Routledge & Kegan Paul.
Huntingdon, Richard and Metcalf, Peter. 1979. *Celebrations of Death: The Anthropology of Mortuary Ritual*. Cambridge: Cambridge University Press.
Jevons, F. B. 1985. 'Greek Burial Laws.' *Classical Review*, 9.
Kassis, Kyriakos. 1979. *Μοιρολόγια της Μέσα Μάνης Α'*. Athens.
——. 1980. *Μοιρολόγια της Μέσα Μάνης Β'*. Athens.
——. 1981. *Μοιρολόγια της Μέσα Μάνης του 20ου Αιώνα*. Athens.
Keller, Evelyn Fox. 1985. *Reflections on Gender and Science*. New Haven: Yale University Press.
Kurz, D. C. and Boardman, J. 1973. *Greek Burial Customs*. London: Thames & Hudson.
Leges Graecorum Sacrae (eds H. von Prott and L. Ziehen), 1896, 1906. Leipzig.
Leigh-Fermor, Patrick. 1958. *Mani: Travels in the Southern Peloponnese*. London: John Murray.
Levi, Peter. 1984. *The Lamentation of the Dead with 'The Lament for Arthur O'Leary' translated by Eilis Dillon*. London: Anvil Press.
Lévi-Strauss, Claude. 1963. *Totemism*. Trans. R. Needham. Boston: Beacon Press.
——. 1969. *The Raw and the Cooked*. New York: Harper & Row.
Loraux, Nicole. 1986. *The Invention of Athens: The Funeral Oration in the Classical City*. Trans. of *L'invention d'Athènes* by Alan Sheridan. Cambridge: Harvard University Press.
Lutz, Catherine. 1988. *Unnatural Emotions*. Chicago: University of Chicago Press.
Martins, Herminio. 1983. *Death in Portugal*. Studies in Portuguese Anthropology and Modern History. Oxford: JASO.
Mendardos, Simos. 1921. *Historia tōn Lexeōn Tragōdō kai Tragōdia*. Athens.
Messick, B. 'Subordinate Discourse: Women, Weaving and Gender Relations in North Africa.' *American Ethnologist*, 14: 210–25.
Moffat, Mary Jane (ed.). 1982. *In the Middle of Winter: Selections from the Literature of Mourning*. New York: Random House.
Monsacré, Hélène. 1984. *Les larmes d'Achille: Les héros, la femme et la suffrance dans la poésie d'Homère*. Paris: Albin Michel.

Mosse, George L. 1990. *Fallen Soldiers: Reshaping the Memory of the World Wars*. New York: Oxford University Press.

Murnaghan, Sheila. 1987. 'Body and Voice in Greek Tragedy.' *Yale Journal of Criticism*, 2, 1.

Naylor, Gloria. 1988. *Mama Day*. New York: Ticknor & Fields.

Nenola-Kallio, Aili. 1982. 'Studies in Ingrian Lament.' *FF Communications*. Helsinki: Academia Scientiarum Finnica.

Neuburg, Matt. 1990. 'How Like a Woman: Antigone's "Inconsistency".' *Classical Quarterly*, 40 (i) 54–76.

Ober, Josiah and Strauss, Barry. 1989. 'Drama, Political Rhetoric, and the Discourse of Athenian Democracy', in *Nothing to Do with Dionysos?: Athenian Drama in its Social Context* (eds J. Winkler and F. Zeitlin). Princeton: Princeton University Press.

O'Riain, Padraig. 1972. 'Study of the Irish Legend of the Wild Man' *Eigse*. vol. XIV.

Ortner, Sherry. 1974. 'Is Female to Male as Nature is to Culture?', in *Women, Culture and Society* (eds Rosaldo and Lamphere).

Ortner, Sherry and Whitehead, Harriet (eds). 1981. *Sexual Meanings: The Cultural Construction of Gender and Sexuality*. New York: Cambridge University Press.

Palamas, Kostis. 1960. *Άπαντα*, v. 1, 4. Athens: Μπήρης.

Partridge, Angela. 1979. 'Wild Men and Wailing Women.' *Eigse*. vol. XVIII. Dublin: National University of Ireland.

Pasayianis, K. 1928. *Μανιάτικα Μοιρολόγια και Τραγούδια*. Athens.

Paz, Octavio. 1961. *The Labyrinth of Solitude: Life and Thought in Mexico*. Trans. L. Kemp. New York: Grove Press.

Petropoulos, D. A. 1959. *Ελληνικά δημοτικά τραγούδια*, 2. Athens: Βασική Βιβλιοθήκη.

Petrounias, Vasilios. 1934. *Μανιάτικα Μοιρολόγια*. Athens: Βιβλιοπωλείο Εστίας.

Pitt-Rivers, Julien. 1977. 'The Fate of Schechem or the Politics of Sex.' *Essays in the Anthropology of the Mediterranean*. Cambridge: Cambridge University Press.

Politis, Nikos. 1978. *Εκλογαι από τα Τραγούδια του Ελληνικού Λαού. Εκδοσις 6'*. Athens: Εκδόσεις Βαγιονάκη.

Prevelakis, Pantelis. 1983. *Ο Ποιητής Γιάννης Ρίτσος*. Athens: Εκδόσεις Κέδρος.

Pucci, Pietro. 1980. *The Violence of Pity in Euripides' 'Medea'*. Ithaca: Cornell University Press.

Radcliffe-Brown, Alfred R. 1964. *The Andaman Islanders*. New York: Free Press of Glencoe.

Rich, Adrienne. 1984. *The Fact of a Doorframe: Poems Selected and New 1950–84*. New York: Norton.

Richards, Janet Radcliffe. 1990. 'Why the Pursuit of Peace Is No Part of Feminism', in *Women, Militarism and War* (eds J. B. Elshtein and S. Tobias). Maryland: Rowman & Littlefield.

Ritsos, Yiannis. 1936. *Επιτάφιος*. Athens: Κέδρος.

Rose, Hilary and Rose, Stephen. 1970. *Science and Society*. Harmondsworth, Penguin.

Rosenblatt, P. C., Walsh, R., and Jackson, A. 1976. *Grief and Mourning in Cross-Cultural Perspective*. New Haven: Human Relations Area Files Press.

Ruddick, Sara. 1990. 'The Rationality of Care', in *Women, Militarism and War* (eds J. B. Elshtein and S. Tobias). Maryland: Rowman & Littlefield.

Sacks, Peter. 1985. *The English Elegy: Studies in the Genre from Spenser to Yeats*. Baltimore: Johns Hopkins University Press.

Said, Edward. 1978. *Orientalism*. New York: Vintage Books.

Schadewalt, W. 1932. 'Der kommos in Aeschylos' Choephoren.' *Hermes*. Stuttgart.

Schenck, Celeste. 1986. 'Feminism and Deconstruction: Reconstructing the Elegy.' *Tulsa Studies in Women's Literature*, April, 13–25.

Schieffelin, Edward. 1976. *The Sorrow of the Lonely and the Burning of the Dancers*. New York: St Martin's Press.

Seaford, Richard. 1987. 'The Tragic Wedding.' *JHS* CVII: 106–30.

Segal, Charles. 1971. 'Andromache's Anagnorisis: Formulaic Artistry in *Iliad* 22, 437–436.' *Harvard Studies in Classical Philology*, 75.

——. 1985. *Dionysiac Poetics and Euripides 'Bacchae'*. Princeton: Princeton University Press.

Seremetakis, C. Nadia. 1990. 'The Ethics of Antiphony: The Social Construction of Pain, Gender, and Power in the Southern Peloponnese.' *Ethos* 18 (1).

——. 1991. *The Last Word: Women, Death, and Divination in Inner Mani*. Chicago: University of Chicago Press.

Sifakis, G. M. 1988. *Για μια Ποιητική του Ελληνικού Δημοτικού Τραγουδιού*. Heraklion, Crete: Πανεπιστημιακές Εκδόσεις Κρήτης. Greek University Editions.

Skopetea, Sophia. 1972. *Τα Μανιάτικα Μοιρολόγια*. Athens.

Steiner, George. 1984. *Antigones*. New York: Oxford University Press.

Sultan, Nancy. 1991. 'The Hero's "Other" Voice.' *Journal of Modern Greek Studies*, 9 (2), October.

Swerdlow, Amy. 1990. 'Motherhood and the Subversion of the Military State: Women Strike for Peace Confronts the House Committee on Un-American Activities', in *Women, Militarism and War* (eds J. B. Elshtein and S. Tobias). Maryland: Rowman & Littlefield.

Theros, Aghis. 1942. *Τα Τραγούδια των Ελλήνων, Β'*. Athens: Βασική Βιβλιοθήκη 47.

Thomson, George. 1946. *Aeschylus and Athens*. London: Lawrence & Wishart, (2nd ed.).

Tiwary, K. M. 1975. 'Tuneful Weeping: A Mode of Communication.' *Working Papers in Sociolinguistics*, 27.

Tong, Diane. 1989. *Gypsy Folktales*. New York: Harcourt Brace Jovanovich.

Trypanis, Constantine (ed.). 1971. *The Penguin Book of Greek Verse*. Harmondsworth: Penguin Books.

Tsouderos, Yiannis Efthivoulos. 1976. *Κρητικά Μοιρολόγια*. Athens: Karavias.

van Gennep, Arnold. 1909. *Les rites de passage*. Paris: Emile Nourry. Trans. by M. B. Vizedom and G. L. Caffee (1960) as *The Rites of Passage*. Chicago: University of Chicago Press.

Vermeule, Emily. 1979. *Aspects of Death in Early Greek Art and Poetry*. Berkeley: University of California Press.

Vernant, Jean-Pierre. 1980. *Myth and Society in Ancient Greece*. Trans. J. Lloyd. Sussex: Harvester Press.

——. 1988. 'Tensions and Ambiguities in Greek Tragedy', in *Myth and Tragedy in Ancient Greece* (eds. J.-P. Vernant and P. Vidal-Naquet). Trans. J. Lloyd. New York: Zone Books.

Vizyenos, G. 1954. *Ανά τον Ελικώνα*. Βασική Βιβλιοθήκη, v. 68. Athens.

Vovelle, Michel. 1983. *La mort et l'Occident de 1300 à nos jours*. Paris: Gallimard.

Winkler, John J. 1990. *The Constraints of Desire: The Anthropology of Sex and Gender in Ancient Greece*. London: Routledge.

Zei, Alki. 1991. Achilles' Fiancée. Trans. G. Holst-Warhaft. Athens: Κέδρος.

Zeitlin, Froma. 1978. 'The Dynamics of Misogyny: Myth and Myth-making in the Oresteia.' *Arethusa*, 11.

Index